PRIMARY Creative Bible Learning Activities for Sabbath School

An Illustrated Encyclopedia of Bible Learning Activities for Children

North American Division Children's Ministries Department

Creative Bible Learning Activities for Sabbath School—Primary

Copyright ©2005 General Conference Division of the Seventh-day Adventist Church—North American Division.

No part of this publication may be reproduced in any form or by any means, electronic, photocopying, recording, or otherwise, without prior written permission—except where noted.

Authors: Noelene Johnsson, Trudy Morgan-Cole
Editorial Assistance: Lehai Allen, JeNean Johnson, Tompaul Wheeler
Design: Genesis Design
Cover Photos: Digital Vision
Graphics: Ginger Calkins
Production Manager: Christal Gregerson
Publisher: Advent*Source*
Type set: Bodoni Book, Stone Sans

Texts credited to NIV are from the Holy Bible, New International Version. Copyright ©1973, 1978, 1984, International Bible Society. Used by permission of Zondervan Bible Publishers.

To order additional copies:
Advent*Source*
5040 Prescott Avenue
Lincoln, NE 68506
1-800-328-0525
www.adventsource.org

Publication Data

Noelene Johnsson
Creative Bible Learning Activities for Sabbath School—Primary
ISBN# 1-57756-138-4
 1. Church work with children
 2. Christian education of children

Printed in the United States of America

Table of Contents

Introduction ... 1
Arts and Crafts Activities

Book Mark Activities
Corner Bookmark ... 9
Friendship Bookmark ... 9

Collage Activities
Mission Map Collage ... 10
Service Collage ... 10
Diversity Quilt ... 11
World Family Quilt ... 11

Diorama Activities
Pop Bottle Diorama ... 12
Shoe Box Diorama ... 13

Drawing Activities
Moving Pictures ... 13

Egg Carton Craft Activities
Egg Cup Animals ... 14
Egg Cup Basket ... 14
Egg Cup Characters ... 15
Egg Cup Flowers ... 15

Miscellaneous Craft Activities
Antiqued Pencil Holder ... 16
Bumper Sticker ... 16
Doorknob Hanger ... 17
First Place Award ... 17
Forgiveness Covers ... 18
Helpful Hand Reminder ... 18
Paper Bag Baskets ... 19
Pinwheel ... 19
Profile Silhouettes ... 20
Scented Sachet ... 20
Windsock ... 21
Word Pictures ... 21
Word Sculpture ... 22
Yarn-Decorated Pencil Holder ... 22

Nature Craft Activities
Seed Pod Pet ... 23

Paper Plate Craft Activities
Children of the World ... 23
Resist Plate ... 24
Mission Map ... 24
Paper Plate Wreath ... 25

Painting Activities
Sponge Painting ... 25
Traditional Painting ... 26
Collage and Paint ... 26
Spatter Painting ... 26
Stenciling ... 26
Decorative Shoelaces ... 27

Papier-Maché Activities
- Balloon Basket 28
- Banquet Cups 28
- Bible Character Masks 29

Picture Activities
- Tissue Picture. 30
- Touch Mosaic. 30
- Pussy Willow Picture 31
- Seed Pictures. 31

Printing Activities
- Apple Print Gift Bag. 32
- Leaf Print Poster 33
- Tin Can Prints 33
- Yarn Print Card. 34
- Hand Print Rainbow. 34

Weaving Activities
- Board Weaving 35
- Fruit Basket Weave 36
- Ladder Weave 36
- Place Mats 37

Language Related Activities

Acrostic Activities
- Special Name Acrostic 38
- Bible Character Acrostic 39
- Lesson Theme Acrostic. 39

Bulletin Board Activities
- Bulletin Board Mail Center 40
- Bulletin Board Display 41

Greeting Card Activities
- Baby Dedication Collage Card 41
- Drizzle Painting Invitations. 42
- Leader Appreciation Card 42
- Grace Card 43
- Get-Well Card 43

Key Word Activities
- Key Word Pick 44
- Key Word Bumpers 44
- Glitter Glue Keys 44
- Calligraphy Keyword 45

Letters and Notes Activities
- Hug-of-War 45
- Encouragement Blizzard 46
- Bible Times Thanks 46

List Activities
- Event Lists 47
- Growing Up Lists 47
- Pay Day at Church 48
- Time Wasters 48

Magic Writing Activities
- Egg Magic 49
- Invisible Writing 49

Poetry Activities
- Rhyming Stories 50
- Bible Limericks 50
- Write a Song 51

Postcard Activities
- Bible Postcard 51
- Mission Memories 52

Recipe Activities
- Healthy Favorites 53
- Recipe Writer 53

Drama Activities

Charades Activities
- On Your Feet Charades 54
- Doing our Best Charades 55
- Sabbath Charades 55

Clown Ministry Activities
- Cleaning Up for Jesus Skit 56
- Humor Clinic 57
- Gentle Hands 57
- Model Servants 58
- Awards Ceremony 58
- Clown Birthday Card 59

Costume Activities
- African "Man Cloth" 59
- African Women's Costume 60
- Angel Wings 60
- Sheepy Head 61
- Jericho Armor 61
- Bible Times Robe (An adult project) 62
- Bible Times Robe (Student project) 62
- Bible Times Belt 62
- Girl's Headband 62
- Bible Times Tunic 63
- Twisted Yarn Belt 63
- High Priest Costume 63

Improvisation Activities
- Bible Treasure Box Mime 64
- Live Statues 64
- Mirror Image 65
- Setting the Scene 65
- Animal Sculptures 66

Interactive Activities
- Key Word Echoes 66
- Active Echoes 67
- Dramatized Story 67

Puppet Activities
    Finger Puppets... 68
    Necktie Snakes... 68
    Paper Bag Animals... 69
    Muscle Man Contest... 69
    Life-size Bible Puppets.. 70
    Life-size Child Puppets.. 71

Experiential Activities
Bible Times Activities
    Bible Times Tablet... 72
    Bible Times Oil Lamp.. 73
    Coil Pottery.. 73
    Money Pouch and Coins... 74
    Bible Times Potpourri.. 74
    Bible Times Communion... 75

Food Related Activities
    Breakfast in Bed... 75
    Butter Fingers... 76
    Candy Sparks.. 76
    Impossible Bottled Egg.. 77
    Pudding Shaker.. 77
    Fill My Cup.. 78

Health Related Activities
    Blind Touch and Talk.. 78
    Health Check.. 79

Nature and Outdoor Activities
    Earth Watch... 79
    Meet a Tree... 80
    Nature Squares... 80

Relational Activities
    Egg Babies.. 80
    Candy Mold... 81
    Mailman's Mission.. 81
    Post-It Quotes.. 82

Science Activities
    Penny Polish.. 82
    Bubble Works... 83
    Growing to the Light.. 83
    Floating Picks.. 84
    Mobius Links... 84
    Perfect Flip... 85
    Ouch Bags.. 85

Trust Activities
    Blind Walk.. 86
    Human Camera... 86
    Nerf Test... 86
    Treat Teaser.. 87
    Trust Chair... 87
    Trust Maze... 88

Team Building Activities
    Affirmation Circle... 88

    Balloon Circle... 89
    New Name Game... 89
    Teamwork Puzzle... 89

  Miscellaneous Experiential Activities
    Popcorn Time Saver... 90
    Balloon Stomp... 90
    Marble Scoop... 91
    Egg Timer Watch... 91
    Body Wrap... 92
    Sober Sides... 92
    Minute Minders... 92
    The Weakest Link... 93
    Trampled Rose... 93
    Trinity Cord... 94
    Trinity Streamers... 94

  Team Activities
    Balloon Burst... 95
    Balloon Circle... 95
    Team Sculpture... 95
    Team Story... 96
    Airplane Accident... 96

  Witnessing Activities
    Sharing Balloon... 97
    Sharing Flower... 97
    Neighborhood House of Prayer... 98
    Fist Topple... 98
    Waters of Forgivness... 99

Class Management Activities

  Attention Getter Activities
    Rhythmic Signals... 100
    Echo Signals... 100
    Tune Snatches... 101
    Jonah Says... 101

  Boredom Chaser Activities
    Stop and Pop Bible Story... 101
    Disguises... 101
    Balloon Smileys... 102
    Balloon Chuckles... 102
    Class Cheer... 102
    Giggle Wipers... 102
    Magnetic Pull... 102
    Popcorn Answers... 102
    Giggles Buster... 102
    Hello, Partner... 102
    If You Hear Me... 102
    Paper Cut... 102

  Crowd Manager Activities
    Hats Off... 103
    Puzzle Grouper... 103
    Count Off... 103
    Grab Bag Grouper... 103
    Team Line Ups... 103

    Team Circles 103
    Clusters 103
    Mystery Chairs 103
    Stand If 104
    Jelly Bean Count 104

Ice Breaker Activities
    Name-Caller Cheer 105
    Name Game 105
    Shuffle Hoops 105
    Newspaper Pileup 105
    Odd or Even 105
    Who Has the Bug? 105

Memory Motivator Activities
    A Maze Verse 106
    Add a Word 106
    Around the World 106
    Books of the Bible Run 107
    Ball of Yarn Reminders 107
    Beanbag Toss 107
    Hang-a-Word 107
    Balloon Pop 107
    Color Code 107
    How Many Friends? 108
    Last One Standing 108
    Memory 108
    Memory Hunt 108
    Memory Verse Songs 108
    Muffin Cup Flowers 108
    Memory Tray 109
    Pop Up 109
    Walk the Talk 109

Prayer Activities

Prayer Experience Activities
    Prayer Partners 110
    Hand-Squeeze Prayers 110
    Prayer Walks 110
    Church Prayer Prowl 111
    ACTS Prayer 111
    PART Prayers 111
    ACTS Hats 111
    Prayer Journal 112
    Prayer Maps 112
    Apple Prayers 112
    Prayer Vespers 112
    Prayer Letters 112
    Sensory Prayers 112

Group Prayer Activities
    Warm Water Prayers 113
    Popcorn Prayers 113
    Prayer Chains 113
    Thanks Banks 113
    Lord's Prayer Chain 114
    Names of Jesus Chain 114
    Intercessory Prayer 114

Telephone Prayer Chain (Primary-Teen) 114
Pocket Prayers 114
Memory Verse Prayer 115
Add-on Prayers 115
Empty Chair Prayers 115
Position Prayers 115
Moving Prayers 115
M&M™ Prayers 115
Prayer Collage 115

Inventories

About Me 117
Favorite Things 119
Friends 121
Fearful Stuff 123
Feelings Inventory 125
I Give Thanks 127
My Bible and Me 129
Power Play 131
Prayer Inventory 133
Temperaments 135
Spiritual Gifts Treasure Hunt 137
What a Pain! 139
What I Know About God 141

Appendix 143

Introduction: *Understanding Ourselves and How God is at Work in Us* A1
Introduction: *Faith Development* A2
Doorknob Hanger: *doorknob hanger pattern* A3
Mission Map: *photocopiable maps* A4
Pay Day at Church: *church pattern* A10
Tin Can Prints: *dove pattern, angel pattern, Jesus pattern* A11
Paper Bag Animals: *animal faces* A12
Money Pouch and Coins: *pouch pattern & coins* A14
Bible Times Potpourri: *circle pattern* A15
How Many Friends?: *spinner pattern & assembly instructions* A16

GraceLink Curriculum Index 159

Bible Story Index 162

Introduction

How to Use This Book

Creative Bible Learning Activities for Sabbath School—Primary is packed full of simple Bible learning activities (BLAs) that involve children in hands-on learning. These creative options will help each teacher teach in the way that children learn best. Each activity in this book includes suggestions to plug into one or more GraceLink Sabbath School lessons. Use the comprehensive index to find specific activities recommended for your lesson—or choose and adapt some other activity that better fits the needs of your group.

The activities are designed with a line beneath the title, indicating where in the lesson the activities best fit—at the beginning as readiness, as part of the Bible story telling/memory verse, or as application—sharing and witnessing. A description of the activity follows, along with "Let's talk," a list of questions to guide the class discussion.
The "Use with" paragraph lists the GraceLink Bible stories that could be enhanced by the activity and an additional comment to guide the discussion. Remember, the real learning comes after the activity is completed, when students have a chance to reflect on what they did and connect their reflection to the lesson.

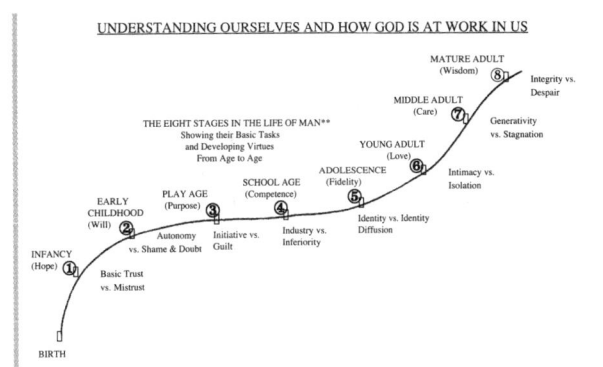

UNDERSTANDING OURSELVES AND HOW GOD IS AT WORK IN US

THE EIGHT STAGES IN THE LIFE OF MAN**
Showing their Basic Tasks and Developing Virtues From Age to Age

- BIRTH
- INFANCY (Hope) — Basic Trust vs. Mistrust
- EARLY CHILDHOOD (Will) — Autonomy vs. Shame & Doubt
- PLAY AGE (Purpose) — Initiative vs. Guilt
- SCHOOL AGE (Competence) — Industry vs. Inferiority
- ADOLESCENCE (Fidelity) — Identity vs. Identity Diffusion
- YOUNG ADULT (Love) — Intimacy vs. Isolation
- MIDDLE ADULT (Care) — Generativity vs. Stagnation
- MATURE ADULT (Wisdom) — Integrity vs. Despair

* Developed by Dr. Paul Irwin, Professor of Religious Education at the School of Theology in Claremont, CA.
** Adapted from Erik Erikson in his book, *Childhood and Society*.

see Appendix A1

Understanding Primary Children

Primary children (ages 6-9) typically range from first-graders to fourth-graders, but being in school or being able to read is not mandatory. A 6-year-old in the first grade may resent being in a Sabbath School class called "Kindergarten." He or she needs to be in Primary. Churches large enough to divide primaries into two classes may separate children into Primary I (ages 6-7) and Primary II (ages 8-9). By mixing the primary ages together we give older children an opportunity for leadership and service. Readers assist non-readers and cliques are split up, avoiding potential discipline problems.

Developmentally, primaries have learned to trust adults in authority, and are proud to do things for themselves. But they may still need help with taking initiative. When they fail to use their self-starters, primaries feel guilty. However, they appreciate teachers who, by promising something fun, offer strong motivation to get started.

Older primaries are expanding their understanding of the world, learning the basic skills required for success in school, and learning to set and attain personal goals. When they fail to complete an assigned task, they feel inadequate.

Research on life-stage development tells us that a child's successful mastery of each successive life task depends on their mastery of the previous task. Tasks not mastered at the appropriate age will be more difficult to master later.

Physically, primaries are characterized by growth spurts, high energy, and frequent restlessness. The wise teacher takes note when children begin to sigh—a sure prelude to restlessness—and changes the activity. The younger primary's large motor skills develop ahead of their fine motor skills. They may be able to run and balance quite well, but may still be awkward with scissors and pencils.

Socially, primaries enjoy playing with their peers, but can be selective with playmates. They particularly enjoy sharing secrets with special friends and joining clubs. They seek the approval of adults and imitate adult behavior.

Emotionally, primaries are usually joyful, but can easily become fearful, mirroring the emotions of their parents and teachers. Primaries do not sustain strong emotions, such as anger and grief, but experience them in short, recurring bursts. When a grieving child laughs, adults may wrongly conclude that the child is coping with his loss, whereas in reality he is unable to sustain grief. Strong emotions not processed tend to explode later and put the child at risk for antisocial behavior.

Mentally, primaries are imaginative and curious, asking lots of questions. Their reasoning powers are developing, but most do not think abstractly yet. They can, for instance, feel loved and talk about how love feels, but they cannot understand love as a motivation for good behavior. Being concrete thinkers, they think about things they can see, touch or experience—or things they have already seen, touched, or experienced. Primaries are becoming interested in the long ago and far away, but they have trouble understanding another person's point of view.

Spiritually, primaries accept God as their Friend and want to please Him. They worship with spontaneity and joy. This age group has no problem believing in miracles. They know right from wrong and feel guilty when they do wrong. Deeply sensitive, they are easily influenced by the attitudes of parents and teachers. At this point, they are moving from a participatory faith toward a belonging faith that values membership in the church community.

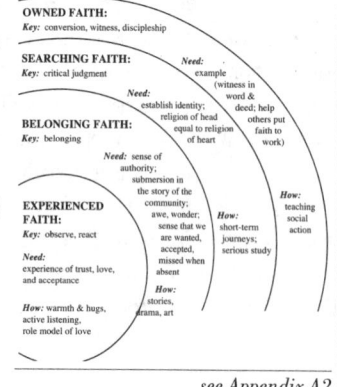

OWNED FAITH:
Key: conversion, witness, discipleship

SEARCHING FAITH:
Key: critical judgment
Need: establish identity; religion of head equal to religion of heart

BELONGING FAITH:
Key: belonging
Need: sense of authority; submersion in the story of the community; awe, wonder, sense that we are wanted, accepted, missed when absent
How: example (witness in word & deed; help others put faith to work)

EXPERIENCED FAITH:
Key: observe, react
Need: experience of trust, love, and acceptance
How: warmth & hugs, active listening, role model of love
How: stories, drama, art
How: short-term journeys; serious study
How: teaching social action

see Appendix A2

How Children Learn

Not everyone learns in the same way. Preschool-aged children and younger primaries learn through the senses—especially when more than one sense is brought to bear on a lesson. For instance, some children like to learn by listening. However, they remember something longer if they both hear and see it.

The Four Modes of Learning

While primaries usually rely on one sense more than the others, they can draw on any of the following four modes, depending upon the situation.

Visual (seeing)—Visual learners say, "Look here!" So use pictures and objects to reinforce the concepts you teach.

Auditory (hearing)—Auditory learners say, "Listen to this!" Music and sound effects help them remember things.

Kinesthetic (manipulating)—Kinesthetic learners say, "What do you make of this?" So provide something for them to make or do as part of the learning experience.

Experiential (experiencing)—Experiential learners say, "Try this." Plan activities that help them experience the lesson; real-life situations can help them do something that brings meaning to an abstract concept or emotion.

Preferred Learning Styles

Children generally have one learning style that they prefer to use. Again, they make use of the others, but to lesser extents. There are four types of learners.

Style 1: Innovative Learners. These students rely on their senses and observation. Conscious of feelings and relationships, they are imaginative, creative, artistic, sensitive and caring. They want to know, "Why should I learn this?"

Style 2: Analytic Learners. These students prefer to learn by thinking and observing. They like facts. So ask them to research information in dictionaries, maps, and the Bible. Style 2 learners tend to think about a task before performing it. They want to know, "What do you want me to know?"

Style 3: Common Sense Learners. These students are thinkers who like hands-on involvement. Problem solvers and decision makers, they like to get straight to the point and work by the clock. They want to know if theories work in real life. Style 3 learners ask, "How does it work?"

Introduction

Style 4: Dynamic Learners. These students prefer to learn by doing. They often begin work on a project before reading instructions or analyzing the task. They will work tirelessly to achieve a goal, time being no object for them. They ask, "What if we do this (or view this) differently?"

Teaching Primaries

The Learning Cycle

By considering the needs of each learning style in numerical order and answering their learning questions, we follow a natural learning cycle. To set up your own learning cycle, divide your lesson time into four approximately equal segments (usually about 15 minutes each in Sabbath School) and start on time, for the sake of style 3 learners who may walk out if nothing seems to be happening. Each 15-minute segment of a one-hour lesson contributes to the cycle as described below.

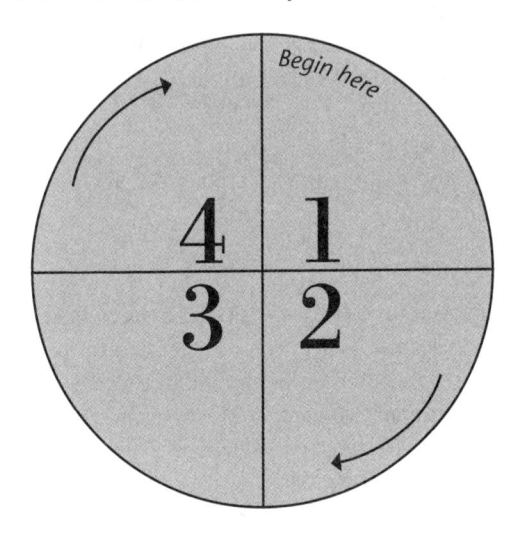

Style 1: Readiness. Readiness helps prepare students for the lesson concept by connecting with something in their life—something they know. Readiness also helps students feel comfortable and accepted in the learning environment. The readiness activity shows them why the lesson is important and gets them talking and working with each other. Students appreciate being given a choice of activities during readiness time. Remember, Style 1 learners may not mind starting late, but the more practical Style 3 learner needs the class to start on time.

Style 2: Learning the Lesson Content. The thinking student is anxious to get into the lesson itself; in addition to a Bible story, this student wants facts, orientation with a map, definitions for new words, and a chance to ask questions. This section of class time is devoted to teaching the lesson and memory verse, and making the main point. Students are more likely to remember new material if they are actively involved in the learning. For instance, if they looked up a map or concordance during readiness, the teacher can ask them to report what they learned.

Style 3: Application. Style 3 learners enjoy the readiness and the teaching of the lesson content, but they get impatient to apply the lesson to life. They want to know how it will work for them. Scenarios—situations from everyday life—are a favorite way of applying the lesson to the student's life. The application of the lesson may involve students in problem solving or giving advice. Application, often overlooked by Style 2 teachers, helps kids focus on how they feel about God and the main idea of the lesson.

Style 4: Sharing Time. This final section of lesson time gives students a chance to respond to the lesson. Their response may involve celebrating a personal decision or sharing the lesson's message with someone outside the class. Students make or do something to help them witness naturally, teaching someone else what they learned. Sharing may be in the form of a class service project. Whatever they do, the sharing should be real and allow freedom for children to ask, "What if I do it this way (my way)?"

Bible Learning Activities

Children with different learning styles prefer different kinds of learning experiences. However, their likes and dislikes are not always predictable. Offering a choice of activities not only gives the learner some control over the learning situation, but also ensures that her needs will be met.

Style 1. Innovative Learners like creative writing (non-readers can draw a picture or talk instead of writing), group projects, activities that allow them to express feelings, trust walks, arts and crafts, role plays, drama and charades. They often dislike personal inventories, and reporting to the whole group.

Style 2. Analytic Learners like reading maps and researching in a dictionary, concordance, or Bible. They enjoy memorization games, quizzes, coded messages, written reports, and reading assignments where they work alone. They often dislike role-plays and skits, listening to oral reports (unless done by an expert) and group projects.

Introduction

Style 3. Common Sense Learners like experiments, coded messages, arts and crafts activities, making up skits, creative writing, quizzes, rebuses, scenarios, and working against the clock. They tend to dislike busy work and predictability, editing their own writing, reading assignments, and rote memorization.

Style 4. Dynamic Learners like experiential activities, physical competition, real life simulation, and activities where they plot the strategy. Style 4 learners also enjoy producing a drama or big event, taking leadership of group activities, decorating, and caring for details. They tend to dislike working against the clock, being hurried, step-by-step procedures where each step is checked by the teacher, as well as rigid boundaries and copying.

Knowing the likes and dislikes of each learning style can help teachers understand where students are coming from. Students should be expected to take part even in activities they dislike, but teachers can help them participate in a way that fits their style. For instance, Style 2 learners who do not wish to act in a skit can help with narration or props. When allowed to choose among several activities, students will choose something that fits their learning style.

Outings and Field Trips

Going outside the regular classroom space can be a powerful learning experience for primary children. Field trips should be held sparingly—perhaps once a year—but do not rule out a field trip just because you have not done one before. Remember the following steps.

- Plan well in advance
- Provide adequate supervision
- Delegate responsibilities to other adults and hold them accountable
- Get church board approval; explain your request ahead of time to the chairperson and to individual board members, if possible. Board approval is necessary for church insurance coverage.

Common field trip ideas include observation trips, such as visiting a nature park, zoo, or planetarium to learn about God's creation. Primaries also enjoy outreach and service trips, such as delivering gift bags to a children's hospital, doing yard work, or visiting senior citizens in the community. Students learn a lot from preparing food bags for the homeless, then delivering them in person.

Facilitating Activities

Crew Leaders. When involving children in hands-on learning, lots of opportunities arise for a large Sabbath School to get out of hand. One way to stay ahead of your game is to divide the children into crews—five students plus a crew leader. Every week the crew leader sits with the crew and encourages them to listen to the class leader's instructions and to complete activities, projects, and assignments. Crew leaders operate behind the scenes; they have no scripted speaking part and no preparation is required of them. But their love and attention to the students can be a real ministry with eternal results.

Class Teachers. The class teacher, the leader-teacher up front, gives the lead in overall group activities for the class. He prepares careful directions, written as well as oral, and sees to it that all of the materials are available; he affirms student efforts and asks students to show or tell what they accomplished.

The most common mistakes leader-teachers make when facilitating up front include these.

1. Talking too much
2. Spending too much time on one activity
3. Failing to give clear directions
4. Failing to debrief activities

Talking too much. Teacher-talk that goes too long can become like static to the class—something to tune out. Because students remember about 80 percent of what they do and only 10 percent of what is heard, replace those mini-lectures with activities. Then stand back and allow students freedom to complete the task. When they are done, ask questions and allow adequate time for students to think and respond. Good leaders are more like coaches than lecturers. They encourage from the sidelines with a word or two as needed, but they don't step in and play the game.

Spending too much time on one activity. Before giving directions, tell students how long they will have to complete the task. To encourage your group to work quickly, state a short and unusual length of time, such as 90 seconds or 2 minutes and 35 seconds. You can allow a little flex time if you wish, but not so much that some of the students will be waiting around. If everyone finishes an activity, chances are that you spent too long on it. Students don't have to finish an activity to learn from it. So when several students are done, move on and begin the discussion. This will help your group form the habit of getting down to business quickly. And for those who get bent out of shape because they want to finish, offer the option of coming back later.

Failing to give clear directions. Giving clear directions can help prevent behavior problems. Before starting an activity, students need specific instructions.
- How they will work—will they work alone, with a partner, in groups of three or four, or in crews?
- Who will do what—everyone in the group or just one person?
- When to start following the directions—"When I give the signal. . ."
- How the directions will be carried out—quietly, without running. . .
- What will be done—bring the materials, make a poster like "this one" . . .
- The signal to start—"Begin," or "You may start."

Failing to discuss activities. Learning does not come automatically from participating in an activity; teachers must encourage students to talk about what happened, how they felt about it, and what they learned. They should accept and affirm each response. Good discussion starters are questions, that may include those listed below.
- What happened? What did you make?
- How did you feel about the activity?
- What does this activity tell you about our key Bible verse (or the lesson's message)?
- What might God be telling you through this verse (or this lesson)?

Encourage different responses; people are not the same, and the Holy Spirit speaks to each mind in unique ways. If nobody mentions the point that you were intending to emphasize, say, "I also think that...." Large classes can discuss the questions in their crews and then two or three crews can report to the entire class.

Bible learning activities often involve supplies that the leader-teacher must gather ahead of time. This will be quick and painless if materials are kept in a well-organized cupboard or supply closet. Twice a year, take inventory, and make a list in the church bulletin or on a bulletin board of the things that are running out. Invite church members to purchase several items to donate to your class when they do their weekend shopping.

Materials To Keep On Hand

Plan to keep the following materials on hand
Bibles (preferably New International Version)
Clear tape, masking tape
Construction paper
All-purpose liquid or gel glue, glue sticks
Index cards
Markers
Paper towels
Pens, pencils, crayons
Scissors
Stickers and/or pictures of Jesus
Typing paper, scrap paper

Other materials to have on hand if possible
Aluminum foil
Balloons
Baskets, bowls, jars
Beanbags
Bible-times costumes (robes, head dress, large T-shirts, ties, cords, scarves)
Blindfolds
Brown bags—lunch and grocery size
Cardboard shoeboxes, empty tissue boxes
Chalkboard or dry erase board
Cotton balls
End-roll of newsprint
Extension cord
Flashlight
Glitter, glitter glue, puff glue
Hole puncher
Magazines, catalogs, newspapers, copies of *Adventist Review* (used/current)
Magnets
Nature specimens
Paper clips
Paper or plastic cups
Poster paint and brushes
Post-it notes

Rhythm instruments
Sealable plastic bags, sandwich size and quart size
Small, inexpensive gifts for children
Tape player/CD player
Yarn (several colors), ribbon, string, rickrack braid

For quick distribution, store materials in such a manner that children do not require adult help to reach them. Pack frequently-used materials (such as scissors, markers, pens/pencils/crayons, glue sticks, and glitter glue) into one basket per crew or class group.
Ask a teacher or volunteer to take responsibility for keeping materials organized from week to week.

Displaying Students' Work

Children feel their work has value and meaning if it is noticed. At the conclusion of an activity, find a way for students to show or tell what they have done. If students worked individually, they can show or tell their class what they did (or would have done had time allowed). If a crew worked together on the activity, they report as a group to the whole class.
Student projects deserve to be put on display for their classmates and others to view. Plan to use students' drawings, crafts, posters, etc., in bulletin board displays around the classroom. If you do not have a bulletin board, post students' signed work either on the classroom wall or out in the hallway where the rest of the church can enjoy it.

Understanding GraceLink

GraceLink is the Seventh-day Adventist church's official Sabbath School curriculum for children. The Primary GraceLink lessons consist of a 4-year series designated by letters A, B, C and D. Year A always occurs for Primary during election year (or Olympic year)—the years divisible by four, such as 2004, 2008, etc.

The Four Dynamics

Each GraceLink lesson is centered on one of four dynamic principles of the Christian faith—grace, worship, community, and service. Each month, the children's divisions study different stories, but all focus on the same dynamic. When a story is repeated in an older age level, it may be viewed through the lens of a different dynamic.

Grace: "God loves me." Lessons based on this first dynamic emphasize what God has done for us—Christ's life and death, and the love, forgiveness, and acceptance He offers us.

Worship: "I love God." These lessons center on our response to God's grace. Worship is presented as a total commitment that includes praise, obedience, lifestyle, Sabbath keeping, tithes and offerings, etc.

Community: "We love each other." These lessons stress the idea that members of God's family love and care for each other without reference to the way a person looks or how smart they are. Nobody is left out because they are different in any way.

Service: "We love you too." These lessons teach children that serving non-believers helps show them that God loves them too—and often presents an opportunity for us to tell the good things Jesus has done for us.

The Message

Children learn best when we focus on a single concept each week. The GraceLink lessons call this the message. Teachers re-state the message when debriefing each activity.

For a truly integrated approach, we focus everything in Sabbath School to the message, even the mission story and Prayer & Praise time.

Making GraceLink Work for You

The GraceLink materials are designed to introduce the lesson on Sabbath morning, so that students will be interested and inspired to study that same lesson throughout the following week. Encourage them to find opportunities to share activities from Sabbath School with their family during the week.

Many parents are motivated to study the Sabbath School lesson with their children only if they think the child will need it to make a good showing at church. Furthermore, more than any other age group, primary children enjoy checklists and competition—the feeling that they are earning their way towards something.

So while you continue to challenge children to study because it is the best way to grow a relationship with God, you may also choose to reward the children with stickers each week for answering the following questions.

1. How many days did you study your lesson? (Affirm any response, encouraging them to try for daily study.)
2. Did you read the lesson from the Bible? (This is an important part of lesson study.)
3. Can you remember last week's text? (Affirm their effort; assist them if necessary.)
4. How did you do the sharing activity for last week's lesson? (Remind them what it was.)

Prayer & Praise

The GraceLink leader-teacher guide provides suggestions for each of the four segments of the learning cycle. Information is also provided for an additional 15 minutes of Prayer & Praise time. This includes fellowship and prayer time, suggested songs related to the lesson, offering, and the mission story from *Children's Mission* magazine (available free; contact your conference Sabbath School department to place an order, or go to http://adventistmission.org and click on "stories". Prayer & Praise time is not recommended for the beginning of Sabbath School. Begin with a readiness activity to give students a reason to be on time. Prayer & Praise works well if it comes after readiness or before the application.

Steps To Choosing Jesus

Ellen White counsels Sabbath School teachers: "Never rest till every child in your class is brought to the saving knowledge of Christ" (*Counsels on Sabbath School Work*, p. 125). We bring children to that saving knowledge by taking them through the following simple steps.

a. Begin with God's love. Jesus always loves us, no matter what we do.
   (John 3:16; 1 John 4:8, 10)

b. Explain the need. All have sinned (done wrong); the wages of sin is death.
   (Romans 3:23, 6:23; Revelation 21:27)

c. Jesus is the Way. He died for us to save us from forever death; those who believe and receive Him are His children.
   (John 3:16, John 1:12, 1 Corinthians 15:3-4).

d. Help them receive Jesus. Then pray the sinner's prayer that recognizes each of the above points: God's love, their need, believing that Jesus is the Way, inviting Jesus into their life.
   (John 1:12; Revelation 3:20)

e. Give assurance of salvation. When we are in God's family, we have a room in His house. We do not have to knock or wonder if He will let us in. We belong there and will go home with Him when He comes. (John 14:1-3; 3:36; Hebrews 13:5)

After primary children have made that commitment, take time to mentor them to grow in Jesus. They will need to know that they will sometimes do wrong things and need to ask forgiveness. If they feel far from God, they can go through the steps to Jesus again. As they grow through prayer and Bible study, primaries will want to share with others how to invite Jesus into their hearts and become children of God. This is the time to help them get plugged in to outreach projects.

An inexpensive, child-friendly booklet, *Coming to Jesus; Growing in Him* (Advent*Source*) is recommended as a give-away to help children understand and remember their commitment to Jesus.

Introduction

Arts And Crafts Activities

Art activities, such as paintings, banners, dioramas, mosaics, diagrams, cartoons, and sculpture, appeal to innovative (Style 1) learners and get students actively involved. Use them when students first enter the classroom, especially those activities that need minimal teacher supervision. Displaying their work on walls or bulletin boards makes for a colorful decor.

Art and craft activities can also work as "sharing" activities at the end of a program. But those that take more time may need to be started at the beginning of class. Select these activities for their appropriateness to the learning situation and for their application to a specific lesson. Many of these projects are messy and will require children to wear protective clothing, such as an oversized shirt or trash bag, to cover their Sabbath clothes.

BOOKMARKS

The easiest way to make a bookmark is to cut a 3x8-inch strip of poster board, construction paper, or wallpaper (from a book of samples, available from an interior decorating or hardware store). Bookmarks make great gifts that also share the lesson's message.

Students decorate one side of the bookmark with an art form and write a message or Bible verse on the other. Bookmarks can be as decorative—or as simple—as the occasion and class resources allow. For durability, cover back and front of the bookmark with wide, transparent tape, often available at a dollar store. The tape should overlap the bookmark all the way around so that it adheres to itself at the edges. You may need to trim the bookmark to fit the size of the tape.

Corner Bookmark
A sharing activity

Materials
- Envelopes, recycled or new
- Scissors
- Markers or gel pens

Activity
Students cut a three-inch triangle from the bottom corner of an envelope as shown. This bookmark fits down over the corner of a page. Write a message on the bookmark and decorate.

Let's talk
How do you feel about the message on your bookmark? With whom will you share your bookmark?

Use with
- Paul and Silas in prison (Draw footprints, write: "I'm Following Jesus")
- Manna in the wilderness (Write: "Sabbath—My Best Day")
- Gabriel visits Mary (Add a Jesus sticker; write: "God's Best Gift")
- Elisha and the axe head (Write: "God Cares")
- Jesus heals a leper (Write: "Time Alone With God")

Friendship Bookmark
A sharing activity

Materials
- Heavy paper, cut to size (directions in box)
- Crayons/markers
- Stickers, glitter, yarn
- Scissors

Activity
Students write a friendly message, such as, "Be my friend" or the memory verse on one side of the bookmark. On the other side, they either decorate with a combination of stickers, glitter, and yarn, or draw a simple picture.
Optional: Wrap the bookmark in clear contact paper.

Hint
Decorative scissors give bookmarks a special edge.

Let's talk
When did a friend encourage you? To whom will you give the bookmark as a sign of your friendship?

Use with
- Animals enter the ark (Friends work together)
- Stephen and the seven deacons (You're my friend)
- Daniel among lions (Wait on the Lord)
- Shepherds visit Jesus (Joy to the World)
- Any time you want to share God's love (Kids write their own message, the day's theme, or the memory verse)

Arts and Crafts Activities

COLLAGE

Collages are artistic compositions created by gluing various fragments of pictures, words, cloth, fiber, or wood to a background in a close, often overlapping fashion. Some children will prefer to randomly overlap the items, while others may use them to form a pattern. Because collages take time, primaries in Sabbath School will accomplish more in the time available by working as a group with adult help on a 17x12-inch background. Allow 10-15 minutes.

Mission Map Collage
A mission activity

Materials
- Poster board or newsprint
- Markers
- *National Geographic* magazines

Ahead
Cover a large section of wall with poster board or newsprint taped down at the edges. Using an overhead projector, project the outline of the quarter's mission map from Children's Mission to fit the paper, and draw the outline with a black marker. Collect *National Geographic* magazines with articles on countries featured in the mission stories.

Activity
Students fill in the land portion of the map with a collage of pictures of people from these countries and entitle them with headlines and descriptions. Trim the edges to preserve the country boundaries. Title the collage, "Serving others, making friends."

Let's talk
What would you like about living in one of these places? What can we do to help them?

Use with
- The mission emphasis any quarter
- Wedding at Cana

Service Collage
A readiness activity

Materials
- Construction paper or recycled file folders
- Scissors and glue
- Newspapers and news magazines

Activity
Students make a collage, using construction paper or a recycled file folder as the background. Their collage will show pictures and headlines of needs that they could serve in their neighborhood, town or country.

Let's talk
What opportunities to serve do you see in these pictures? What one opportunity would you like to do this week?

Use with
- Jacob serves Laban seven years (Caption: "Learning to Serve")
- Feed my sheep (Caption: "We find ways to serve")

Arts and Crafts Activities

Diversity Quilt
An application activity

Materials
- 8-inch precut squares of wrapping paper or cloth in several different colors and patterns
- Pinking shears (optional)
- Banner paper, cut and taped to form a square
- Black construction paper
- Glue sticks

Activity
Students trim squares before gluing them on the banner paper to simulate the effect of a patchwork quilt. Older students can cut out extra squares for younger children to paste. They cut letters from black construction paper for the caption, "All are precious in His sight!" and glue them over the finished quilt.

Hint
Leaders in small churches might plan ahead to have the Adult Sabbath School help the children with their quilt. They can all talk about it together.

Let's talk
How do you feel about the different squares of the quilt? What can we learn about each other from making the quilt? Could you have finished the quilt in the same time working alone as you did working in the group?

Use with
- The early church serves all
- The lost coin
- The Tower of Babel
- Jericho falls (We all work together)

World Family Quilt
An application activity

Materials
- Lift off masking tape
- Scissors, glue sticks
- Full-page magazine pictures from *National Geographic* or similar magazines, portraying people of different countries
- Black marker

Activity
Students pair up; each student selects a picture and cuts it lengthwise into 2-inch-wide strips. Students lightly number their strips in order from left to right. The object is to arrange their strips to form one continuous line, with no space between strips. The trick is to keep laying them in numeric order, but with their partner's strips in between. To form a quilt, students tape their mingled collages on the wall.

Let's talk
How is our quilt like our world? Can you see in your picture? What do you suppose God sees when He sees our world?

Use with
- Solomon dedicates the temple (Caption: "We worship with God's family around the world")
- The Tower of Babel "(We help people—even those who are different")
- A wife for Isaac ("God wants everyone to join His family")
- Esau sells his birthright ("I can love people who are different from me")

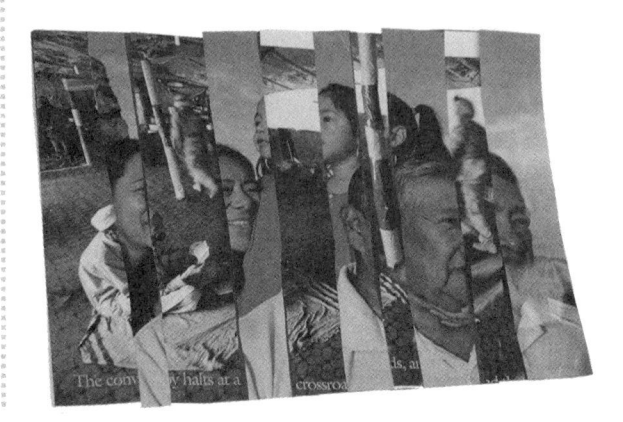

Arts and Crafts Activities

DIORAMAS

A diorama is a three-dimensional representation of a scene or event. Usually it is housed inside a box or other container, and may include a wide variety of materials, such as: figures cut from used pages of the student Bible study guide or figures sculpted from clay; nature objects such as twigs, rocks, sand; cardboard structures furnished with fabric scraps; objects fashioned from aluminum foil, etc. Dioramas help make things real to kids and capture their imagination.

Pop Bottle Diorama
An application activity

Materials
- 2-liter soda bottles, one per child
- Clear packing tape
- 3x5-inch pieces of cardboard
- Glue, clay
- Small twigs
- Colored tissue paper

Ahead
Wash and dry the bottles, removing any labels. Carefully cut around the bottom of each bottle, right above the base, to make a removable "lid."

Activity
Students make trees and bushes by tearing off tiny bits of tissue paper and gluing them to the branches of the twigs. Using the clay as a base, students stand the twigs inside the bottle, as shown. Cut out people figures from recycled Bible study guides, tape them to tooth picks, and stand them up in a clay base. Add other structures that fit the Bible story. Using the clear packing tape, tape the lower end of the bottle back in place.

Let's talk
You have just made a Bible story in a bottle; who is willing to use their bottle to tell the story to the class?

Use with
- Moses at the burning bush (Add only one large bush with red and yellow tissue "flames.")
- Jonah and the whale (Instead of cutting the bottle, fill it 2/3 full with water. Cut Jonah and whale figures from craft foam and insert them through the mouth of the bottle. Add tiny grains of coarse sand and a tiny plastic boat from a craft store.)
- Jesus and the storm (Make as for Jonah, but adding people instead of fish.)

Arts and Crafts Activities

Shoe Box Diorama
An application activity

Materials
- Shoe boxes (one per child)
- Modeling clay
- Scissors, glue, construction paper
- Natural objects: twigs, dry grass, moss, rocks
- Fabric pieces, facial tissue, yarn, etc.

Activity
Students turn the carton on its side and imagine the scene they are building. They may want to draw a background on the back panel of the box. Using materials provided, they build a scene to illustrate the Bible story. Items can be kept in place by pressing their base into clay balls and then pressing the ball to the base of the diorama.

Let's talk
If you were a tiny person in your diorama, what would you like best about living there?

Use with
- Noah's ark (Either make an ark from construction paper or clay to sit in the center of the scene, or imagine the box as being the inside of the ark.)
- The Sanctuary (Divide with construction paper curtains into three parts: the Holy and Most Holy places and the courtyard. Don't worry about proportions. Make altars and furniture from clay.)
- Creation (Create a scene with items that can be added for each day of Creation.)
- Birth of Jesus (Use a half-pint milk or juice carton for the nativity scene.)

DRAWINGS
Drawings are so simple and universal that we need not detail the directions. Just provide the materials and ask for a drawing of the Bible story or of a situation in real life. Students may use paper and pencils/crayons/markers, damp sand and wood scraps, or a sidewalk and chalk. Children enjoy making freehand drawings, especially if they can combine them with a variety of other materials. Drawings give children a means of communicating without words and a way to express their feelings. When asking students to draw something, encourage them to use their imagination and provide an accepting environment where they know their efforts will be appreciated. Drawings are appropriate for any lesson—but do not overuse them.

Moving Pictures
An application activity

Materials
- Lightweight construction paper, white or beige
- Crayons

Activity
Students fold the page in half, vertically, three times. They then draw some feature of a nature scene (a mountain range or river), running across the entire page. The picture will change a little in each section to reveal what happens as the story progresses. If the story requires more than 8 frames, they combine some sections of the story in one frame or leave part of it out.

Let's talk
Who is willing to tell the story with pictures to your group? With whom could you share this picture story this week?

Use with
- Ten Plagues (Illustrate 8 of the 10 plagues as follows. Draw the river flowing through all frames. Add grass and trees in earlier pictures. In section 1, the river is half blue and half red; in section 2, the frogs are near the river; in section 3, flies cover the panel, etc. Tape on two additional panels to complete the story the next week.)

Arts and Crafts Activities

EGG CARTON CRAFTS

Egg carton crafts are projects made from empty egg cartons. Many of these crafts require the egg carton to be cut up—some into two-piece, hinged eggcups, and some into half cups. The result provides a creative reminder of the Sabbath School lesson, an appealing way to share the lesson's message.

Egg Cup Animals
An application activity

Materials
- Egg cartons, enough for one per child
- Beige yarn, glue sticks, scissors
- Brown paint and brushes
- Construction paper
- Masking tape

Activity
Students trim the edges of their eggcup and paint the outside of the cup brown. While it dries, they draw the animal's face and cut it out. To make a lion's mane, apply the glue stick in a circle around the edge of the face and lay down 1-inch pieces of yarn, side-by-side, creating a fringed circle. To make a lion tail, cut a slit at the back of the eggcup, insert one end of a 4-inch piece of yarn, and secure it inside the cup with masking tape. Fringe the other end of the tail, combing it with a plastic comb until quite fluffy. (The mane can also be combed, but pinch the edge of face and glue yarn first.) To make a pig's tail, cut a spiral from construction paper. Finally, glue the animal's face onto the cup.

Use with
- Noah and the animals
- Daniel and the lions
- Creation

How to cut a pig's tail

Egg Cup Basket
An application activity

Materials
- Egg cartons, one per group of 6 students
- Construction paper, blue and green
- Glue sticks, scissors, tape
- Cotton balls
- Facial tissue
- Modeling clay

Activity
Students cut a 6-inch square of blue construction paper as a base for the craft (or use a blue unlined index card). Cut several 4-inch tall rows of rushes from green construction paper, folding under the lower half inch. Trim a cup from an egg carton to make a basket for baby Moses; glue the bottom of the basket to the blue base. Glue the underneath fold of the rushes to make them stand up behind the basket. Use another cup to make a lid for the basket; attach the lid with tape (or yarn glued to top and bottom). Pull apart a cotton ball to line the basket and form a baby from clay. Wrap the "baby" in facial tissue, and place it in the basket.

Let's talk
Do you think a baby could live long in a basket without getting wet or drowning?

Use with
- Baby Moses (Who made sure that Moses was safe?)
- Baby Jesus (Make a manger, with baby as above; use dry grass for hay)
- Jonah in the whale (Cut two adjacent cups from a Styrofoam egg carton, leaving them connected. Fold one over the other for the whale's body; glue on eyes, fins and tail; put a cutout of Jonah inside.)
- Lost sheep (Make a cotton ball sheep to place inside the basket as a reminder of this lesson.)

Arts and Crafts Activities

Egg Cup Characters
An application activity

Materials
- Egg cartons
- Styrofoam balls, 3/4-inch size
- Glue, markers
- Craft sticks (optional)

Activity
Students cut out a single eggcup, trim the open edges and invert to form the body of their Bible character. Glue a Styrofoam ball on top for the head, and make facial features with markers or yarn. Fashion clothing from scraps of cloth or tissue.

Hint
Glue a craft stick inside each eggcup and turn the character into a puppet. Each student in the class can make a different character from the story; retell the story with puppets.

Let's talk
Whom will you show your character to this week? What story will you tell about the character?
(*They practice telling the story.*)

Use with
- Birth of Jesus (Make an eggcup shepherd; glue a 4-inch pipe cleaner crook to his side.)
- Abraham and Melchizedek (The men wear flowing robes.)
- Birth of Jesus (Make Mary, Joseph, wise men and/or shepherds to go with the eggcup manger. See Eggcup Basket.)
- King Hezekiah
- Enoch

Egg Cup Flowers
A sharing activity

Materials
- Egg cartons (enough for 2-3 egg cups per child)
- Small pom-poms, buttons or beads
- Scissors, glue, hole punch
- Index cards
- Green construction paper
- Pipe cleaners

Activity
Cut an eggcup as shown to form the petals of a flower. (For a fuller look, nest two cups together.) Use a pencil to poke a small hole through the bottom of the cup. Insert the tip of a pipe cleaner through the hole and secure it with a rolled knot or with glue.
Glue pom-poms, buttons or beads in the center of each flower, and add construction paper leaves to the pipe cleaner stem. Write the lesson's message on an index card, punch a hole in it, and fasten the card to the flower's stem.

Let's talk
How can we use our flowers for worship? Do we have to be in church to worship?

Use with
- Jesus and the children
- Dorcas
- Bezaleel
- Jesus does good on the Sabbath

Arts and Crafts Activities

MISCELLANEOUS CRAFTS

The following crafts make great gifts that can be used for sharing Jesus or for other gift giving opportunities, such as: Mother's Day, Father's Day, baptisms, pastor appreciation, teacher appreciation, member appreciation, etc.

Antiqued Pencil Holder
A sharing activity

Materials
- Small jars (one per student)
- Masking tape
- Brown wax shoe polish
- Soft rags
- Spray shellac (optional)

Activity
Students cover the outer surface of the can with overlapping 1.5-inch pieces of masking tape. Rub the surface with brown shoe polish to bring up the grain of the tape. When the polish is dry, buff the surface with a soft dry cloth.

Let's talk
How might you use your pencil holder project to serve others and make friends for God?

Use with
- Jacob works for Rachel
- Jesus turns water to wine
- Jesus feeds the 5,000
- Esther saves her people

Bumper Sticker
A sharing activity

Materials:
- Construction paper or other heavy paper
- Pencils
- Glue or glitter glue
- Toothpicks or yarn (pre-cut latch-hook yarn works well)

Ahead
Bumper stickers give kids a chance to convey a short, pithy message without saying a word. While this project is not suitable for display on the outside of the family car, it may be posted in a window or hung on a wall or refrigerator.

Activity
Students cut a sheet of paper in half lengthwise. On one half of the paper, write in block letters a word or phrase that captures the main idea of the lesson, such as, "FRIENDS SHARE." Form the letters by gluing yarn or toothpicks in place.

Hint
Bumper stickers can also be made with crayon resist (see p. 24), or simply use markers, crayons, or glitter glue.

Let's talk
What can you do to cheer someone up with your bumper sticker?

Use with
- Moses grows up (Write: Praise the Lord!)
- Abraham pleads for Sodom (Write: Serving others)
- The Exodus (Write: God cares for me)
- Jesus and the Samaritans (Write: Jesus is my friend)
- The lost sheep (Write: Jesus found me)

Doorknob Hanger
A sharing activity

Materials
- Door hanger pattern (see Appendix A3) photocopied onto heavy paper, one per child
- Markers, glitter glue, stickers and trim (optional)

Activity
Students cut out a door hanger. Using glitter glue, crayons, or markers, they write a message, such as, "SERVICE ZONE!" and decorate it. They take it home to hang on the doorknob of their bedroom.

Let's talk
How can you make your bedroom a service zone?
A. By keeping it tidy?
B. By gladly helping anyone who asks for help there?
C. By sleeping in?
What kinds of service do you enjoy most?
A. Helping someone?
B. Doing the job by yourself when asked?
C. Surprising someone by doing something for them.

Use with
- The first Passover (Write: Praise Offered Here)
- God calls Abram (Write: Service Zone)
- Joshua meets the Captain (Write: Prayer Zone)
- Isaiah sees God's throne (Write: Forgiveness Found Here)
- The lost sheep (Write: Jesus Found Me)
- Cain and Abel (Write: PEACE)

see Appendix A3

First Place Award
An application activity

Materials
- Facial tissue
- Strong thread, glue
- Scissors, construction paper, a quarter
- 6" strips of blue construction paper
- Masking tape

Activity
To make the rosette, students cut one facial tissue in half along the fold line. Make half-inch accordion pleats in it, as shown. Pinch the tissue in the middle to tear in half. Lay both halves side by side and tie tightly with thread. Lightly glue the split edges together until you have an unbroken circle. Now tease the two layers of the tissue apart all the way around. Place the quarter on the construction paper and draw around it. Write "#1" inside the circle and cut it out. Glue the circle over the center of the rosette and the rosette to the top of the 6" strip, on which students will write, "God has first place." Add a loop of masking tape at the back so they can wear the rosette on their jacket or shirt.

Let's talk
Read Daniel 6:10. How do we know Daniel made God number 1? (He prayed so much that no matter what happened, he obeyed God.) What does it mean to make God number 1? (You do things His way; you do what is right even when you don't feel like it.)

Use with
- Daniel prays three times daily

Arts and Crafts Activities

Forgiveness Covers
An application activity

Materials
- 6-inch squares of aluminum foil, one per student
- 4-inch squares of cardboard, one per student
- Construction paper in bright colors
- Scissors and glue sticks

Activity
Students crumple the foil while the teacher talks about how we hurt each other. After repeating the memory verse, they smooth out the foil over the cardboard, as shown. They cut flower shapes from construction paper and tape them to the foil before covering the entire picture with the plastic wrap.

Let's talk
In what way is crumpling the foil like hurting a person? Saying sorry is like smoothing the foil. But what do you notice about the smoothed foil?

Use with
- Adam and Eve sin (God forgives but we still live with consequences. What were the consequences for Adam and Eve and for us?)
- Forgiving 70x7 (They work in pairs, smoothing each other's cover.)

Helpful Hand Reminder
An application activity

Materials
- Styrofoam plates or trays
- Yarn, glue
- Pencils, markers (test on surface—permanent markers work best on Styrofoam)

Activity
Students trace a pencil outline of their hand on the tray. In the center of their hand, write the memory verse or the message. Glue yarn around the hand outline.

Let's talk
Read Galatians 6:2. What things can you do with your hands to show people you care about them? What do you imagine Jesus' hands would have looked and felt like? Why?

Use with
- Lazarus' death and resurrection
- Rachel at the well (Write inside the hand, "Learning to Serve.")
- Naaman (Outline a large heart with yarn, lace, or rickrack; inside write, "Grace is for everyone.")
- Esther becomes queen (Outline a large crown by making a double M at the top, and without cutting the yarn, continue into a large circle that comes back to the beginning of the M; inside write "Chosen to Serve.")

18　　　　Arts and Crafts Activities

Paper Bag Baskets
An application activity

Materials
- Brown paper grocery sacks
- Scissors, stapler
- Crayons and stickers

Ahead
Challenge the students to fill the basket with like-new clothing and toys for Community Services or with socks for a homeless shelter.

Activity
Students trim the length of the bag halfway back to the desired height of the basket, and fold the sides down until the cut edge meets the base of the basket. Crease the fold to make a crisp edge. Make a handle from a 3-inch strip of the trim, folding down the edges of both sides so that they meet on the under side; tape or staple the handle to the center of the sides. Decorate the finished basket.

Let's talk
Now that you have made the basket, what do you want God to fill it with? Imagine that you are a basket; what does God want to fill your life with? (Happiness, cheerfulness, peace, love, etc.—all the things you cannot buy.)

Use with
- Elijah fed by ravens
- Resurrection

Pinwheel
An application activity

Materials
- 5x7-inch index cards (cut to 5-inch squares) or other heavy paper
- Scissors, ruler
- Pencils with new erasers
- Markers, thumb tacks, or pushpins

Activity
Using a ruler, students draw lines from corner to corner of the paper square. In each corner, make a dot to the left of the line, as shown. Cut each line 2 ½ inches from the corners—take care not to cut all the way to the middle! Use a thumbtack to poke a hole in the center, then decorate the paper and write the memory verse in the four sections as follows: *I will come back * and take you * to be with * me.* They add a sticker of Jesus in the fourth section. Finally, push the thumbtack through one of the corner dots and bend the paper so the pin is over the center. While holding it there, one by one, they bend each paper corner so the dot comes close enough for the pin to push through it. When all corners are on the thumbtack, push the pin through the center hole of the pinwheel and into the eraser of their pencil.

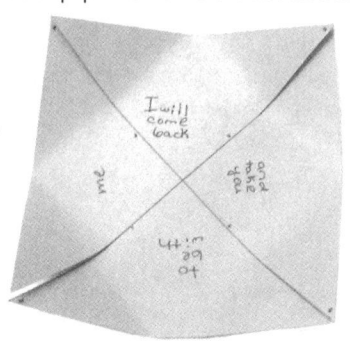

Let's talk
Repeat John 14:3 together. Whenever you blow on this pinwheel, what are you going to remember? (That Jesus is going to take us to be with Him.) What is good news about living with Him? (No death, no tears, no night, maybe even no bedtime.) How do you feel about a God like that?

Use with
- Death of Moses
- Creation of people (Write in the sections: *God * created * you * in His likeness.*) Put a Jesus sticker in the first section and a square of shiny foil in the third. Challenge them to remember this when they blow on the pinwheel.

Arts and Crafts Activities

Profile Silhouettes
A readiness activity

Materials
- Construction paper, 1 sheet each, in both black and white
- Scissors, pencil, glue
- A bright light

Activity
Students sit sideways between the light and their sheet of black paper while an adult draws their profile in pencil. They cut out the profile and glue it to the center of the white sheet. Underneath, they write the monthly theme: "We learn about God together."

Hint
Cut through two sheets of black paper; pin the extra profile on the bulletin board.

Let's talk
What did you learn from seeing each other's profile?

Use with
- Peter and John before the Sanhedrin
- Peter's Denial (We are God's family; He wants me in His family)

Scented Sachet
An application activity

Materials
- 4-inch squares of light cloth
- Cotton balls, vanilla extract
- Needles and thread for older students
- Narrow ribbon for younger students

Activity
Students dab some vanilla onto the cotton ball and place the cotton in the center of the cloth. Stitch a wide circle with large running stitches, removing the needle from the thread when done. Pull both ends of the thread together, pushing back the cloth. As the cloth starts gathering tighter, keep the cotton ball inside. When the thread is tight, tie the two ends into a knot. For younger children, gather up the corners of the cloth and tie them with the ribbon. They give it to someone in church whom they feel gets left out.

Let's talk
Have you ever been left out? Tell me about it. How does it feel to be left out? (Bad, like you don't have friends, etc.) How does God treat people who get left out? (He made Mary His best friend.)

Use with
- Mary anoints Jesus

Windsock
An application activity

Materials
- Heavy paper, string
- Stapler, masking tape, hole punch
- Crepe paper streamers of different colors

Ahead
A windsock is a tube of lightweight material, usually cloth, opened at both ends. It is hung to indicate wind direction. Windsocks make unique decorative items. With their connection to wind, they can be reminders of Creation day 2 or the Holy Spirit.

Activity
Children decorate a piece of heavy paper (8.5 x 14 inches) and tape or staple it into a tube shape. They choose and cut different colored streamers (about 36 inches long), then tape or staple them so they hang from the bottom of the tube. Reinforce the top of the tube with masking tape. Punch three holes in the top and tie string for a hanger.

Let's talk
What in today's lesson will our windsocks remind us of? (The wind and tongues of fire, the Holy Spirit, prayer.) What had the disciples been doing before they heard the wind? (Praying for the Holy Spirit to come.) What would the Spirit bring into our lives? (Power, comfort, guidance.)

Use with
- Rainbow promise
- The Sabbath in Genesis, Exodus (They take the windsock on their Sabbath walk.)
- Pentecost

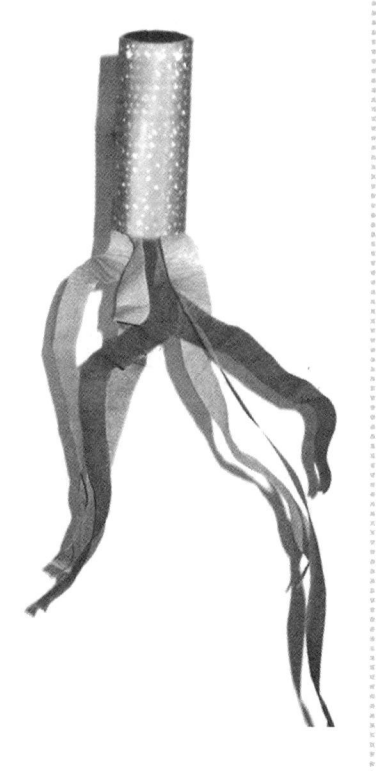

Word Pictures
An application activity

Materials:
- Typing paper
- Markers or crayons

Activity
Students write the word "LOOK" in large block letters that almost fill the page. Draw and color the face of David in the first "O," and the lion inside the second one. Children hold up their paper and say to each other, "Look! I can't save myself; Jesus saves me."

Let's talk
Read Psalms 23:1. Who looks out for us as if we were lambs? How does that make you feel knowing He looks after us?

Use with
- David the shepherd boy ("LOOK," with David and a lion)
- Jesus calls disciples ("FOLLOW," each letter with arms and legs as if following a sticker of Jesus they have placed to the right of the page.)
- Sabbath ("PRAY," with the P given kneeling legs and praying hands)
- Peter heals the lame man ("SHOW," with a picture of Jesus inside the O)
- Dedicating the temple ("WORSHIP," with the O made to look like our world)
- Esther gives a banquet ("COURAGE," with a picture of Esther inside the O)

Arts and Crafts Activities

Word Sculpture
An application activity

Materials
- Modeling clay or salt dough (recipe provided)
- Washable poster paint
- Clear varnish or shellac

Activity
Students roll the clay into fat tubes, bending and molding them to form the letters of their name. The letters stand upright on their own with no space between them. Set sculptures aside to dry.
The week after making name sculptures, paint them and spray with clear varnish for protection.

Let's talk
Just as Jesus' parents dedicated Him to God, many of you were dedicated by your parents and given a special name. What do you think are your parents' hopes for you? Read 2 Thessalonians 2:16. What things do you have to hope for because Jesus lived and died for you?

Use with
- Baby Jesus' dedication
- Sabbath (Sculpt the name, Sabbath)
- Jesus feeds the five thousand (Sculpt the name Jesus)
- Jesus heals a blind man (Jesus)

Salt Dough Recipe

Materials
1 c. salt   1 c. flour   1 T. alum
Water (enough to make dough workable consistency)
Shaped cookie cutter

Directions
Mix salt, flour, and alum. Add water until the mixture is the consistency of putty. Roll out dough to ¼ - ½" thickness. Cut out shaped cookie cutter. Allow to dry before painting.

Note: Ornaments may be made ahead of time. Children can then paint them and string the ribbon through the hole. Or this project may be completed on two separate occasions.

Yarn-Decorated Pencil Holder

Materials
- Empty juice or soda cans, clean and dry
- Yarn in assorted colors
- Scissors, clear tape
- Pencils, 2-3 per child, highlighters

Ahead
Completely remove the top of the can and check for smooth edges.

Activity
Students tape the end of the yarn to the can and then wind the yarn neatly around the can and over the tape until it is covered. To begin a new stripe, they cut the yarn they are working on and tuck it under the strands of their stripe. They then begin the second stripe as for the first. Continue making stripes until the can is completely covered. Give each child two or three pencils or highlighters to put in their pencil holder.

Let's talk
As you take this special pencil holder home what will it remind you to do? (To study their Bibles.) What will you use the pencils/markers for? (To mark special Bible verses.) Read Psalm 119:105.

Use with
- Josiah's revival

Arts and Crafts Activities

NATURE CRAFTS

All kinds of interesting and creative bric-a-brac can be made from natural materials. For long-lasting results, thoroughly wash and dry the materials and paint with lacquer, either before using them or after completing the project.

Seed Pod Pet

Materials
- Small pieces of poster board or cardboard
- Acorn caps, unshelled peanuts
- Plastic moveable eyes
- Glue

Activity
Students cut out modified heart shapes for the pet's feet, as shown. Glue the peanut to the feet with the widest end down. Glue on the eyes and the acorn cap. Work with a partner to make several pets.

Let's talk
How many pets did you and your partner make? How do you feel about working as a team? Read Philippians 1:27. In God's family we work together.

Use with
- Animals enter the ark
- The fall of Jericho
- Nehemiah rebuilds the temple

PAPER PLATE CRAFTS

A variety of simple crafts may be made using paper plates. These can be used as sharing activities to illustrate lesson stories or themes.

Children of the World
A readiness activity

Materials
- Paper plates, dessert size
- Scissors, crayons or markers, glue
- Scraps of yarn, cloth, buttons, etc.

Activity
Students draw and color a face in the middle of a paper plate, then cut a hat and collar from fabric scraps or construction paper to fit a specific nationality or culture (see illustrations).

Let's talk
What is the same about the faces you made? What is different? What does that tell you about people?

Use with
- The day of Pentecost
- Tower of Babel
- Use for mission emphasis

Arts and Crafts Activities

Resist Plate

Materials
- Paper plates
- White crayons
- Transparent water color
- Brushes, cup of water, saucer or lid

Activity
With a white or light-colored crayon, students write in the center of the plate, "Listen to God" and draw a picture of an ear. Paint the plate with a strong color so that the crayon stands out.

Let's talk
Read Isaiah 30:12. What in this activity is most like God's gentle voice? (The picture or the white crayon.) What kinds of things can we do today to help people hear God more clearly? (Be kind, cheerful; live a good life, etc.) Options: Use paper instead of a plate.

Use with
- God speaks to Elijah
- Saul's conversion

Mission Map
A readiness activity

Materials
- 8-inch paper plates, one per child
- Glue, scissors, markers or crayons
- Photocopies of a mission map
- Children of the world stickers

Ahead
See Appendix A4-A9 for a selection of mission maps. Additional maps are available at www.adventistmission.org.

Activity
Students color the bottom of the plate blue; cut out the map pattern and glue it to the plate. Glue children of the world stickers to the rim linking them with yarn or ribbon to their country on the map.

Let's talk
How many people are in your church? (They may guess in the hundreds.) Your church is bigger than the people who meet here; we worship God every week along with millions of members around the world.

Use with
- Solomon dedicates the temple
- Crowd worships Paul (Use the map of Paul's missionary journeys; draw his boat)
- Abraham's journey from Ur

see Appendix A4

Arts and Crafts Activities

Paper Plate Wreath
An application activity

Materials:
- 8-inch paper plates
- Scissors, glue
- Red and green construction paper
- Hole punch

Activity
Students write the memory verse in the center of a plate. Cut out about 20 holly leaves by folding a 3-inch rectangle of green construction paper in half; cut scallops as shown. Glue the leaves around the rim of the plate, overlapping slightly. Cut a red bow as shown and glue to the wreath. Cut small circles of red paper for berries; glue them in groups on the wreath.

Let's talk
Read Luke 2:17. The circle of the holly wreath never ends; it goes round and round. What Christmas gift goes on giving all year? (God's gift of Jesus, the gift of love.)

Use with
- Animals enter the ark
- The tower of Babel (Make wreath with multi-colored handprints)
- Shepherds tell the good news
- Creation (Make wreath with dry leaves, flowers, bark, pine cones, etc.)

PAINTING
Provide large sheets of paper and tempera paint, thick brushes and oversized shirts to cover their clothing and children will oblige with a picture of the Bible story. For best results, have the paint fairly thick and encourage the children to touch the brushes to the side of the paint pot to shed excess paint before touching brush to paper. For variations of painting, use sponges and other materials in place of brushes. Besides painting pictures, children can enjoy using paint in other creative ways. The following types of painting can be used either to make pictures or to decorate other crafts, greeting cards, gifts bags, gift wrap, and bookmarks.

Sponge Painting
An application activity

Materials
- Washable poster paint,
- Kitchen sponges, each cut into several pieces
- Black paper
- Trash bags or oversized shirts to protect clothing
- Optional paint brushes

Activity
Students make pictures of their Bible story using pieces of sponge to paint the background. Paint the people with either sponge or brushes.

Let's talk
Imagine that you are in your painting. Where would you be? Who would you be?

Use with
- Peter walks on water
- Birth of Jesus
- Bible lessons with water, storms, sunsets, sky, or hills
- Water from the rock
- Noah's ark rests

Arts and Crafts Activities

Traditional painting

Children paint as described above, creating pictures of the Bible story the way they imagine it to have been. If paint that is too watery runs down the paper, blot it with the edge of a paper towel. Let the paint dry and paint over.

Collage and paint

Children paint the picture, except the details they have problems with, such as faces, hands, feet, etc. These can be cut from magazine pictures and glued on.

Spatter painting

Rubbing a paint-filled toothbrush over a piece of fine mesh creates spatters of paint that fall on the paper below. The spatter can be given special meaning when a leaf or some other object is placed on the paper. After the paint dries and the object is removed, its silhouette remains.

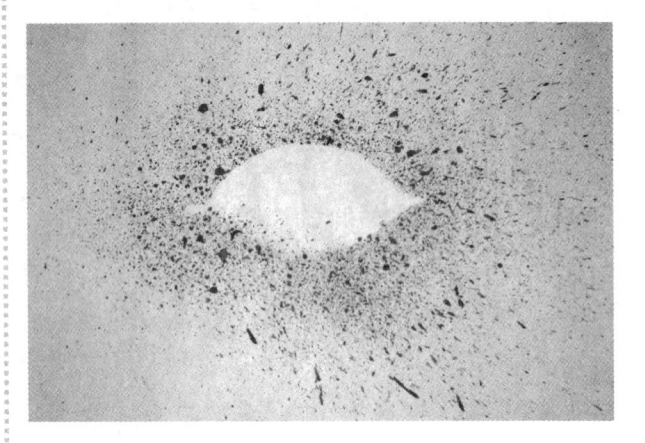

Stenciling

Stenciling is done by dabbing a short-haired, stubby brush into the paint and then touching it repeatedly to the paper. (Do not wipe the brush on the paper; use an up and down motion only.) To make a stencil, take a second piece of paper the same size as the piece on which the student is stenciling. Cut out a shape, such as a church, heart, cross, or crown; place the stencil over the paper and tape the edges before applying the paint with the stubby brush. A sponge can be used in place of the brush.

26   Arts and Crafts Activities

DRIBBLE
Take some latex house paint and dribble it from a coffee stirrer or a paintbrush. Dribble often looks like the paint equivalent of scribble. It can be used as a technique in its own right and as an alternative to prints or stencils.

Decorative Shoelaces
A sharing activity

Materials
- 2-3 bright colors of latex house paint
- Large trash bags or oversized shirts to protect clothing
- Stir sticks or paint brushes
- New, white shoelaces

Ahead
Ask each child to bring a pair of new, white shoelaces. Spread newspaper or garbage bags to protect furniture.

Activity
Students decorate a pair of shoelaces using one of the following techniques.

Drizzle design.
Lay a pair of laces side-by-side on several layers of protective newspaper. Dribble latex paint over the laces as described above.

Quick stripes.
Spiral the laces around a pencil, without any overlap. Tape both ends. Draw lines with a permanent marker, the length of the wrapping on the pencil, spacing the lines 1/4-inch apart. When unwrapped the lace appears striped.

Let's talk
Giving gifts is fun; to whom could you bring joy by giving the shoelaces you made? Whenever you see shoelaces, what will you remember?

Use with
- Angel visits Mary, Zechariah
- The Exodus (If you were in there, and if you were wearing tennis shoes, you would not need extra laces for your sneakers. Why not?)
- Peter escapes from prison (What was Peter wearing on his feet when released from prison? Read Acts 12:8.)

PAPIER-MACHÉ
Papier-maché is made by covering an object or frame with a thin layer of petroleum jelly before covering it with one-inch pieces of paper (or cloth) dipped in glue that has been diluted to a soupy consistency and placed in shallow bowls or pie pans for easy access. The paper pieces are criss-crossed and overlapped, building up three layers. The work is then left a week so the glue dries thoroughly and the object is easily removed from inside. The following Sabbath students paint the now hard papier-maché with colorful tempera paint and when the paint dries finish by painting with lacquer or shallac. This craft lends itself to making baskets, bowls, and other household ornaments that can be given as gifts. This craft can be messy, so provide oversized T-shirts to protect Sabbath clothes.

Papier Maché glue
Use any prepared glue; dilute with water until a soupy consistency. Pour into pie plates so students can drag their paper strips through it.

Cooked Flour & Water Glue
Start with one-third cup of white flour. Stir in cold water until the mixture reaches a soupy consistency. Add mixture to one quart of boiling water. Stir until the glue thickens. Allow to simmer 5 minutes. Pour into pie pans and allow to cool.

Balloon Basket
An application activity

Materials
- Round balloons, one per child
- Scraps of yarn, ribbon, pipe cleaner and string
- Glue, heavy paper

Ahead
Prepare papier maché glue.

Activity
Students blow up a balloon and tie it off (with adult help, if necessary). They cover the lower half of the balloon with strips of ribbon, yarn, and scraps of cloth. When the project is thoroughly dry, pop the balloon and peel it away. Trim the upper edge of the basket in a smooth or scalloped fashion. Form a circular base by stapling together the ends of a 1/2-inch-wide strip of construction paper. Squeeze glue along the top edge of the circle and set the basket on top.

Hint
Draw a line around the balloon to mark the top of the basket. Bring ribbon to this edge.

Let's talk
How could you use this basket to share today's Bible story with a friend?

Use with
- God sends manna (They can place paper in the basket and partly fill with dry cereal to look like manna.)
- Dorcas (How can you use your basket to help others this week?)
- Solomon builds the temple (How can you use your basket for worship at home? In church?)

Banquet Cups
An application activity

Materials
- Disposable plastic cups, one per child
- Petroleum jelly
- Newspaper, glue, scissors
- Yellow paint, optional gold spray paint
- Plastic "gems"

Ahead
Prepare the glue as described above.

Activity
Students cover their cups with papier-mâché and when dry, paint the cup yellow. A teacher can later spray-paint the cups with a touch of gold and/or cover them with shellac. Option: Glue on plastic "gems" or other decorations.

Let's talk
What stories might this cup tell had it been at Esther's banquet (Or in Rebecca's kitchen or in Abraham's backpack, or at Belshazzar's feast) ?

Use with
- Jacob and Esau reunited
- Abraham and Melchizedek
- Esther's banquet
- Belshazzar's feast

Arts and Crafts Activities

Bible Character Masks
An application activity

Materials
- 1" squares cut from newspaper
- Flour and water glue
- Balloons, one per child
- Poster paint, brushes, lacquer

Ahead
Prepare Cooked Flour and Water glue and let cool

Activity
Students make a mask that represents someone in the story. They blow up a balloon to about the size of a person's head and tie it off, with an adult's help, if necessary. They cover half the balloon with three layers of papier-mâché, adding extra layers to shape eyes, nose, and mouth. Allow the mask to dry. The following week, when the project is thoroughly dry, students pop their balloon and peel it away. Paint the mask and staple on hair or headgear. Staple a paint stir-stick to the bottom of the mask for a handle. These masks will take at least two weeks to finish. A teacher can lacquer the masks or spray them with shellac when the paint is dry and no students are around.

Let's talk
Are masks real? Why do we use them? (For pretending—to make it seem real.) Was Daniel's prayer life like a mask that he used—was it just pretend or was it real? And how do you know?

Use with
- Jacob and Rachel
- Daniel prays three times a day
- Esther

PICTURES
Children can make pictures in many creative ways besides the usual line drawings. These ideas can be used with different lessons and themes. Pictures make good sharing activities, bulletin board displays, and take-home reminders of the Bible lesson.

Collage pictures
Collage pictures are made by cutting out the various parts of the picture from magazines or newspapers and gluing them in place. The student completes the picture by drawing and/or painting the background and any missing elements. The elements within a collage picture, such as people, trees or houses, usually are not correctly proportioned or uniformly colored.

Crayon Resist
Crayon resist is done by covering a crayon picture with black crayon strokes and then scraping away the black in places so that the colors show. The scraping can form yet another picture.

Mosaic Pictures
Students combine small pieces of colored construction paper to form a picture, filling in any mass with pieces of the same color. Mosaics look great when the colored pieces are glued to black paper. The larger the background paper, the larger the pieces need to be. Use ½ inch pieces to fill an 8½ x11-inch sheet.

Tissue Pictures
Figures or shapes appropriate to the finished picture are cut from tissue paper of several different hues. The resulting pieces are overlapped and glued to the paper, creating additional shades and hues.

Tissue Picture
An application activity

Materials:
- Small sheets of construction paper
- Colored tissue paper
- Scissors, glue

Ahead
Cut the tissue paper in 4-inch and 2-inch shapes.

Activity
Students cut out shapes or use the tissue as is. They overlap the pieces to enrich the colors and finish by writing a caption suggested by the lesson message.

Let's talk
What happened when you overlapped the colors? What will you tell people about the Bible story when you share this artwork with them?

Use with
- Moses and the burning bush
- Ten bridesmaids
- Tree of Life

Touch Mosaic
An application activity

Materials
- Colored construction
- Glue sticks, scissors

Ahead
Cut 8-inch squares of black construction paper for each student.

Activity
Students use small pieces torn or cut from colored construction paper to form a word or a picture on the black paper. They lightly glue each piece in place, leaving a little black showing around each, for a stained glass look. Surround the design with a border made from paper pieces of a contrasting color.

Let's talk
Read Luke 2:10, 11. What reasons do you have to be joyful at Christmas? How is God's Word like a mosaic? (There are lots of pieces—each Bible story tells a piece of the story.)

Use with
- The first Sabbath (Make the word "JOY", or a picture of an angel)
- Simon carries the cross (Make three crosses)
- Angels speak to shepherds (Make an angel)
- Mary's song (Make the word Joy)

Pussy Willow Picture
An application activity

Materials
- Green or black construction paper
- Q-Tips or similar cotton swab sticks
- All-purpose glue, scissors

Activity
Students draw several stems on the paper and break or cut off cotton "buds" to glue, on alternating sides of each stem. Write the memory verse underneath.

Let's talk
Read Genesis 1:1. How do you feel when someone doesn't appreciate a gift you made for them? What are some created things that you want to thank God for?

Use with
- Creation
- Aaron's rod buds
- Any lesson that has a comforting memory verse

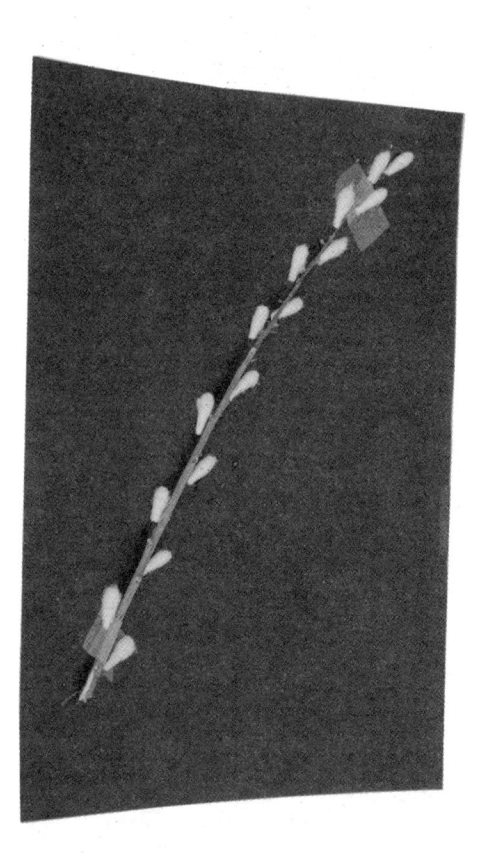

Seed Pictures
An application activity

Materials
- Variety of colored seeds and beans (e.g. popcorn, green/yellow split peas, pinto beans, red beans, sunflower seeds, rice, etc.)
- Construction paper
- All-purpose glue

Activity
Students draw a whale on a piece of construction paper and write the memory verse underneath. Cover the whale outline with a thin layer of glue and press seeds into the glue. If time allows, add waves and other details. Don't attempt to pick up the picture until the glue is dry.

Let's talk
Later, whenever Jonah smelled fish, what do you think he thought of?
1 John 1:9 (What lesson do you think Jonah learned from his experience?)

Use with
- Moses and the bush
- Cities of Refuge
- Jonah and the whale
- To the unknown God

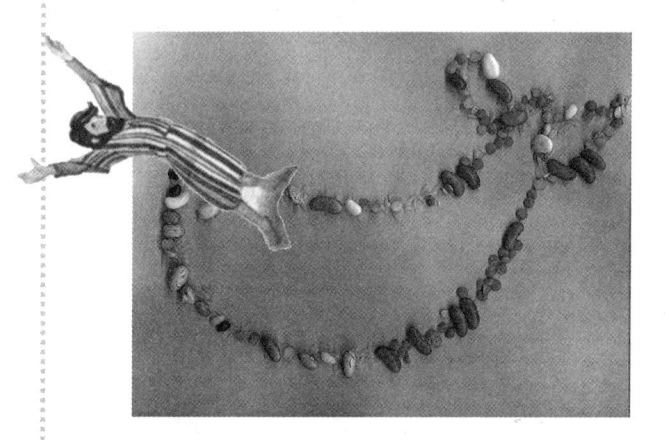

Arts and Crafts Activities

PRINTING

A print is made by dipping an object in tempera paint and pressing it on paper to leave a print. Primaries enjoy making repeated prints that form a border or a pattern to fill the page. Prints can be made of any one (or a mix) of the following: leaves, segments of fruit or vegetables, wadded paper, hands, thumbs, Christmas shaped or heart-shaped cookie cutters (the cutter print will be an outline only), shapes cut from sponge, felt pieces cut into a shape and glued to a small block of wood. Use prints to decorate wrapping paper, homemade book covers, greeting cards, bookmarks, or painter's caps, T-shirts, paper napkins and aprons. Provide protective gear, such as over-size T-shirts or garbage bags with holes cut for head and arms, to cover the student's clothing and newspaper to protect tables.

Potato print

Draw a large shape on the flat surface of a half potato. Using a plastic knife cut away the potato either outside the shape or inside it. Use the potato as if it were a rubber stamp and the paint, the stamp pad.

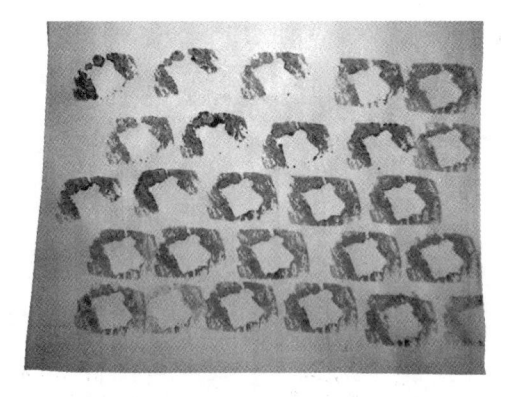

Vegetable prints

Print with cross sections of various vegetables, such as: celery, carrot, apple (wedge or half apple), orange wedge, pea pod, etc.

Apple Print Gift Bag
An application activity

Materials
- Paper bags (plain), one per child
- Apples cut in half, core removal optional
- Washable poster paint
- Shallow dish or plate, sponge
- Paintbrushes
- Large trash bags or oversized T-shirts to protect clothing

Activity
Students press an apple onto a paint-soaked sponge, then onto the paper bag. Print a row of apples across the top of the bag or make a cluster in the middle, refreshing the paint often. Use a paintbrush to draw seeds in the center of each apple and write "A Gift of Love" on the bag. Take the bag home to fill with non-perishable food items for a Thanksgiving food drive.

Let's talk
How do you feel about your creation? Think of someone you want to cheer up. What could you do with your bag to make a happy Thanksgiving (or Christmas) memory for that person?

Use with
- Any lesson prior to Thanksgiving, Easter, or Christmas

Arts and Crafts Activities

Leaf Print Poster
A sharing activity

Materials
- White construction paper
- Small leaves, such as ivy
- Tempera paint, green and purple
- Protection and clean up materials, listed above

Activity
Students write the memory verse in the center of their paper. Draw a winding border all the way around the paper about one inch from the edge and stamp a leaf at various intervals along the border. Add bunches of berries by dipping the eraser end of a pencil in purple or green paint; print in bunches. When the prints dry, take them home to share with a neighbor.

Let's talk
When you give away your poster, what will you say to share the lesson or memory verse?

Use with
- Any Communion Sabbath
- Worship in Heaven
- Parable of vineyard
- The Sabbath
- Onesimus (Cut the paper into a large heart; write, "Serve with your whole heart.")

YARN AND CAN
Ahead, wrap thick yarn around a can several times; space the yarn and glue it down with waterproof glue in wavy lines for effect. Roll the can on a paint-soaked sponge before rolling it over the paper. Refresh the paint when the print gets too light.

Tin Can Prints
An application activity

Materials
- Frozen juice cans, one per student
- Yarn, 18" per student
- White paper and index cards
- Dove template
- Washable tempera paint, sponge
- Glue, scissors

Ahead
Dilute blue or green paint to a soupy consistency in a pie pan or shallow bowl. Place a sponge in the paint, and turn it over for a fresh soak each time a child rolls their can on it. Copy templates from Appendix A11.

Activity
Students make the yarn print, rolling the can horizontally, and leave their work to dry. They draw the appropriate shape on an index card and cut it out. When the paint dries, they glue the cutout over the tin can print.

Let's talk
Read Matthew 3:17. Why did Jesus want to be baptized? He already belonged to God's family. (He wanted people to know it; He wanted to be a good example so that we would get baptized too.) How do you feel about belonging to God's family and being baptized?

Use with
- Jesus' baptism (dove)
- Angels visit the shepherds (angels)
- Jesus ascends to heaven (Jesus)

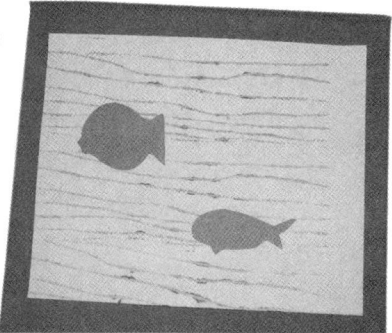

Arts and Crafts Activities

Yarn Print Card
A sharing activity

Materials
- Typing paper
- Wood blocks (2 x 2 inches or larger) or flat bowl
- Thick string, water-proof glue
- Red or pink tempera
- Markers, glitter glue, scissors
- Large trash bags or old T-shirts to protect clothing

Activity
Students glue the string onto the woodblock in a heart shape. While the glue dries, fold the typing paper in half twice. Inside write a loving message for a family member or friend. Decorate the card by stamping it with the woodblock. Give the card to a friend or neighbor as a reminder of God's love.

Let's talk
How do you feel when someone sends you a card? Why might you want to send cards to people? Who do you know who needs to know that you love them? What could you say when you give them the card?

Hint
Use a small flat-bottomed bowl instead of a wood block

Use with
- Creation (Write: "God is love")
- Use the week before Valentine's Day ("I love you")

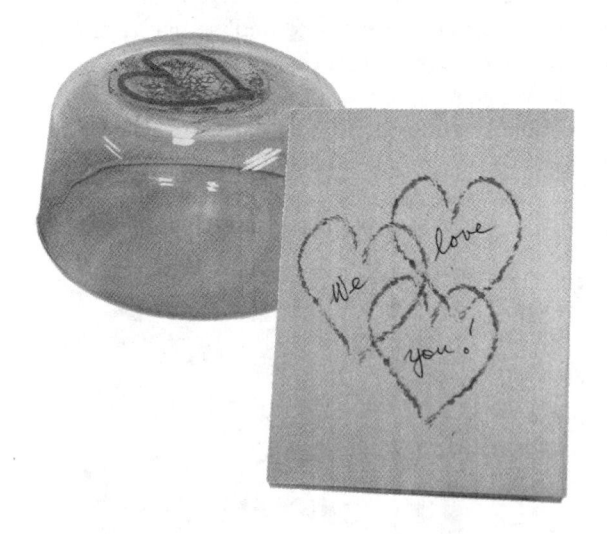

Hand Print Rainbow
An application activity

Materials
- Large sponges
- Tempera paint in green, yellow, orange, red, purple, and blue
- Pie pans, one for each color paint
- Banner paper
- Protective and clean up supplies

Ahead
Pour paint into the pans and place a sponge in each pan to soak up the paint. Draw on a large sheet of banner paper, a huge arch. Students will use this penciled arch as a guide when they lay down their hand prints.

Activity
Students press both hands in the green paint and then stamp them side by side on the paper, just above the arch to form a row of green. Repeat, making a row for each color of the rainbow, as shown. Small churches may want students to stamp their hands several times in each color, large churches, just once.

Let's talk
What did you like most about making our rainbow? What if we had only one color of paint in the rainbow? Which color do you like best? Which does God like?

Use with
- The rainbow promise
- Peter and Cornelius (Instead of rainbow colors, use flesh colors made of pudding: chocolate, chocolate and vanilla mixed, vanilla, and strawberry)
- Mordecai saves the king

Arts and Crafts Activities

WEAVING

Weaving crafts require some patience and skill as children work yarn, ribbon, paper strips, and/or string over and under a fixed set of strings to create a pattern. Weaving can illustrate how clothing was made in Bible times and it can create an interesting take-home reminder of the lesson theme.

How to weave

Tie the fixed strings to a tight frame of some kind or wind them around a stiff piece of cardboard. Thread a length of yarn/ribbon/string or paper strips over and under the fixed strings to create a line of weaving. Weave in reverse to make a second line, going under the strings that you went over in the previous line. Repeat lines 1, 2, tying another length of yarn or a strip of ribbon to the end of the yarn as it becomes shorter. Continue weaving until you reach the bottom of the frame or until time is up. Slip or cut the strings away from the frame and tape them behind the weaving.

We recommend limiting the weaving to six strings or bars, so that the project can be finished during class time.

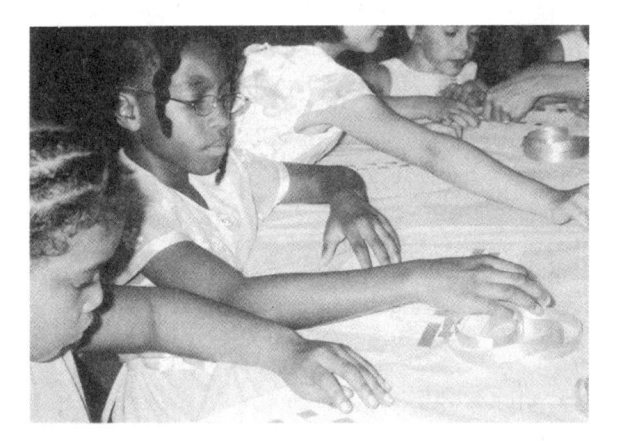

Board Weaving
An application activity

Materials
- 12-inch lengths of yarn in more than one color
- Styrofoam food trays or cardboard squares
- Scissors, tape
- Large paper clips

Activity

Students trim the edges from a Styrofoam tray so it lies flat. Make half-inch slits along the top and bottom edges as shown. Tie a knot in one end of a long piece of yarn and secure the knot in the first slit at the top, fastening it with tape. Take the yarn down to the slit directly below the first slit, and around the back of the tray to the second slit and back up to the top, as shown. The yarn winds back and forth from top to bottom as shown and is taped behind the last slit. Tying a fresh piece of yarn to a key or paper clip, they begin weaving, as described above. When one piece of yarn runs out, tie on a new piece in a different color, so the resulting weave will be multicolored, like Joseph's coat.

Let's talk

People in Bible times did their own weaving. How might they have shown love by their weaving?

Use with
- Joseph's coat
- Offerings build tabernacle
- Boy Samuel's coat

Arts and Crafts Activities

Fruit Basket Weave
A sharing activity

Materials
- Plastic strawberry baskets
- Assorted colors of yarn and ribbon

Ahead
Cut lid from basket and increase the length of the slits in the bottom.

Activity
Students cut 24-inch lengths of yarn, taping one end to make a "needle." They tie the other end of the yarn to the fruit basket and weave in and out through the holes until the basket is covered. Pour some dry breakfast cereal into the completed baskets to eat while debriefing the project.

Let's talk
How do you feel about the basket you made? This basket is for collecting good things that God gives you; what will you put in the basket?

Use with
- Lazarus' death & resurrection (What might have been in Lazarus's basket?)
- Manna in the wilderness (What kinds of good things had God given the Israelites?)

Ladder Weave
An application activity

Materials
- Recycled Styrofoam trays in which baked goods were packaged
- Blue construction paper
- White chalk or glitter glue
- Yellow yarn, scissors
- Table knife, tape

Activity
Students cut the construction paper to fit the inside of their tray, and draw angels with chalk or glitter glue on it, as shown. In the top center of the tray, cut a 1/2-inch slit and one on either side of it. Repeat on the bottom edge of the tray. Children slip one end of a piece of yellow yarn behind the left slit at the top of the tray, taping it down at the back. Pull the yarn down to the first slit at the bottom and then up to the center top slit and down to the center bottom; finally pull the yarn up through the center right slit and down to the lower right so that three lines of yarn are in place. Cut excess length from the yarn and tape the loose end behind the tray. Zigzag yellow yarn in a loose weave over and under the vertical strings of yarn, finishing by slipping the yarn into a slit and taping it at the back. Children glue their sheet of angel drawings inside the tray, underneath the ladder, so that it looks like angels going up and down the ladder.

Hint
Tie one end of the yarn for weaving to an old door key to make the weaving easier for younger children.

Let's talk
What if there really was a ladder that reached from here to heaven? What would you do with it? What was the most special thing about Jacob's ladder?

Use with
- Jacob's ladder

Place Mats
A sharing activity

Materials
- Construction paper
- Printed paper (gift wrapping, colorful magazine, or calendar pages), cut in 2-inch strips
- Scissors
- Glue

Activity
Students fold a sheet of construction paper in half and cut 6-7 slits through the fold to within 2-inches from the other end. (Don't rule lines first. And don't worry about spacing.) Open out the paper and weave picture strips over and under the slits. When the weaving is finished, cut two pieces of contact paper that are 1/2-inch larger than the place mat. Trim and glue down the ends of the strips.

Let's talk
What are you going to do with your place mat? How could you use it to share Jesus with a friend? (With parent's permission they might invite a child home and set their place with the placemat.)

Use with
- Paul's call to Macedonia
- Esther gives a banquet

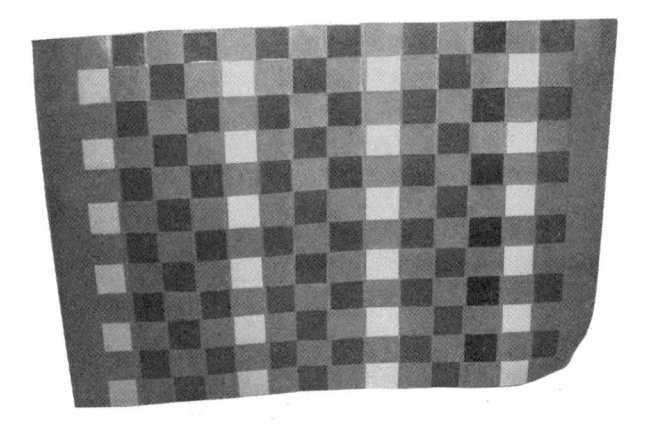

Language Related Activities

Primary age children vary widely in their language skills. More than half are functionally neither readers nor writers. They need teachers to set them up for success, by doing the following.

- Tell instead of expecting students to read directions or stories
- Assign activities in crews; groups of 2-5 children with a crew leader to assist
- Accept group responses and efforts, but allow also for individuals who prefer to work independently
- Pair readers with non-readers
- Accept responses given orally, or in pictures instead of in writing

ACROSTICS

Acrostics feature a key word or name that is written vertically down the left of the page. These letters now become the first letter of words or phrases, written horizontally. The words not only start with the given letters, but they are chosen because they tell something about the word or name written vertically. Sometimes the words and phrases are chosen to make a sentence. Read in order from the top, they make sense, helping to explain the key word. Acrostics like this are used as a review or sharing activity to reinforce the message.

Special Name Acrostic
A readiness activity

Materials
- Paper, pencil

Activity
Students write their names vertically on their paper and add words or phrases describing themselves, beginning with each letter of their name. Older children may choose words that make sense when read one after the other. When time is up they read their acrostics in groups.

Let's talk
How do you feel about your name? Today's Bible story tells about a person with a special name.

Use with
- Dedication of Jesus (Jesus)
- Esther (Esther or Mordecai)
- Any story with a main character new to the class.

B—Bursting with
E—Energy and
N—News of
J—Jesus
I—Invitation

Bible Character Acrostic
An application activity

Materials
- Pencil and paper

Activity
Students write the name of a Bible character from the day's lesson story. They then think of words that remind them of what the Bible character did in the story.

Let's talk
In what ways would you want to be like this Bible character? In what ways do you want to be different?

Use with
- Isaiah's vision of the temple
- James & John asking to be first
- Creation
- Gideon

I—Inspired
S—Surprised
A—Adores God
I—In vision
A—A prophet
H—Helps God

Lesson Theme Acrostic
An application activity

Materials
- Paper, pencil

Ahead
The teacher writes vertically the lesson theme word—grace, worship, community, service—or a more specific key word, such as trust, happiness, etc.

Activity
Students write the word down the left side of their paper. Then they make an acrostic of it. Younger students can work as a group, thinking up words with an adult's help; the adult writes them on the board. When time is up, children share their acrostics and tape them on the wall or bulletin board.

Let's talk
What did we learn about (*the key word*) from today's lesson? What did this activity teach us about God?

Use with
- Jesus welcomes the children (Keyword: Children)
- David shares the victory (Keyword: Winners)
- Philip and the Ethiopian (Keyword: Bible)
- Why we worship on Sabbath (Keyword: Sabbath)
- Moses' last words (Keyword: Moses)

G—God
R—Rescues me
A—And I
C—Cannot
E—Ever repay Him

Language Related Activities

BULLETIN BOARDS

Bulletin boards can make a major contribution to the décor of a room, keeping the lesson theme before the students and displaying their work. And in the case of the mail center, the bulletin board becomes a communication center for building a sense of community. Students enjoy having a part in putting together the bulletin board displays and will bring their parents to see it. Bulletin boards take effort; students will enjoy them for a month or more.

Tips for designing a bulletin board
- Use large colorful letters
- Make the background a darker color than the lettering
- Cut letters from felt and use them more than once
- Give your board a caption based on the lesson theme or message
- Keep the caption short and to the point
- If you need lettering on the sides of the board, keep the letters side-by-side, not one above another

Bulletin Board Mail Center
A project for readiness and prayer time

Materials
- Empty tissue boxes of various shapes and sizes
- Markers and decorative materials
- Thumb tacks or staples

Activity
Students bring empty tissue boxes to serve as personal mailboxes. Decorate the top of the box with their names, glitter glue, stickers, etc. The boxes are attached to the class bulletin board with their oval openings out. This bulletin board can function until students tire of it.

Hint
To inaugurate the mailboxes, teachers stuff the mailboxes with encouraging notes.

Let's talk
How do you feel when someone says something nice about you? When they say something bad? What kind of messages do we always want to write for the mailboxes?

Use with
- Peter escapes from prison
- As an ongoing activity, use the mailboxes to encourage students to affirm each other and share Jesus. You may also connect the mailboxes with class prayer time—students leave notes in someone's box requesting them to pray for something specific. The replies to such notes can be prayers or messages of encouragement and prayer promises.

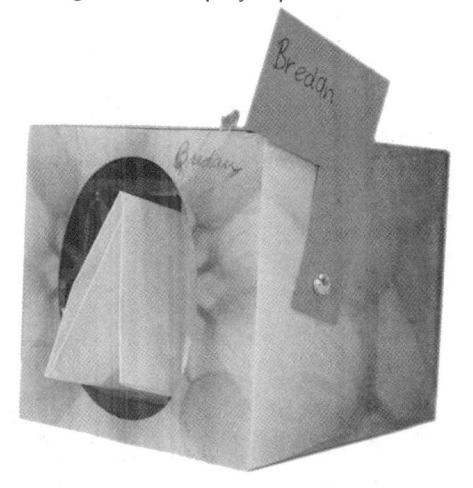

Language Related Activities

BulletinBoardDisplays
An ongoing activity

Materials
- Bulletin board or a wall space
- 4" bulletin board lettering
- Thumb tacks, pins, masking tape, etc.

Activity
Students make or collect display items suitable to the chosen theme topic, including news clippings, where appropriate. Some of the material they can collect from their family and from seniors in the congregation. Students mount and label the display items before attaching them to the bulletin board. Display a caption based on the lesson theme.

Hint
Put an invitation in the church bulletin for members to view the finished display.

Let's talk
Who brought this item? Tell us about it.

Use with
- Jonathan defeats the Philistines (Display winner ribbons, trophies, certificates)
- Creation (nature specimens and collections)
- Jesus serves his disciples (Caption: *We can serve like Jesus.* Feature photos of children involved in a service project)
- Spiritual gifts
- Moses at the Red Sea (Feature desert objects)
- Any prayer story
- Jonah story (Caption: *Don't tell God how big your storm is; tell the storm how big your God is.* Feature huge paper waves.)
- Peter & John before Sanhedrin (Caption: *We Learn About God Together.* Add student silhouettes)
- Peter's denial (Caption: *Wanted—in God's Family.* Use student photos or silhouettes.)

GREETING CARDS
Children can make greeting cards for almost any occasion in church life: baby dedications, baptisms, promotions, transfers, weddings, Mother's Day, Father's Day, etc. Cards can be a way to deliver affirmation, congratulations, friendship, get-well messages, invitations, and teacher appreciation. Make greeting cards from paper in any size, weight, and color. Older students can write their own simple message after talking about it. Younger children will copy a message from the white board. They decorate the cover in an art style chosen by the teacher, such as: collage, crayon drawing, crayon resist, sponge painting, basket weave (on cover only and with only 4-5 precut slits), mosaic, seed picture, yarn print, apple print, etc.

Baby Dedication Collage Card
A sharing activity

Materials:
- Typing paper
- Writing materials
- Used magazines
- Scissors, glue

Activity
Students fold the paper in half twice and write a simple message inside the card, such as, "Welcome Baby" and sign their name. On the cover they glue words and pictures relating to babies.

Let's talk
How do you think Jesus feels about babies? What in the Bible leads you to believe that?

Use with
- Jesus' dedication
- Any time there is to be a baby dedication at church
- Baby John (Adapt to make a welcome baby card.)

Language Related Activities

Drizzle Painting Invitations
A sharing activity

Materials:
- Construction paper
- Small tubs of poster paint, in at least three colors
- Coffee stirrers or Popsicle sticks
- Sponges, cut into 2-inch pieces
- Newspapers, paper towel, aprons to protect clothes

Ahead
Write: "You are invited" followed by the who? what? where? when? information for an imaginary event that someone in the Bible story might have organized, or for a real event your class is planning. Stir dribbles of water into the poster paint, as necessary to bring it to a soupy consistency.

Activity
Students fold the construction paper in half and copy the invitation message inside. When done, they close the card and decorate the cover by dipping the stick or stirrer in the paint and dribbling the paint over the card. They repeat to a lesser extent with a second color and follow up with just a blot or two of the third color. Leave to dry.

Let's talk
What have you learned from this activity? How can you use invitations to serve God?

Use with
- Parable of the wedding banquet
- Elijah on Mt. Carmel
- Priscilla and Aquila
- Josiah
- Any real event your class is planning

Leader Appreciation Card
A sharing activity

Materials
- Paper
- Writing materials
- Materials for chosen art work (see sidebar)

Activity
Students write a message to a church leader they appreciate, such as the pastor, a teacher, greeter, storyteller, or song leader. The message might begin, "Thank you for the way you ..." or "I like it when you ..."

Let's talk
How do you feel when someone appreciates you? How do you feel when you appreciate somebody else?

Hint
Work in groups on large cards for a leader in your conference. Mail the card to them.

Use with
- Crossing the Jordan (Appreciating leaders)
- Raising the widow of Nain's son (Appreciating Jesus, doctors, etc.)
- Mary anoints Jesus (Appreciating someone who works unnoticed)
- Deborah and Barak (Some leaders work unnoticed)
- Aaron's rod buds (Write to someone in authority.)

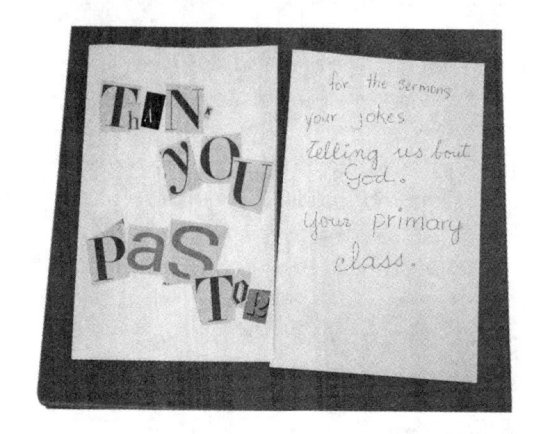

Language Related Activities

Grace Card
A sharing card

Materials
- Heart-shaped paper "lace" doily
- Pink and red construction paper
- Scraps of yarn and ribbon
- Scissors, glue

Activity
Students glue the doily to a piece of construction paper that is larger than the doily and trim the paper to one-half inch all the way around. From the other color of construction paper they cut a smaller heart to glue in the center of the doily. They tape yarn to hang like streamers from behind the doily. Finally, they place a Jesus sticker inside the smallest heart and write the word "GRACE" beneath it.

Let's talk
What do you want people to know when they see your heart? What do you hope they will ask you about? What could you reply?

Use with
- Crucifixion
- Saul's conversion
- Any grace story

Get-Well Card
A service activity

Materials
- Construction paper
- Markers/crayons
- Glitter glue

Ahead
Check with your pastor for names of sick or shut-in church members.

Activity
Students write a message or Bible text inside the card, sign it, and decorate it with the chosen art style. On the cover they might write "Get Well" in glitter glue. They either deliver the cards in person, or return them to a teacher for distribution.

Hint
Make get well cards as a readiness activity any week, building up a supply to use as needed.

Let's talk
For whom did you make your card? How do you hope they feel when they read it?

Use with
- Apostles heal and preach
- The Golden Calf
- Feed my sheep (Make a card for someone who needs cheering up.)
- Any time a class member is sick

Language Related Activities

KEY WORD ACTIVITIES

Key Word Activities are quick, time-filler activities that can reinforce the theme message of the Bible lesson. By focusing on one key word, the children also focus on the main point of the lesson and have something they can easily remember and share. The following will work for any keyword. When used as quick fillers, they need not be debriefed.

Key Word Pick
A listening activity

Materials
- Paper or construction paper
- Pencil/marker/glitter glue or toothpicks
- Invisible ink, optional

Activity
Students listen for what they consider to be the most important word in the lesson, such as "PRAISE," and write it with the materials provided. If using toothpicks, they may need to break some toothpicks in half but no smaller. When time is up they compare their choice of words.

Hint
Display their signed efforts on a wall or bulletin board.

Let's talk
Who will you share your key word with? What can you tell that person about your key word and about God?

Use with
- Cities of Refuge
- Belshazzar's feast (write with invisible ink)
- With any Bible story, any time attention is lagging

Key Word Bumpers
A sharing activity

Materials
- Typing paper divided in half, vertically
- Glue, yarn

Activity
Students make bumper stickers by writing the key word, such as "PRAY," with glue on their paper, pressing colored yarn over the glue, and decorating.

Hint
This works best with cursive writing. Younger children can print in lower case but join the letters with the yarn.

Let's talk
With whom will you share your key word today? Let's pray for that person now.

Use with
- Adam & Eve hide from God
- Finding a wife for Isaac
- Any time attention is lagging

Glitter Glue Keys
An application activity

Materials
- Construction paper
- Scissors, glitter glue

Activity
Students cut a large key from the construction paper and write the key word on it with glitter glue.

Let's talk
What in your life might this word be a key to:
1) Sleeping soundly, 2) Making friends, 3) Being happy, 4) Getting to know God, 5) Something else.

Use with
- Ten Bridesmaids (pray)
- Jacob makes peace with Esau (peace)
- Moses cannot enter Caanan (trust)
- Any time attention is lagging (class chooses keyword)

44   Language Related Activities

Calligraphy Keyword
An application activity

Materials
- 6" x 4" index cards, one per child
- Calligraphy pen, optional
- Markers

Activity
Students write the key word in decorative letters, adding a decorative border.

Let's talk
Where do you think God wants you to serve this coming week?

Use with
- Titus visits Corinth (Key word: either *willing* or *serve*)
- Mordecai saves the king (Key word: *accept* or *everyone*)
- Any lesson with a service theme (Look in the lesson message to find a key word.)

Willing Servant

ACCEPT EVERYONE

LETTERS AND NOTES
Letters are more formal messages than notes. Both have a salutation, a message, and a close, followed by the writer's signature. Children can write letters to God, to a friend or family member, or imaginary letters from one Bible character to another. Letters give children the opportunity to express their feelings or ask questions about the lesson. Younger children can draw a picture and tell what their letter says.

Hug-of-War
An application activity

Materials
- Note paper
- Pens/markers, stickers

Activity
Students think of ways they can support specific people in their church family with notes of appreciation and promise of their prayer support. They think of their message as a hug that they all give.

Hint
Students look in a community newspaper to find someone who lost a family member to violence of some kind.

Let's talk
How is this hug-of-war different from a tug-of-war? How might you team up with the person for whom you wrote your note?

Use with
- Water in the desert
- David the shepherd boy
- Peter's denial
- Any lesson with a community theme

Language Related Activities

EncouragementBlizzard
An application activity

Materials
- Note paper
- Pens/markers, stickers

Activity
Students write encouraging notes to each other. They share with the class the encouraging messages they receive.

Let's talk
How do you feel about receiving encouragement? What could we do to start a blizzard of encouragement?

Hint
Teachers also write notes so nobody is overlooked. Use in connection with the Mailbox Bulletin Board.

Use with
- Any lesson in February (Make them into Valentines)
- Apostles escape prison
- Speck & plank parable (To a person in their family who has irritated them)
- Steven & deacons
- Peter & Cornelius (To a person not a member of your church family)
- Cripple at Pool of Bethesda (To a leader in their church)

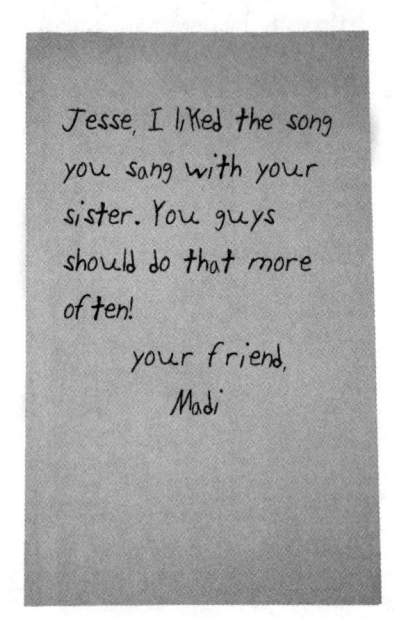

Bible Times Thanks
An application activity

Materials
- Construction paper or fancy note paper
- Pens/markers

Activity
Students fold the construction paper to form a card and write an imaginary thank-you note that a Bible character might have written to someone in the story. After reading their finished cards to the class, they display them on the bulletin board or wall.

Let's talk
People feel invisible and need to check in the mirror to see if they are really there when someone forgets to say, "Thank you." Whom do you need to thank this week?

Use with
- Animals enter the ark (Noah thanks a family member for a job well done)
- Josiah leads a celebration (Josiah thanks someone who helped with the celebration)
- Creation of man (They thank God for creating them and tell Him what they truly appreciate about themselves)
- Zacchaeus (A little boy in the crowd thanks Zacchaeus)
- Joseph and Potiphar's wife (God's letter to Joseph)

46   Language Related Activities

LISTS

Lists are a great way to get children imagining themselves in a situation or story. As organizers of an event or activity, for instance, they would list the tasks or materials needed. Lists are quick and generally fun to do and can stimulate children to think about the lesson story as if they were actually there. Lists can also be used to prioritize values, and for other purposes.

Event Lists
A readiness activity

Materials
- Paper, pencil

Activity
Students each think of 2-3 things they would need to do or organize in preparation for a big event, such as Communion, a wedding, a baby shower, or a party. They list these things on their paper or share them with a partner.

Hint
The point here is to help kids think in terms of serving, not to be practical or to remember everything.

Use with
- The Last Supper (List things needed for foot washing or Communion)
- Party on Sea of Glass (Things needed for a birthday party)
- Rahab & the spies (Things needed to pack an emergency kit)
- Solomon builds temple (Ways kids can help with a church building project)
- Raising the widow's son (What you have to do so God will love you more. Note: Nothing— because He already loves you extravagantly)
- The ten bridesmaids (List things needed to prepare for a wedding)

Growing Up Lists
A readiness activity

Materials
- Paper, pencil

Activity
Students list five things that they wanted for their fifth birthday and in a separate list, write the five things that they most want now. They then compare the two lists.

Let's talk
Were your two lists the same? Why are they different? Even adults need God to help them grow up and change their attitudes.

Use with
- Simon tries to buy power (List what they wanted and now want for Christmas)
- Finding Isaac a wife (Five things a child wants in a friend; five that Isaac may have wanted in a wife)
- God heals Hezekiah (List promises people made when you were little; promises you make to your parents now)
- The Sabbath (Favorite Sabbath things you did when little and now)
- Elisha and the borrowed axehead (List things little kids worry about; your worries now)

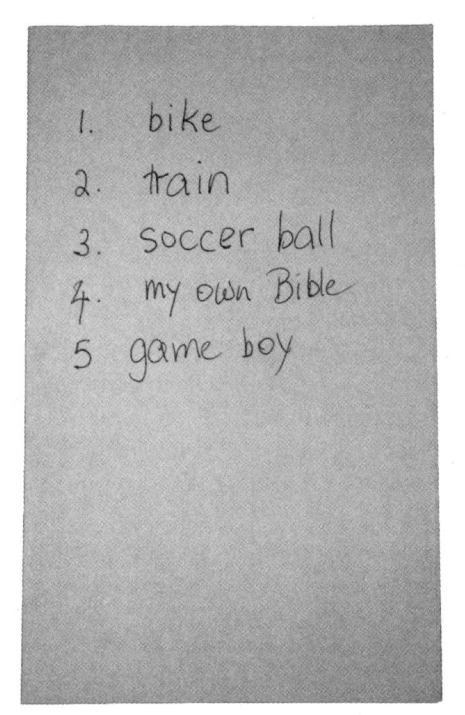

1. bike
2. train
3. soccer ball
4. my own Bible
5. game boy

Language Related Activities

Pay Day at Church
An application activity

Materials
- Photocopies of church pattern
- Pencils

Activity
Students list, inside the drawing of the church, all the expenses the church has to take care of (e.g. lights, heating, pastor's salary, etc). They read their lists and compile a "master list" on the board before discussing where their offerings go.

Let's talk
What can this activity teach us about ourselves? About our church? How does it feel when you give a generous offering?

see Appendix A10

Use with
- The wilderness sanctuary
- The magi worship with gifts (gift box outline, list the types of things that we give God; debrief: Giving at church is giving to Jesus)
- Abraham and Melchizedek (outline of a suitcase, list expenses involved with sending a missionary to China)
- Joseph becomes ruler of Egypt (outline of a crown; list things a ruler must be faithful with, talk about ways that God helps us to be faithful in giving)

Time Wasters
A readiness activity

Materials
- Paper, pencil

Activity
Students list things that waste time for somebody their age. They then list tips for saving time.

Let's talk
Many people say that they don't have time to read their Bible and pray every day; how could they make time?

Use with
- Enoch spends time with God
- Daniel prays anyway (Debrief: Giving God first place means giving Him time, too)
- Jesus spends time in prayer (Debrief: I have time to pray when I save time)

My Time Wasters
1. TV
2. Video games
3. Teasing Sister
4. Messy closet

48   Language Related Activities

MAGIC WRITING

Magic writing at first seems invisible, and only appears after a certain treatment has been applied. The fascination of seeing invisible words appear helps make the lesson theme or text memorable for children.

Invisible Ink recipes

Use straight lemon juice or milk (not quite as effective as the juice). When this ink is dry, iron the back of the paper or hold over a warm lamp or candle; the heat brings color to the ink.

Exotic alternative

Mix Cream of Tartar in water for the ink. When dry, brush the paper with wet sponge that has been dipped in water that has had violets soaking in it. Try this out ahead.

Egg Magic
An application activity

Materials
- White crayon
- White, hard-boiled eggs
- Pre-made dye (a cup of boiling water, a teaspoon of vinegar, and some food coloring)

Activity
Students write on their egg with white crayon and dip their eggs in the dye until the name appears.

Let's talk
What invisible things can people hide in their heart?

Use with
- Elijah fed by ravens (Write their name; debrief: Nobody knew where Elijah was, but he was in God's memory)
- The Easter story (Jesus' name; debrief: We hide God in our hearts)

Invisible Writing
An application activity

Materials
- Invisible ink (see sidebar)
- Toothpicks
- 6" square tissue paper

Activity
Students write a short message to someone in their group, using invisible ink on paper. Exchange papers and with teacher's supervision, apply heat or sponge as described in the sidebar.

Hint
If the toothpick fails to hold the "ink," bite the tip a couple times to soften the point, and try again.

Let's talk
What invisible messages about God do people write? (Their kind deeds show God's love.) Tell one kind of invisible message about God you want to send this week.

Use with
- Jesus heals a blind man
- Belshazzar's feast
- Elisha & the invisible army
- Paul's blindness healed

Language Related Activities

POETRY

Poetry has been popular since the beginning of human language because it makes ideas memorable and fun. Take advantage of the power of poetry and challenge primaries to create their own poems. Poems usually have four lines or more, with the last word of each line rhyming with the last word of another line. Rhyming lines often occur in pairs, one following the other, or as alternate lines. Another endearing characteristic of poetry is its rhythm. Making poetry is a great worship activity for sharing time.

Rhyming Stories
A sharing activity

Materials
- Paper, pencil

Activity
Students as a group, with adult help, choose a word that occurs a lot in the lesson, (such as "LOVE") and for which they can make a list of rhyming words (*above, dove*). They then try to make a 4-line verse using these rhyming words. They can say their poem together for the whole class.

Hint
This works best for primaries when you give them the first line and ask them to complete the second.

Use with
- The Good Samaritan
  *A bleeding man lies in the road
  On the way ....
  The priest and Levite, stare from above
  But the Samaritan gets down and....*
- Nicodemus
  *Nicodemus talked to Jesus at night;
  He wanted to get into heav'n.
  Jesus said he could... (rhyme with line 1)
  But first he must.... (rhyme with line 2)*

Bible Limericks
An application activity

Materials
- Display board, marker or chalk
- Pencil, paper

Ahead
The teacher writes on the board a sample limerick, as shown below.

Activity
Students read the limerick and notice that there are five lines; lines 1, 2, and 5 are longer and have the same rhythm and rhyme schemes. Lines 2 and 4 are short with a new rhyme scheme. Working together with adult help, students develop a limerick based on the Bible lesson.

Let's talk
With whom can you share your limerick? When someone tells you they like your limerick, what could you say to share God's love?

Use with
- Elijah on Mount Carmel
  *Elijah told the prophets of Baal
  Their prayers would certainly fail...*
- Creation of Man
  *When life on this earth first began
  God created a woman and man...*
- Feeding the 5,000
  *The crowd was so hungry that day
  As they heard what the Lord had to say...*

*God hears us whenever we pray.
Though everything looks cold and gray,
When we call to the Lord
And trust in His word,
He sends something to brighten our day!*

Language Related Activities

Write a Song
An application activity

Materials
- Display board, markers

Activity
Students, with the teacher's help, take a familiar carol or song, and write their own worshipful words for it. When the song is finished, they sing it together for the whole class.

Let's talk
How do you feel about our song? What makes it a worship song? How does God feel about our worship?

Use with
- Shepherds worship Jesus (*Tune: "Joy to the World"; first line: "Today a tiny babe is born."*)
- The Christmas story (*Song—"Silent Night," opening line: "Tiny babe, God's own Son."*)
- Jesus does good on Sabbath (*Song: "Sabbath is a Happy Day," first line: "Sabbath is a day for …."*)

POSTCARDS
Postcards are messages, brief and to the point, usually coming from a specific town or tourist attraction. Postcards may require students to check the Biblical setting in a Bible atlas, or they can draw from imagination. Students who do this as a readiness activity can share it their cards with the class at an appropriate stage in the telling of the Bible story.

Bible Postcard
A readiness activity

Materials
- 4" x 6" index cards or construction paper
- Markers or pens, crayons

Activity
Students draw on one side the Biblical location as they imagine it or as it appears in a Bible map or encyclopedia. On the other side they write a message that the Bible character in their lesson might have sent to a friend. For instance, Saul might have written to his friends back home, telling what happened on his journey to Damascus.

Let's talk
If we really could visit Bible lands, what would you most want to see? What would you bring back?

Use with
- Conversion of Saul (Saul's postcard from Damascus to friends in Jerusalem)
- Abram's journey from Ur (His postcard from Caanan)
- Solomon builds the temple (A slave's postcard home after attending the temple dedication)
- The Ascension of Jesus (John's postcard home from the Mount of Olives)

Language Related Activities

Mission Memories
A mission activity

Materials
- Index cards, 6x8-inch size
- Markers, pens
- *National Geographic* magazines

Ahead
Pick out magazines and newspaper articles relating to the countries being studied.

Activity
Students research material on a country featured in *Children's Mission*. They create a postcard featuring something special from that country and write an imaginary message from a missionary to that country.

Use With
- Any mission promotion

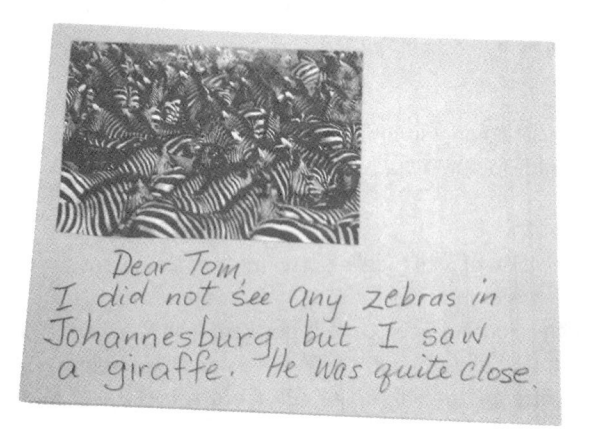

RECIPES
Recipes are step-by-step instructions, with ingredients and their measurements, for making a successful dish. Children can imitate a recipe-writing style to give their instructions for producing a desirable outcome, such as a happy family. Recipes that illustrate a concept are a good way to encourage children to think through an idea. Children's food recipes can be inaccurate, even wild in their measurements, but that is what adults find appealing. Choose one of the following ways to share the recipes:
- Gather the recipes into a little booklet to send home as a gift.
- Show them to the pastor; he might include some in the church bulletin.
- Make a bulletin board display of them, perhaps on a wall outside your classroom.

As with other creative writing projects, some children prefer to work alone, but others will work in groups with a crew leader's help.

Dear Tom,
I did not see any zebras in Johannesburg but I saw a giraffe. He was quite close.

Healthy Favorites
A readiness activity

Materials
- Paper, pencil

Activities
Students think of their favorite healthy foods and write out recipes for them, to be published in a collection titled, "We Give Thanks."

Hint
Resist the urge to edit student's recipes or to question the ingredients

Let's talk
How did you feel while you were writing your recipes? How do you think people will feel when they read them?

Use with
- Daniel and friends at the king's table (favorite healthy food)
- Manna (recipe for a food made with *Kellogg's Special K* or rice bubbles—manna may have been like cereal)
- Christmas (healthy Christmas recipes)

Recipe Writer
An application activity

Materials:
- Paper, pencil

Ahead
Read the sample recipe below so children get the idea.

Activity
Students write a recipe for something abstract, complete with ingredients, measurements, and how-to instructions, as for a food recipe. When they are done, read their recipes to the class.

Let's talk
How did you feel about writing your recipe? What do you hope people will learn about God from reading your recipe? What did you learn about yourself?

Use with
- The Crucifixion (Recipe for Living Forever)
- Simon carries the cross (Recipe for Carrying a Cross)
- Joshua meets the heavenly Captain (Recipe for Winning Battles)
- God heals Hezekiah (Recipe for An Answered Prayer for Healing)

Recipe for Happy Homes

You need happy adults
Growing kids
Sunshine
Fresh air
Mix all together for a long time with prayer and Bible stories.

Language Related Activities

Drama Activities

Drama activities, such as charades, clown skits, improvisation, and puppet plays help to bring the Bible lesson and theme alive for children. Drama can be used for readiness, telling the Bible story, or as an application scenario. Children can also prepare drama activities to share in church or as outreach to other children.

Choose drama activities that children can perform spontaneously without memorizing a script. Children who don't want to act in a drama may work "behind-the-scenes," making or storing costumes, manipulating props, or directing the production.

CHARADES

Charades require children to act out a word, phrase, or scene, while others try to guess what they are portraying. Charades help children remember Bible stories, think on their feet, and work as a team. This activity requires imagination but no extra materials.

Large classes
Divide the children so they do charades in groups of 6-10 and involve more children in the acting.

On Your Feet Charades
A review activity

Activity
Students, after hearing the Bible story, take turns acting out the role of various characters in the story so that others can guess which character was portrayed.

Let's talk
How do you feel about the character you portrayed? Are you like or unlike that character, and in what ways?

Use with
- Jesus serves the disciples (Roles: Jesus, John, Judas, Peter)
- Jairus' daughter (Roles: Jesus, Jairus, servant, the daughter, mourners, disciples; we are like the daughter)
- Jericho's walls (Roles: Joshua, priests, soldier, people, Rahab)
- The Good Samaritan (Roles: Samaritan, Levite, priest, inn keeper, victim)
- Any story that has multiple characters and a developed plot

Doing our Best Charades
A service application activity

Activity
Students take turns acting out tasks a character in the Bible story might have done, or they act out ways that they can serve at home or at school.

Let's talk
Why does God want us to learn to serve?

Use with
- Jacob's long service (Jacob's tasks: carry or feed lambs, shear sheep, lead the flocks to water, keep wolves away)
- Onesimus returns to Philemon (tasks of a slave, in the house or yard)
- Josiah leads a revival (tasks connected with encouraging priests and people to serve God)
- Boy Jesus (helping around home tasks)

Sabbath Charades
A worship sharing activity

Activity
Students act out things Jesus might do on Sabbath or things we can do to learn about or share God's love on Sabbath.

Let's talk
Ask about each charade: In what way is that worship? (*When we help people out of love for God, or when we look for evidences of the Creator outdoors, we are worshiping.*)

Use with
- Jesus does good on Sabbath
- Sabbath (Ways we can worship—at church, at home, in nature, visiting sick, etc)

Drama Activities

CLOWN MINISTRY

Clown ministry is a fun and attention-getting way to involve children in worship and Bible learning. Clown costumes and make-up can be simple or elaborate. Juniors, teens or adults may perform some of the activities that follow for the primary division. Primaries themselves might perform other activities. Clown activities may fit almost anywhere, if done thoughtfully, but consider the climate in your church before bringing clowns to the worship service.

Cleaning up for Jesus Skit
A readiness activity

Props
- A large garbage can
- Clean, paper trash
- A candle and matchbook
- Glass of water
- Bible with one live match inside

Ahead
Mess up the classroom with the garbage can tipped over and papers strewn about. Leave a box of matches and a candle within view of everyone.

Activity
Two clowns enter, see the mess, and enthusiastically pick up and fill the garbage can. Clowns then see the matchbook and start playing with it. They accidentally drop it in the glass of water. They fish it out and try to light it again. After a few, unsuccessful tries, they find the Bible and the dry match hidden in it; they light the candle and turning to leave, wave to students and staff.
–Copyright 1990. Floyd Shaffer. Used with permission.

Let's talk
What did the clowns just do for us? (They got the room ready.)

Use with
- Shepherds visit (Who felt better because of the shepherds' visit?)
- Shepherds spread Good News (What was the good news that the Shepherds spread?)
- Angel announcement (What is good news for you in the angel announcement?)

56   Drama Activities

Humor Clinic
A joyful readiness skit

Props
- Large signs, one each for Check Up Time, Chuckle Check, Merry Eye Test, and Tender Touch Test
- Stethoscope
- Black bag

Activity
A clown doctor enters with his black bag and waves a sign reading, "Check Up Time." When the children don't act overjoyed the clown draws in the air the shape of a smiling mouth and tries to get the kids to smile on cue. He then holds up a sign that reads, "Chuckle Check," and motions for a student to come up front. After shaking hands with the patient, the clown uses a toy stethoscope to listen to various body parts but forgets to attach it to his own ears first. Each time he moves the stethoscope he frowns because he hears nothing. Finally, he puts the stethoscope to the child's heart and to his own ears and breaks into exaggerated, silent laughter. He applauds the patient and gestures for her to return to her seat.

For the "Merry Eye Test," the clown points to a chart that reads: HE HA HO TEE, set out like an eye chart. The clown points to these words in any order, repeating some, such as HE HE, and getting the audience to say them faster and faster. He then applauds everyone. For the "Tender Touch Test," the clown has a student stand, extend arms, and give a back patting hug. Repeat with three or four willing volunteers. Finally, the clown checks his watch, grabs his bag and waves as he exits. –Copyright 1990. Floyd Shaffer. Used with permission.

Let's talk
How did the clown serve God today? Did he make you feel bitter or sweet?

Use with
- God creates the Sabbath (Does God want your Sabbath to be bitter or sweet?)
- Bitter waters made sweet
- Any time the weather is gloomy and kids need something to brighten their day

Gentle Hands
A service activity

Materials
- Clean towels, one each for clowns
- Basin
- Bible

Ahead
Place the towels, basin, and Bible on the front pew.

Activity
Several students dressed as clowns enter, each with smudges on their faces and pretending to have dirty hands, which they try to clean by rubbing them together. They stand facing the audience. The first clown points to a smudge on the next guy's face; he rubs it with his sleeve before asking the third clown if it's clean. Soon all are moving about and wiping their faces with their hands.

Another clown enters, picks up the open Bible, and motions for the clowns to sit on the front row. They try to, but none can bend their knees. They turn around and try repeatedly, even helping each other by pushing down on shoulders and slapping the backs of their knees. The leader scratches his head, trying to figure out what the problem is. Then noticing they all have dirty hands, he fetches the basin, pretending there is water in it, and tenderly cleans their hands with the towel, which he keeps dipping in the basin and wringing out. After showing their clean hands, the clowns are all able to sit. The clown with the towel gently folds it and puts the basin aside. Then all clowns get up and disperse around the room, for two minutes wiping hands and gently patting them. –Copyright 1990. Floyd Shaffer. Used with permission.

Let's talk
How did one clown's act of service help the other clowns worship? Was anyone left out? What can we learn from this?

Use with
- Mary washes Jesus' feet
- Jesus serves the disciples
- The older children could practice this and do it for the children's lesson at the start of the service on Communion Sabbath

Drama Activities

Model Servants
A greeting activity

Activity
Clowns greet children at the door and perform little acts of service for the children: escort them to their seats, help them find materials for the first activity, offer tissue to child needing one, pat heads, straighten ties, etc. They might throw out balloons before they leave.

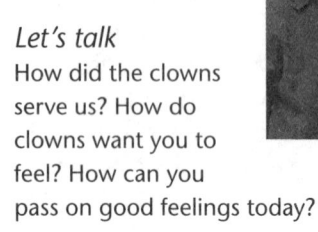

Let's talk
How did the clowns serve us? How do clowns want you to feel? How can you pass on good feelings today?

Use with
- Paul writes to Timothy
- Crowd tries to worship Paul, Barnabas
- Seven deacons
- Apostles healing in the streets

Awards Ceremony
A readiness activity

Props
- Fake certificates
- Costumes for clown
- A series of posters, described below
- Ribbons or award certificates
- Promotion certificates

Activity
On promotion Sabbath, students watch as the clown holds up a poster that says "Awards Time" and claps hands motioning that the applause is for them. He then holds up a poster that reads "Best Smile". He then demonstrates his own smile and encourages the children to compete with their smiles. (She awards a ribbon or certificate to a child who is trying hard to smile.) Other awards might include: Most Athletic (tossing/dropping a ball); Most Intelligent (reading a book upside down); Best Dancer (tries to dance and trips over own feet). After the "clown awards" have been given out, give promotion certificates and hugs to children. –Copyright 1990. Floyd Shaffer. Used with permission.

Let's talk
You have grown so big that we have real certificates that say you successfully completed Primary. Thank you for sharing Jesus with us.

Use with
- Promotion Sabbath
- Heaven (The clown certificates are fake, to make us feel good. But God's award is heaven—and it's real; it's God's way of saying, "Thank you for being My child.")

Clown Birthday Card
Birthday device

Props
- Two inflated balloons
- Large poster board birthday card cover

Ahead
Make a giant birthday card on poster board, as shown. Cut a large neck hole near the top of the card for the clown to put his head through and another near the bottom for his left hand.

Activity
The clown enters, holding the poster board with his right hand. His head and left hand poke through the holes. The left hand clutches two balloons. He sings "Happy Birthday" as he enters. When the birthday child comes up, the clown gives him one of the balloons. If there are other birthday children, the clown will come out again, celebrating for just one child at a time as the program progresses. –Copyright 1990. Floyd Shaffer. Used with permission.

Hint
Adapt this activity so that sometimes a Bible character or angel or a teacher in a huge doggie costume brings out the card.

Let's talk (to God)
Pray for each birthday child separately; the clown assumes an attitude of prayer.

Use with
- Children's birthday celebrations at VBS or Children's Church.

COSTUMES
Students can make many simple Bible-times or mission costumes and accessories out of everyday materials. Making costumes and dressing up in them is done as a readiness activity. The children wearing the costumes will help act out the Bible story or mission emphasis at the appropriate place in the program. Keep the best of the costumes for future use.

African "Man Cloth"
A mission activity

Materials
- 12 yards of white or brightly printed cloth
- Scissors

Ahead
Cut the cloth in half, so you have two 6-yard lengths. Open them out and with right sides together, stitch them together so you have one 6-foot piece of double width. Hem any raw edges.

Activity
Students drape the cloth over a boy's left shoulder so the end in front reaches his knees. They drape the rest of the cloth around his back and under his right arm, across the front and over the left shoulder, leaving his left arm covered with fabric. Pick up the lower hem of the fabric covering his arm, and bring it up to his shoulder. (This has the effect of folding the arm fabric in half.) Most men do not pin or tuck the end in, but hold it with their hand or arm.

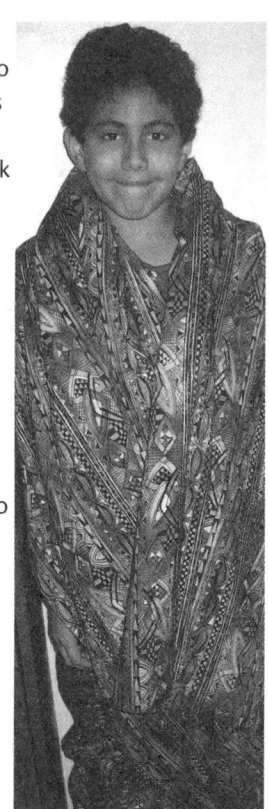

Drama Activities

African Women's Costume
A mission activity

Materials
- 8 yards of bold cotton print
- Scissors

Ahead
Measure and cut a 6-yard length of cloth and hem the raw edges. Cut the remaining yardage in half, lengthwise and hem.

Activity
Students wrap the large piece around one of the girls, tucking in the loose end at the waist to form a skirt. Then wrap one of the remaining pieces under the arms, tucking it in under the left arm, to form an apron. Wrap the head with the last piece.

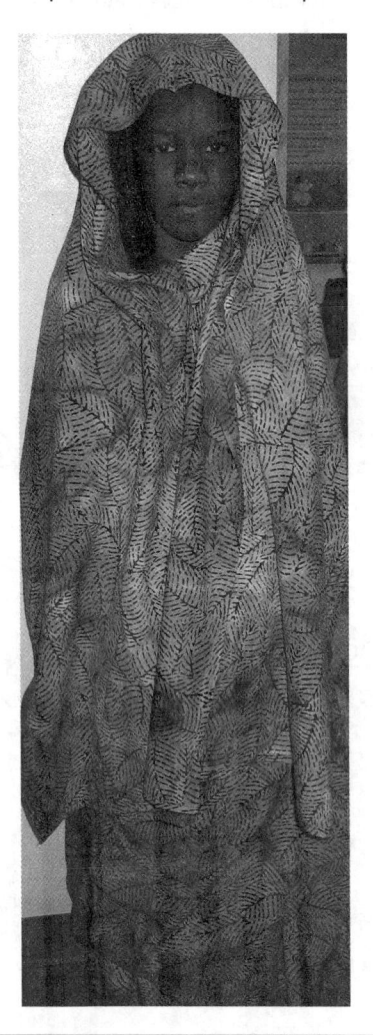

Angel Wings
A readiness activity

Materials (per angel)
- Two wire coat hangers
- Two nylon stockings, bleached white
- Masking tape
- Safety pins
- Angel hair or feathers (optional)

Activity
Students cut the legs off the hose and overlap the hangers so that the necks align, with the hooks inside the triangle of the other hanger. They bind the necks with masking tape, stretch the hose over the coat hangers, and tie the open ends together. (Optional: decorate the wings with angel hair or feathers.) Use safety pins to attach the wings to the child's clothing.

Let's talk
What do you think real angel wings feel like?

Use with
- Jesus' Resurrection
- Heaven
- At Jesus' tomb
- Angels' message

Drama Activities

Sheepy Head
A readiness activity

Materials
- Old baseball hats
- Cotton balls
- Scissors, glue
- Large, moveable eyes (optional)
- Black construction paper, white typing paper

Ahead
Ask families to donate old child-size baseball hats.

Activity
Students make sheep caps by gluing cotton balls to the baseball caps. They add round, black eyes just above the bill of the cap, and glue a 3x5-inch, black or brown nose to the bill. Attach 3x6-inch, floppy ears, under the rim on either side.

Let's talk
The Bible often calls God's people "sheep." We know that sheep wander and get lost easily. They also need a lot of care so they get green grass to eat, clear, calm water to drink, and time to rest. Why, do you think, God calls his people sheep?

Use with
- Shepherd's story
- Sheep and goats

Jericho Armor
A readiness activity

Materials
- Fruit trays, ask at grocery store
- Felt pieces
- Plastic bags
- Aluminum foil, masking tape

Activity
Children work together to create a suit of armor and dress a volunteer in it. For the headband, join a strip of brown felt 3 inches wide. For the coat of mail, two fruit trays forming front and back are joined by a pair of 7x3-inch brown felt shoulder straps. For durability, the back of the trays—the side with round depressions—can be glued to a flat piece of brown felt. The shield consists of a single fruit tray with the corner depressions trimmed off and a stiff paper handle taped or glued to the back.

Let's talk
How strong would you be wearing this armor?
If God were fighting alongside you, how strong would you be then?

Use with
- The Crucifixion
- Fall of Jericho
- Any lesson that requires a soldier
- Spiritual armor

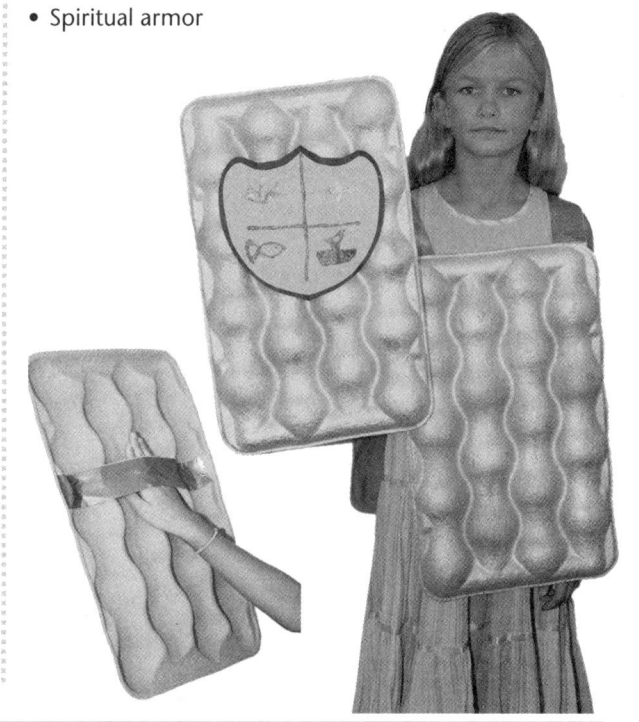

Drama Activities

Bible Times Robe
An adult project

Materials
- Cloth, 5x3-feet
- 2 yards of rickrack trim
- Scissors, sewing machine

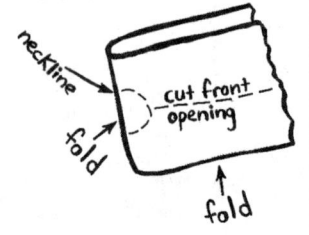

Ahead
Iron out any creases in the cloth, but leave the cloth folded. Bring the two raw edges together, folding the cloth in two (there will be four thicknesses). Cut out the neckline. Open out the cloth to one thickness and cut from the front hem up to the neckline to create the front opening. Trim the entire opening with rickrack. Turn up a hem at bottom and stitch it.

Use with
- Any Bible times man. Wear over a tunic or a loose T-shirt or over their regular clothes. For a laborer or disciple, tie a belt over the robe.

Bible Times Robe
Student project

Materials
- A king-size pillow slip
- Scissors
- Fabric Glue
- Rickrack trim

Ahead
Fold the pillow slip in half, lengthwise, and iron the fold. Students cut out a quarter circle from a point 3-inches down the ironed fold to a point 4-inches along the shoulder seam. They open out the pillow slip and cut up the ironed front fold from the bottom to the neck. They trim off the side seams from the shoulder down by 6-8 inches. They glue the rickrack all the way around the front opening and neck. When the glue is dry, they wear the robe over a tunic, with or without a belt.

Use with
- Any Bible story requiring people

Bible Times Belt
A readiness activity

Materials
- Colorful cloth, 1.5 yards
- Scissors

Ahead
Cut the cloth lengthwise into 30" strips; finish the lengthwise raw edges with zigzag stitching.

Activity
Students cut a fringe or fray both ends of the belt; they may make stripes with fabric paint above the fringed ends.

Use with
- The robes or dresses, tying them at the waist

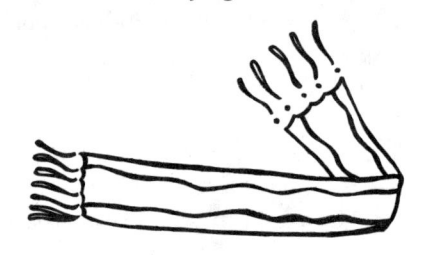

Girl's Headband
A readiness activity

Materials
- Wide ribbon, 24-inches long
- Scissors
- Glitter glue

Activity
Students trim the ends of the ribbon to make a V shape. They then decorate the center of the ribbon with glitter glue and let it dry. The ribbon is worn low across the forehead and tied at the back of the head.

Hint
Headbands can also be made by folding a scarf in half diagonally. Fold the long edge back 2 inches again and again until the scarf is reduced to a band.

Drama Activities

Bible Times Tunic
A readiness activity

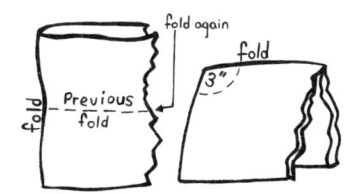

Materials
- 1 yard of 36" wide fabric
- Scissors

Activity
Students open out the cloth and fold it in half twice, They cut out a 3-inch quarter circle on the fold. If the opening is too small, trim an additional ½ " around the neck. Wear with a twisted yarn belt, under a robe.

Twisted Yarn Belt
A readiness activity

Materials
- Colored yarn, four 50-inch lengths per student

Activity
Students pair up and make one belt at a time. They each hold one end of the yarn and stand apart far enough that the yarn is straight. They each then tie a knot in their end of the yarn and begin twisting the yarn in a clockwise direction. When the yarn is twisted tightly, a third person holds the center of the yarn while the pair move side-by-side. The third person slowly walks toward the pair, and the yarn, as it slackens, twists together into a cord. Make new knots 3-inches from either end and trim. Comb the loose ends to make a tassel. Repeat for the second cord.

Let's talk
What happened when you stood side-by-side? How is the cord different from the yarn you started with?

Note
The picture shows just one strand twisted. Twisting four strands together will be more spectacular.

Use with
- The Trinity (Use only 3 lengths of yarn, each of a different color, to illustrate our three-in-one God.)
- Wear as a belt over Bible times robes or tunics

High Priest Costume
A teacher project

Materials
- Blue or white pillowcase
- 1/2 yard blue cotton cloth
- 2 large buttons
- 12 medium buttons of various colors
- Gold braid or yellow yarn
- Scissors, sewing essentials

Activity
EPHOD:
cut a neck opening from the closed end of the pillowcase. Trim off the sides to make armholes and slit the lower side seams. Add an 8" or 10" band of blue cotton cloth to the open edge of the pillowcase to lengthen the ephod. Cut a 5" fringe around the bottom of the band and knot each strip of fringe to look like tassels.

BREASTPLATE:
cut two 10" squares. With right sides together, stitch around 3 sides of the square, 1/2" from the edges. Trim the seams to 1/4" and turn inside out, pressing the seams flat and turning in the edge of the fourth side of the square. Press the edges, then stitch along the folded edge, through both thicknesses. Trim with braid and add buttons. The high priest wore the ephod over his robe and the breastplate over that. Tie the yarn in back to keep the breastplate in place.

Use with
- Stories involving the tabernacle or temple
- Stories about Aaron, the priest
- The Good Samaritan

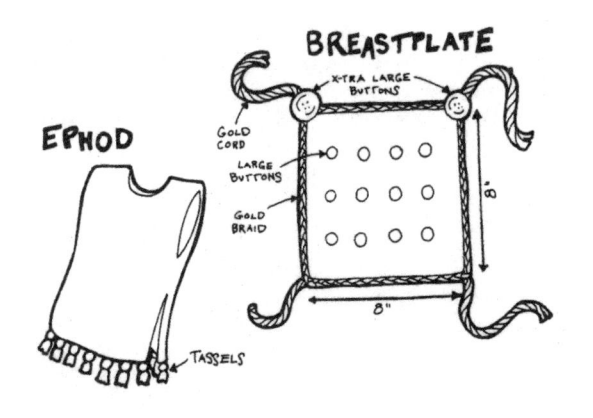

Drama Activities

IMPROVISATION

Improvisation is acting out a story or scene without scripts, costumes, practice or props. This kind of spur-of-the-moment acting is fun for children because it's fresh and spontaneous. Nobody expects perfection when you haven't had time to practice. Improvisation has the advantage of getting children to imagine they are there in the Bible story. Later, they will remember details that were improvised as if they were really there. The following improvisation activities can be used to illustrate a lesson story or idea. They work well during the Bible lesson, or afterwards as an application activity.

Bible Treasure Box Mime
A story review activity

Activity
The class sits in a circle while the teacher pretends to hold an imaginary box. He pretends to take out an object, miming the object's shape, size, weight, etc. and admiring its shape and brilliance (if any). He then passes the object to the person on his right who likewise admires it and passes it on. When a student guesses correctly what the object is, the teacher passes the box to that person to take out the next treasure. Keep the game going until time is up or until the class runs out of objects to mime.

Use with
- The golden calf
- The 12 spies
- Finding a wife for Isaac
- Praise for Red Sea deliverance

Live Statues
An application activity

Activity
A student "sculptor" shapes the other students into live statues to represent the characters in a scene from the Bible story. Without speaking a word, the sculptor places students in position and raises or lowers their arms, tilts or turns their heads, and tweaks facial expressions to match the character and situation being portrayed. The students respond to the light pressure of their "sculptor," holding their positions until the desired effect is achieved.

Hint
Photograph the group for the bulletin board. Large churches divide into groups of 8-10, each group with its own sculptor.

Let's talk
What might God want to sculpt with our lives?

Use with
- The Transfiguration (Characters: Peter, James, John, Jesus, Moses, Elijah)
- Jesus calls Matthew the tax collector (Characters: Jesus and disciples)
- Raising the widow of Nain's son (Jesus, disciples, widow, son, mourners)
- The Second Coming (Sculpt scene of people reacting to the appearance of Jesus in clouds)
- Jonah and the gourd (Jonah, the vine, the sun, the wind, the waves on the shore)

Mirror Image
A readiness activity

Activity
Students stand facing a partner. The child, taking the role of leader, moves hands, face, and body in a variety of patterns, while the other student tries to mirror every move the leader makes. After 45 seconds, switch and let the other child be the leader.

Let's talk
Is it easier to lead or to follow the leader? When does God want you to be a leader? When does He want you to be a good follower?

Use with
- Deborah and Barak
- Disciples prepare to serve
- Crossing the Jordan (By being good followers, we can help God's leaders)
- Joseph made ruler of Egypt

Setting the Scene
An interactive storytelling activity

Activity
As the teacher sets the scene for the Bible story, the children take turns improvising the props she refers to. For instance, if she refers to a cooking fire, a student places the wood, lights a match, blows or fans the flame, and warms his hands.

Let's talk
What did you see, hear, or feel in this story?

Use with
- Jeremiah visits a potter
- Esther's banquet (Examples: the banquet table, the golden pillar supporting the high roof, the couches, the platters of food, etc.)
- Samson

Drama Activities

Animal Sculptures
A readiness activity

Activity
Students, in groups of 4-5, work together to imitate an animal assigned them. The object is for them to show the way it looks, not the way it sounds. Students practice first before showing their animal to the whole class. (*Small class*: Children take turns organizing everyone to form their animal.)

Hint
Animals to form: elephant, porcupine, centipede, kangaroo, cheetah, scorpion, rabbit.

Let's talk
What happened in this activity? Was it easy? Why or why not? What did you learn about working together from this activity?

Use with
- The first Sabbath (Form the animals Adam and Eve saw on their Sabbath walk.)
- Animals come to the ark
- Tree of life (Animals that come to rest in the shade of the tree.)

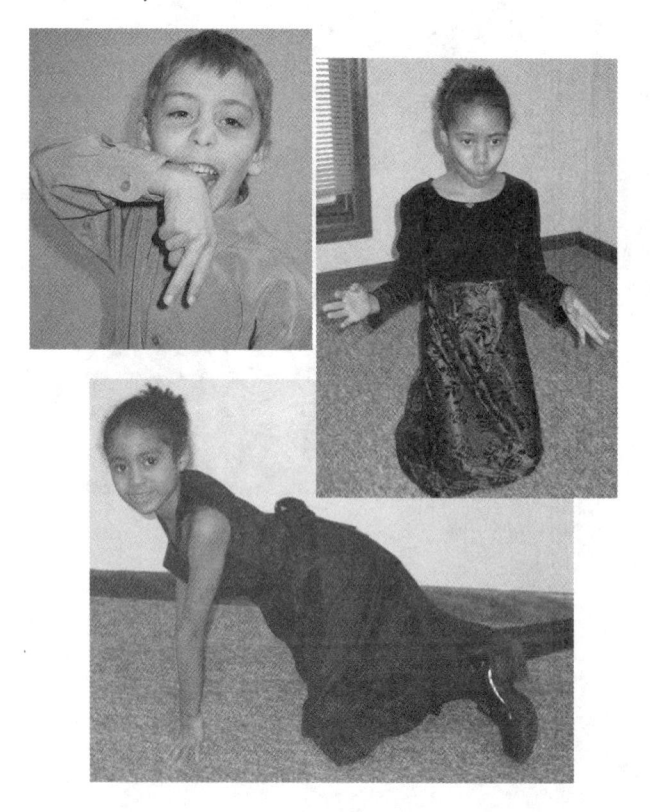

INTERACTIVE STORIES
Interactive storytelling involves children in the Bible story by giving them an action to do or sound effects to make during the story. This kind of storytelling motivates children to listen and participate in the story. When done well, the children imagine that they are there in Bible times, hearing and seeing the event.

Key Word Echoes
A storytelling activity

Ahead
Choose some key words that will occur often in the story and practice telling the story so that the words occur often enough to keep the children involved.

Activity
The teacher tells students which words to listen for and what to do or say when they hear the words. Students listen; when they hear the words, everyone makes the prearranged response.

Use with
- Daniel and friends refuse king's food (words: *king's food* [response-"Yuk" and motion to push it away]; *vegetables, lentils or fruit* [smack lips noisily]; *Daniel* [gesture of praise while saying, "Yea! God's man!"])
- Jonathan's victory (*Jonathan* [gesture of support while saying, "Go, Jonathan!"]; *Philistines* [gesture like you are ashamed of them while saying, *Boo!*]); *run, ran, or running* [motions of running])
- Noah's ark (*rain* [say, "*pitter-patter, pitter-patter*" while motioning to put up umbrella]; *animals* [each child has chosen an animal to imitate with sound and motions])
- Daniel prays (*prayer or prayed* [portray an attitude of prayer, say: "*Amen!*"]; *lions* [imitate the pacing of a caged lion and roar once])

---

66   Drama Activities

Active Echoes
Storytelling activity

Activity
Follow along as for "Key Word Echoes," except instead of speaking, students will do actions. Before beginning the story, tell the children which words to listen for and what actions to do.

Use with
- Zaccheus (*Zaccheus* [jump up and sit again]; *Jesus* [make a drum roll with hands on thighs])
- The bronze snake (*snake* [raise and wiggle right arm, while imitating fangs with two fingers], *Moses* [raise arms to God], *complaining people* [make unhappy faces], *healed people* [jump and wave])
- Healing ten lepers (*leper* [cross arms over chest so hands slap other arm], *Jesus* [both hands extended forward, palms up])
- Jesus' baptism (*Jesus* [hands folded in prayer], *John* [one arm raised], *people* [jump and wave], *disciples* [hand shading eyes and turning head])

Dramatized Story
An active storytelling experience

Activity
Some students represent a character in the story and may or may not dress for their part. The remaining students act out crowd parts or special effects. As the teacher tells the story, elaborating on interesting details, students listen for their character's prompts and whispered instruction on what they say and do.

Hint
Tell the story first and then act it out; children will not need so much prompting.

Use with
- Elijah on Mount Carmel
- Daniel and the lions
- Any story with action in it

PUPPETS
Puppets are hand-held objects that represent characters or animals; they do the acting and/or talking to recreate a Bible story. Puppets capture attention and help the child visualize the story correctly. Children themselves may or may not manipulate the puppets. Teachers may choose from a wide variety of puppets, depending on their budget. To use realistic puppets effectively, one needs to learn the rudiments of puppetry. But sock puppets and potato puppets need little or no prior practice. Puppet stages that the manipulators can hide behind can be made of fabric curtains on a pipe frame, or turning a table on its side may suffice.

Puppets can be used to tell Bible stories, to act out role-plays, or to make a point. Children enjoy making puppets to take home for sharing Bible stories with family, neighbors, and friends. Making puppets is a readiness activity; using puppets can be for experiencing the Bible story or for application. The examples below suggest how four different kinds of puppets could be applied to a specific Primary lesson story.

Finger Puppets
A sharing activity

Materials
- A fine tipped pen or marker, or faces from quarterlies
- Scissors and tape

Activity
Students make puppets by drawing faces on their fingers or by cutting out faces from old Bible study guides, or by drawing one-inch faces on paper and cutting them out. They tape the cutout faces to their fingers. Children manipulate their finger puppets to act out the story as they retell it.

Hint
Encourage children to go home and share their finger puppet story with children their age or younger.

Let's talk
If you were one of the characters in this story, who would you want to be?

Use with
- Zacchaeus (Jesus on left hand, Zacchaeus on right)
- Nicodemus (Nicodemus, Jesus)

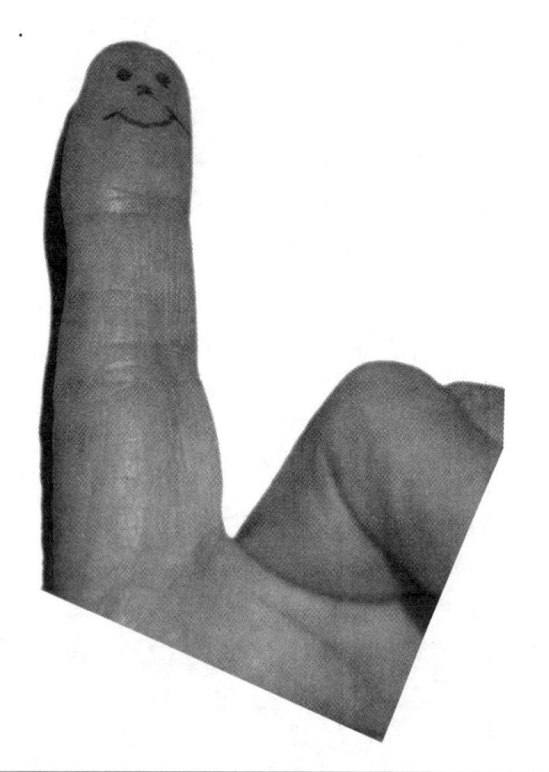

Necktie Snakes
A sharing activity

Materials
- Old neckties
- Glitter glue
- Moveable eyes
- Cotton balls, pencils

Activity
Students stuff an old necktie with cotton balls, poking the balls down with the eraser end of a pencil. As the tie widens, it might be easier to stuff with the legs cut from hose. When the necktie is stuffed, the wide end is glued onto the stuffing so the tip is left to overlap (as shown). Students glue on wiggly eyes or felt circles and make diamonds or spots on the back with glitter glue. Children use the snake to help tell the Bible story.

Let's talk
What were snakes created to be like? What do snakes remind us of?

Use with
- The serpent tempts Eve
- Animals enter the ark
- Bronze snake

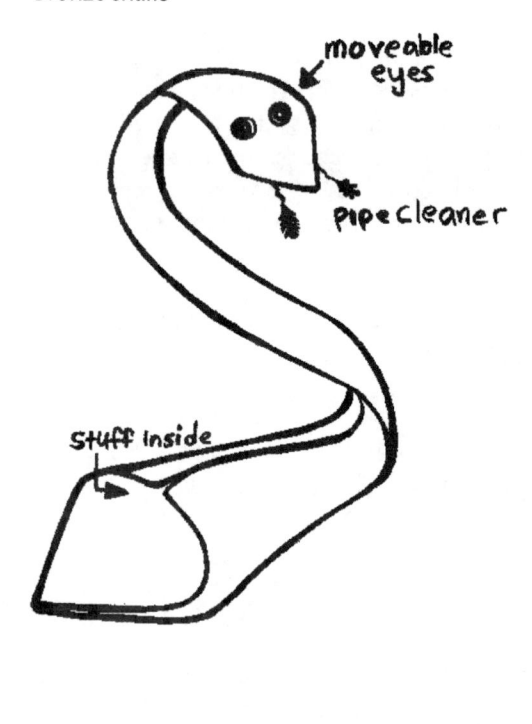

Drama Activities

Paper Bag Animals
A sharing activity

Materials
- Paper bags
- Yarn, scissors, glue
- Markers
- Construction paper

Activity
Students make animal puppets by drawing faces on construction paper and gluing on yarn for hair or fur. Children can use the puppets to tell neighbors the Bible story.

Let's talk
How will you use the puppet to tell someone today's Bible story? (Children pair up; tell them to take turns making their puppets tell the Bible story.)

Use with
- Any lesson, to challenge students to share the Bible story and message with a younger child.

see Appendix A13

Muscle Man Contest
A readiness activity

Materials
- Oversized stretch track suit
- Balloons

Activity
Students volunteer to be a muscle man. (Choose someone not particularly muscular.) Three additional volunteers come up to help the first volunteer do some "muscle building." Everyone else blows up balloons to the size of a grapefruit and bats them forward so the team of three can stuff the first child's tracksuit.

Hint
Use small balloons or tell children not to inflate balloons too much; pick up all balloons and balloon parts afterward as they can be a choking hazard for small children.

Let's talk
What if you really had muscles this size? What would you do with your massive power?

Use with
- Eutychus falls (We don't need to be superheroes to help others in emergency situations; we just need to be willing to serve)
- Samson (Use for telling the lesson story)

Drama Activities

Life-size Bible Puppets
A readiness activity

Materials
- Large sheets of butcher paper
- Tape, stapler
- Fiberfill or newspaper
- Yardsticks
- Sponges and poster paint or markers

Activity
Children lie on a double thickness of butcher paper while others trace around them in pencil. They add lines for Bible times clothing, according to the specific character they are creating. They go over the key lines with black washable markers then color/paint the puppet and cut it out through the double thickness. They glue or tape the yardstick to the back, centered side to side with the lower end positioned for a child to hold easily. They glue or staple the edges of the puppet together, leaving an 18-inch unsealed space on one side to stuff fiberfill or crumpled newspaper.

Hint
Use life-size puppets several weeks in a row. You can stand puppets in a bucket of sand or gravel.

Let's talk
How do you think the person represented by your puppet felt about what happened in this story?

Use with
- James and John want to be first (Make Jesus, several disciples and one additional person)
- Paralytic dropped through the roof (Use figures already made, kids act crowd part) Small church: children hold more than one puppet
- Healing blind man
- Jacob stories

Life-size Child Puppets
An application activity

Activity
Make as for life-size Bible puppets, but clothe in today's school clothing. Give glasses to at least one child puppet. Make at least three puppet children. The puppets can be made for readiness and dressed at the application time.

Hint
Save puppets and use all month for application situations that show the child's reaction to incidents described below.

Let's talk
Would anyone have reacted differently? In what way(s) was your reaction like or unlike what happened in the lesson story?

Use with
- Forgiving 70x7 (Act out reactions to: child cutting line, friend who lies to you, being left out at party time)
- Vineyard workers (Teacher awards a prize to a C student but not to you, the A student)
- Mary's perfume (On a mission trip to Asia, a dirty child touches your feet. After they react, ask: What if you knew that the child was honoring you?)
- Raising Lazarus (You attend a funeral with your mom; a person beside you starts crying. What do you do?)
- Isaiah's vision (Mitchell accidentally bumps Madi and as a result she spills her milk all over you. Mitchell and Madi both apologize, but that doesn't clean up your clothes. What do you do?)
- Hezekiah healed (You promise to give Jacqui the pick of your new litter of prize puppies. When you see Jacqui's family pick her up from school in a big, expensive car, you realize that she can afford to pay for the pup. What do you say to Jacqui the next morning?)
- Jeremiah and the potter (Juanita has saved up to buy new sneakers; her brother Juan needs shoes worse than she does. Her heart is set on an expensive pair, but if she gets them, she can't buy Juan's. What happens on the way to the store?)
- Bible prophecy fulfilled (The evening news reports a strange sight of a cloud the size of a man's hand that is approaching earth)

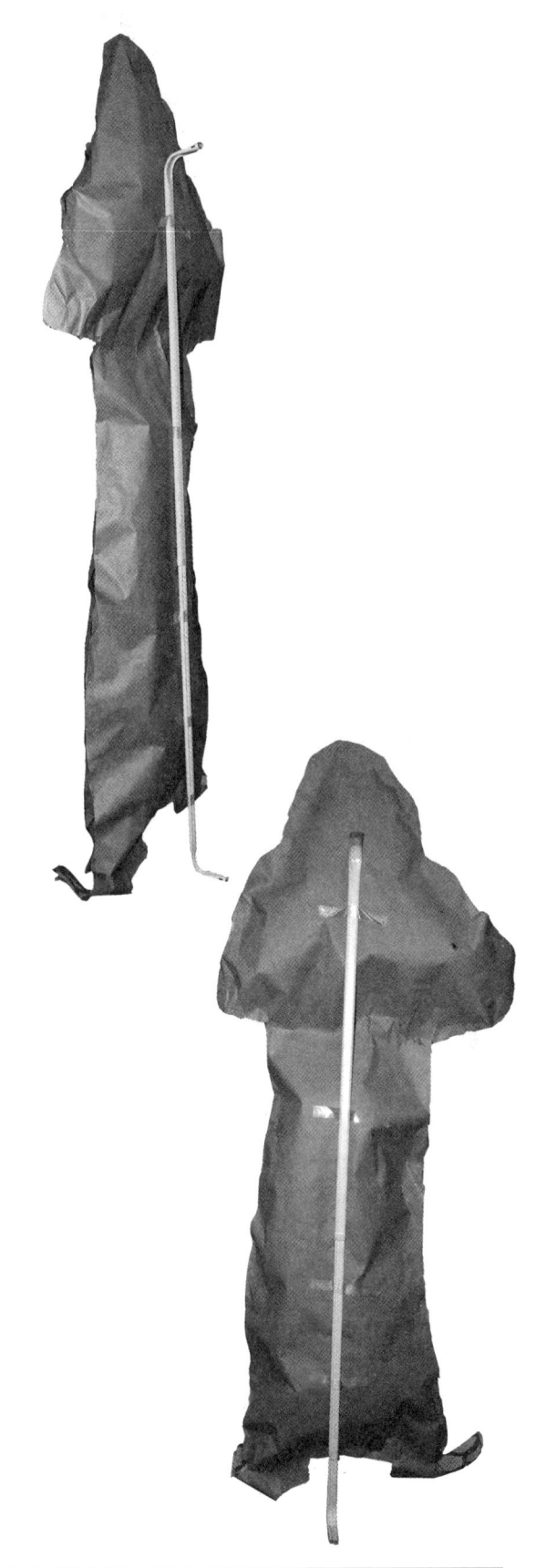

Drama Activities

Experiential Activities

Experiential activities provide hands-on Bible learning to help children experience an abstract concept, such as trust. The emphasis here is not on creating a product but an experience. Typically, experiential activities require few materials to make them work, and make a lasting impression.

BIBLE TIMES ACTIVITIES

Bible times, hands-on activities let children experience everyday living as it was in Bible times. Experiencing one or more of these activities can help bring a Bible story "alive" for children by helping them sense what it would have been like to be there. Begin these activities for readiness and draw on them when you tell the Bible story. Use the products as a craft to take home for sharing the lesson.

Bible Times Tablet
A sharing time activity

Materials
- Paraffin wax
- Corrugated cardboard
- Coarse paintbrushes
- Saucepan of boiling water
- Paper towels
- Coffee can, oiled on inside
- Electric crock pot or a saucepan and hotplate
- Craft sticks, already sharpened with a utility knife

Ahead
Sharpen the craft sticks, cut the cardboard into 5-inch squares, and oil the inside of the coffee can. Place chunks of paraffin into the can, and partly fill the crock pot with boiling water. Place the can of wax in the crock pot, and choose a setting warm enough to keep the water boiling and the paraffin melted.

Activity
Students paint a thick layer of wax over their cardboard square and when it dries, add a second coat. They use sharpened craft sticks to write on the waxed board.

Hint
Students can apply the wax to the cardboard during readiness. Then they write on it for sharing time. Keep the wax melted so they can do touch-ups.

Let's talk
How do you think they recycled this kind of tablet?

Use with
- Zechariah and the angel's prophecy (Zechariah wrote John's name on a tablet like this one.)

Bible Times Oil Lamp
A sharing activity

Materials
- Air-drying clay
- An old pillowcase
- A metal lid from a jam jar
- Olive oil
- Scissors

Activity
Students form clay into a ball and hollow the center with their thumbs. As they work, they press the clay into a hollow oval, pinching either end of the oval into a lip. They write their initials in the clay and leave the lamps to air dry. The following week, after the clay has dried, they make a wick by twisting a strip torn from the pillowcase. They lay the wick inside the lamp with one end resting on a lip. They use the other lip as a handle. NOTE: *These lamps cannot be lit. If you wish to make lamps that can be lit, use pottery clay and have it fired in a kiln.*

Hint
To demonstrate how an oil lamp works, pour a little olive oil into a metal lid. Coil one end of the cloth wick in the bottom of the lid with the other end resting on the rim of the lid. Trim the end with scissors so it does not droop downward. When the oil soaks up to the end, light the wick.

Let's talk
How effective would this lamp be without oil? How easily does oil pour from one lamp to another?

Use with
- The ten bridesmaids (The lamps were not just used as flashlights, but for lighting the wedding.)
- Wedding at Cana (Oil lamps would have provided the lights for this wedding.)

Coil Pottery
A readiness activity

Materials
- Air-drying clay
- Forks, knives
- Sponges
- Shallow containers of water

Ahead
Provide for each child a lump of clay the size of a tangerine.

Activity
Students pinch off their clay into thirds and roll each into a ball. They then roll each ball between their palms to form "snakes" a half-inch thick. They coil the first snake to form a 3-inch base for their pot and the others overlapping the edge of the base. Build up the sides until all the clay is used up. Before overlapping each successive level of clay, they dampen the edge of the coil below with a wet sponge, score the edges with the fork and wipe with the sponge again, moistening and smoothing it. When the coils are finished, they use the moistened sponge to smooth the sides and top of the pot. They leave it to air dry.

Hint
The scoring and dampening helps successive layers adhere to the layers beneath.

Let's talk
Potters in Bible times made small pots in this way, but they used a potter's wheel for bigger pots. The potter's wheel spins the clay like a top. As the potter applies pressure to the spinning clay, a hollow circle quickly takes shape. The wheel makes it quick and easy to form perfectly round pots. Suppose a potter accidentally spoils a pot. Does he need to throw it out?

Use with
- Jeremiah and the potter
- Elijah and the widow's oil

Experiential Activities

Money Pouch and Coins
A readiness activity

Materials
For pouch
- Brown fabric, cut in 12-inch circles, one per student
- Hole punch
- Boot laces (one pair per student) or string, 24-inches long

For coins
- ¼-inch cross sections cut from a small branch
- Nails, one per student
- Silver spray paint

Activity
Students punch holes around the outside of the fabric circle about 1" from edge and 2" apart. They thread laces through the holes starting from opposite sides of the circle, gather all four ends of the lacing together, and knot all ends together (see illustration). Students sandpaper the flat surface of the coins and make depressions with the nails to draw the symbols. An adult can take the coins outside and spray paint them silver. They will dry by the end of class. They place their coins in their pouches as people did in Bible times.

Hint
This activity could take two Sabbaths.

Let's talk
Would you prefer to give all your coins to me or to keep at least one of them? You want to keep a coin because you made it, and because you did a good job. So which coin will you keep? What makes you a keeper for God?

Use with
- Offerings to build tabernacle (We are made for worship; God likes our worship and He loves us.)
- Tithing or any time you talk about giving to God (Make 10 coins. Tithing is a way to show God that we are His servants.)

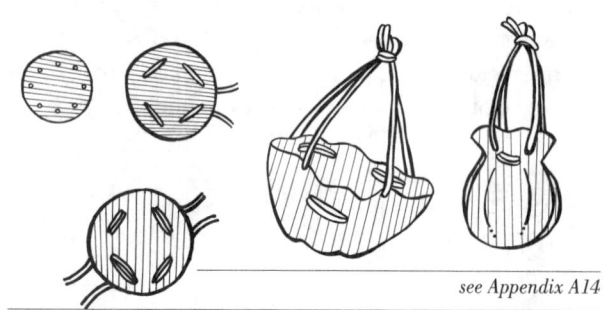

see Appendix A14

Bible Times Potpourri
A sharing activity

Materials
- Flower petals, optional dried lavender
- Wood shavings
- Calico or an old bed sheet cut in 8-inch circles, one per student
- Yarn or ribbon
- Cinnamon bark, cardamom seeds
- Orange oil, cotton balls
- 24-inch lengths of yarn or ribbon, one per student

Ahead
Cut circles of cloth with pinking sheers (optional). Dry the flower petals in the sun or in an oven at low setting. Set out separate containers of flower petals, wood shavings, and spices.

Activity
Students fill the center of their cloth with spoonfuls of petals, shavings, and spice. They add a cotton ball dipped in orange oil before gathering up the edges of the fabric, as shown, and tying with the ribbon.

Let's talk
What will you remember when you smell the fragrance of the potpourri? What might God want you to remember about this activity?

Use with
- Mary perfumes Jesus' feet
- Old Testament tabernacle service

see Appendix A15

Experiential Activities

BibleTimesCommunion
A story telling activity

Materials
- Bible times costumes
- A table set for communion
- Toasted pita bread
- Grape juice
- Small disposable cups
- One bowl of water and a towel

Ahead
Ask the church deacons and deaconesses to set up a table in your room set for communion. Offer to provide crackers and grape juice. Stack the chairs so there is room for everyone to sit on the floor.

Activity
Students remove their shoes at the door and put on Bible times costumes over their Sabbath clothes. They then sit on the floor with their crew leaders for Sabbath School. At lesson time, they look and listen as the leader, who is part of the lesson story, takes a bowl and washes a child's feet. Everyone tastes the bread and juice after the story is done.

Let's talk
How did you feel about the foot washing? Give three reasons why we wash each other's feet. Why do we eat the bread and drink the juice?

Use with
- The Last Supper
- Worship in heaven (The banquet on the Sea of Glass will be our new kind of Communion.)

Communion Bread
$\frac{1}{2}$ cup white flour
$\frac{1}{2}$ cup whole wheat flour
$\frac{1}{4}$ tsp. salt
3 $\frac{1}{2}$ Tbs. corn oil
4 Tbs. cold water

Mix salt and water in a bowl; add water slowly, beating with a fork until emulsified. Pour onto the flour all at once and mix lightly into a dough. Turn onto a floured board and knead, pound with wooded mallet until elastic (5-6 min). Roll to thickness of thin pie crust. Mark with dull knife into squares. Prick each square with a fork and bake 30 minutes at 325 degrees.

FOOD RELATED ACTIVITIES
Be aware that adults will often spark controversy over the use of food in Sabbath School, particularly if children have a chance to eat it. So before introducing food, check with parents to find if any children have food allergies or if parents object to their kids eating. When providing food, offer healthy options.

Breakfast in Bed
A sharing activity

Materials
- Ingredients for making a healthy breakfast
- Photocopies of breakfast recipes

Ahead
One week ahead, the teacher asks students about their favorite breakfast dishes. During the week that follows, she makes up a sheet of simple breakfast recipes and photocopies it for everyone.

Activity
Students prepare the breakfast foods and practice making up a breakfast tray and carrying it. Then they go home and prepare breakfast in bed for their parents.

Let's talk
When you give someone breakfast in bed, what does it tell about you? About the person you make it for?

Use with
- Any lesson that has a service theme
- The lesson right before Mother's Day or Father's Day
- The captive maid

Experiential Activities

Butter Fingers
An application activity

Materials:
- A quart jar with secure lid
- 1 cup heavy table cream
- Squeeze of lemon juice
- ¼ tsp. salt
- Measures: 1 cup, ¼ teaspoon
- Crackers, plastic knife

Activity
Students measure into the jar 1 cup cream, lemon juice, and ¼ teaspoon salt, before tightening the lid. They take turns shaking the jar vigorously while other activities continue. When butter forms, they spread some on crackers to taste as they talk.

Let's talk
What happens when we shake or whip cream? The protein molecules, called whey, separate from the fat molecules, which stick together. And because the fat is lighter, it floats to the top. What can butter teach us about our problems?

Use With
- The floating axe head (God brings good things out of troubles.)
- Noah and family wait in the ark (In times of trouble for our family, we stick together like the fat molecules.)
- Moses' last words (How might Moses' advice be like butter for us if we follow them?)

Candy Sparks
An application activity

Materials:
- Wint-O-Green LifeSavers™ candies, one each

Activity
Students pair up, facing each other with the candy in their mouths. With lights off and the room as dark as possible, they bite down on the candy with their front teeth, producing a blue spark. They can repeat and see how long they can produce the spark.

Let's talk
What happened? The pressure of teeth on the sugar molecules created an electric charge that made a spark. What are some of the things that create pressure in our lives? We may not realize God is there until He sends us a spark of His love.

Use With
- The lost sheep
- Jacob's ladder
- Angel's song

Impossible Bottled Egg
An application activity

Materials
- One hard-boiled egg, shelled
- A glass jar with a mouth smaller than the egg
- Two 1-inch strips of paper
- Matches

Ahead
Assemble the materials and try out the activity so you have a jar that looks impossibly small for the egg but which the egg will fit through when heated.

Activity
Students place the egg upright on the mouth of the jar and try to figure out how to get it inside without damaging either. When children conclude it's impossible, the teacher crumples the paper, lights one end, and drops it into the jar. (Make sure the teacher, not a child, does this since fire is involved!) The flame goes out, and the egg slips into the jar.

Let's talk
What just happened? What could we learn from this experiment?

Use with
- Daniel comes out of the lion's den (God always has a solution for things that seem impossible to us)
- Praise for Red Sea deliverance

Pudding Shaker
A readiness activity

Materials
- Packages of instant pudding, one per group
- Chilled milk, 2 cups per group
- Plastic drinking glasses with secure lids, 2 per group
- Small paper cups, plastic spoons, one per student

Ahead
Measure the milk into the glass and store in the refrigerator until needed.

Activity
Students add the instant pudding to the glass and secure the lid. They take turns shaking the glass vigorously until the pudding thickens. Pour a little pudding into small paper cups so each child can have some.

Let's talk
Name something bad that happened when you were little to shake you up and one good thing God brought out of it.

Use with
- Joseph sold into Egypt
- Daniel prays in spite of decree
- Paul and Silas
- Jacob meets Esau (How was Jacob shaken? Have the shakers share their pudding with everyone else.)

Experiential Activities

Fill My Cup
An application activity

Materials
- Individual cups
- A jug of water
- A jug of orange juice
- An empty gallon milk jug

Activity
Students each hold up their empty cup for the teacher to fill with water. (If someone drinks his water, the teacher refills the cup.) The teacher then produces a large bottle of orange juice and offers the children some in the same cup. They discover that they can't take the juice until they pour out what they have (into the empty gallon jug the teacher provides). Some children will decline the juice and that is OK.

Let's talk
God does not have any favorite people, right? So how come He gets closer to some people than others? How do people make room for God? When people refuse to empty their cup and receive God's blessings, what do they miss out on?

Use with
- Disciples want first place (Serving others makes room for Jesus)
- Pentecost (To make room for God's Spirit, we empty our lives of distractions, such as TV)
- Paul and Barnabas go to Cyprus (Sharing God's grace makes room for more grace)
- Jesus' childhood of service (Serving others made room for the Spirit of God to fill His life)
- Elisha and the Shunammite (We make room for blessings by sharing)

HEALTH RELATED ACTIVITIES
Bringing health and Adventist lifestyle into Sabbath School helps some primaries learn for the first time how their lives can be healthier and happier. Such activities also reinforce values that faithful parents are teaching. We do not need to preach or offer personal views; just convey the impression that living healthfully is the cool thing to do. As with other concepts and values, health is best learned through active participation and demonstration.

Blind Touch and Talk
An application activity

Materials
- Blindfolds torn from a sheet, one per child
- A brown bag with nature objects: leaf, seed pod, flowers, thorns, bird nest, egg shell, bark

Ahead
Collect the materials and place in a brown bag.

Activity
Students sit with blindfolds on in tight circles of 5-6 people, passing around, one at a time, objects from nature. They use their senses of smell, touch, and hearing to discover something about the object. The object of the lesson is for each person to tell one thing they have learned about the secret object before passing it on. (They may not repeat any observation already stated. Only people who have not held the object may guess what it is.)

Let's talk
What have you learned this morning about your eyes? (That seeing is a quick way to learn; that there is more to learn than meets the eye, etc.) What if this was the only way you could learn? How would you feel about that? What can we do to keep our eyes healthy?

Use with
- Jesus heals a blind man
- Samson (Samson understood God's plan for him after he lost his sight)
- Mission, any time (Do with objects from a specific country that is featured in mission offering promotion)

Experiential Activities

Health Check
A readiness activity

Materials
- Pencil/paper
- Mercury-free thermometers
- Stop watch
- A health-care professional with blood pressure cuff

Ahead
Arrange with a health-care professional to show the children how to do simple health checks.

Activity
Students perform simple health checks on themselves and on each other and learn the "normal" values as well as acceptable variations from the norm (not everyone has to have the exact same temperature or heart rate).

- Pulse: Place two fingers in the hollow at the base of the neck and count how many heartbeats they feel in 30 seconds, then multiply by two. (The norm for children is about 90 beats per minute.)
- Temperature: Using a non-mercury thermometer, demonstrate how to take temperature and how to read it. (The norm is 98.5 degrees Fahrenheit.)
- Blood pressure: A health-care professional checks their blood pressure and tells them what it is. (The norm for children is about 110/70)
- Exertion: Children run on the spot for 3 minutes and check their pulse again. It should have increased over their resting pulse.

Let's talk
Why do you want to be healthy? Why does God want us healthy?

Use with
- Daniel and friends (Nobody is perfectly healthy, but we should be as healthy as is possible for us)
- Adam and Eve created (Good health is one of the gifts God surrounds us with)
- Heaven

NATURE AND OUTDOOR ACTIVITIES
Nature fascinates most primary-age children, especially when they experience it hands-on. Nature is best observed outdoors, so take primaries outside to the church parking lot, lawn, or garden areas. Or bring nature inside by giving them a chance to hold specimens and observe them with a magnifying glass. The object of bringing nature to the classroom is always to learn a spiritual truth or to worship our Creator God. Help them appreciate God's attention to detail and to beauty, but be ready to acknowledge that we are seeing creation after the entrance of sin.

Earth Watch
A special event activity

Ahead
Suggest that children bring play clothes for this activity.

Activity
Students lie down in the woods while teachers cover them with leaves, sticks and pine needles. They stay as quietly as possible, looking upward until they hear the signal to come out. This activity will take at least 15 minutes.

Let's talk
What happened? What did you see? What did you hear? What did you feel? What if you were lying here when God created birds and animals? What might you have seen?

Use with
- Creation
- Heaven
- Any worship or stewardship lesson that focuses on God as Provider/Sustainer

Experiential Activities

Meet a Tree
An outdoor readiness activity

Materials
- Blindfolds, one per pair of students

Ahead
Choose a level area outdoors, among trees, where the group will assemble.

Activity
Students pair up, one blindfolding the other. The sighted students lead their blind partners each to their own tree where they explore the tree using senses other than sight. After being lead back to the starting point, the blind students remove their blindfolds and try to find the same tree. Students then switch roles and repeat the activity.

Let's talk
What helped you identify your tree? What, if anything, made it hard for you? Suppose that you were there at creation and God said, "This is your tree." What would you do to take care of it?

Use with
- Creation
- Creation day 6

Nature Squares
A readiness activity

Materials
- Duct tape, cut in 8-inch strips
- Masking tape

Activity
Use masking tape to attach the duct tape to the front of students' shirts, sticky side out. Students go for a nature walk, picking up things they find beautiful or interesting: flowers, twigs, leaves, etc. They touch the objects to their sticky paper. When they get back, they pair up to show what they found.

Let's talk
What is the one most interesting thing you or your partner found? Did anyone find something that they had never seen before? What if you had been there to do this when the earth was brand new; what might you have found then?

Use with
- Creation days 1-5
- Heaven
- Any worship lesson that focuses on praise

RELATIONAL ACTIVITIES
Activities that relate to family and friendship are loosely grouped together. Family activities place children in the role of another family member—an interesting and instructive experience for primaries. Friendship activities help children develop relationships and feel comfortable and confident about their ability to get to know people. Team activities teach children that we need each other in working together. In the process, children also learn to value individual differences, to discover that we are more alike than we are different, to realize that differences bring variety and richness to their world.

Egg Babies
An application activity

Materials
- Eggs, one per student
- Yarn, glue sticks
- Moveable eyes, large (optional)
- Markers
- Brown bags
- Tissue paper or shredded paper

Ahead
Boil the eggs and arrange them in a basket or bowl.

Activity
Students decorate their eggs with yarn hair, moveable eyes, and other features drawn with a marker. They make little brown bag baskets and line them with tissue paper or shredded paper so they can carry around their egg babies for an entire day. They will care for them as they would a baby, not leaving them unattended—and, of course, not cracking the shell.

Let's talk
What will you name your baby? How will you care for your baby so it does not break? Why does God ask parents to take special care of their babies?

Use with
- Samson
- Baby Jesus (Mary and Joseph give Baby Jesus lots of care and attention)

Candy Mold
An application activity

Materials
- Small candy molds
- Cream cheese (3 oz.)
- Powdered sugar (2 cups)
- Flavoring, mint or lemon (2 or 3 drops)
- Food coloring
- Sandwich bags

Activity
Students mix candy ingredients until they can easily be rolled into small balls and pressed into the candy molds. They flex the candy molds until the candy pops out, and then compare the candy with the original mold. They take candies home in sandwich bags to share with neighbors as a way to share about the importance of being like Jesus.

Let's talk
How was your candy like the mold? How was it different? Are people all alike the way your candies are alike? What does that tell us about God?

Use with
- Peter, John heal lame man (How was Peter's ministry like that of Jesus in this story? How was it different?)
- God creates Adam, Eve (Illustrates being made in God's image. Note that some candies come out of the mold imperfect.)
- Josiah restores true worship (When I let Jesus mold me, He can help others see Jesus in me.)

Mailman's Mission
A readiness activity

Activity
Students form groups of three. They choose who will be the spotter, thinker, and mailman. The object is for the spotter to choose someone in another group to whom they will send a compliment; the writer thinks up a sincere compliment, such as, "We like it when you giggle"; the mailman runs to tell the compliment to the person spotted. Each group sees how many compliments they can deliver before time is up.

Let's talk
How did you feel about this activity? How is this like what missionaries do? What messages does God want us to give the world?

Use with
- Any mission promotion
- Philip and the Ethiopian
- Solomon and the Queen of Sheba
- Hezekiah and the visiting Babylonians
- Any time you need to build team spirit

Experiential Activities

Post-It Quotes
An application activity

Materials
- Sticky notes
- Pencils

Activity
Students and adults think about what they admire about other students, write it on a sticky note, and then place it on somebody's back.

Let's talk
After students pair up to pull off and read each other's notes, they tell how they feel about the activity. What messages might God want you to share with your neighbors who do not know Him?

Use with
- Jonah preaches to Nineveh
- Saul's conversion
- Apostles escape from prison
- Jesus on trial (Write the notes they would have written for Jesus when he was alone on trial.)
- Any time kids need confidence building

SCIENCE ACTIVITIES
Primaries enjoy science activities because they get to see the results of what they do. They enjoy learning the reasons underlying a cause and effect situation. Remember, children do not do science in church to learn about science, but to learn more about God and about themselves. When doing experiments, make sure to provide lots of supervision and keep harmful substances out of reach of students.

Penny Polish
An application activity

Materials
- Tarnished copper pennies, two per student
- 2 metal pie pans
- Vinegar
- Salt

Activity
While the lesson story is told, students soak their pennies, one in a solution of vinegar and salt, and the other in vinegar alone. Later they come back and see the difference the salt made to the shine.

Let's talk
What difference did the salt make? Jesus said that His followers are like salt—they make a difference. What kinds of difference might He have been thinking of?

Use with
- Boy Jesus in the temple
- Daniel and friends taken captive

Experiential Activities

Bubble Works
An application activity

Materials
- Bubble solution
- A large round fry pan
- 12-inch length string, one per student
- Drinking straws, one per student
- Scissors

Ahead
Mix the bubble solution according to the recipe.

Activity
Students cut their straws in half, then thread string through both halves and tie the ends together. After submerging the string and straws in the bubble solution, they grasp the straws to open the string and either blow or wave the string to make a huge bubble.

Let's talk
Of what are bubbles made? Why do they always burst? What in our Bible story will the bubbles help you remember?

Use with
- Death of Moses (The bubbles we made will not last, but we will worship God forever.)
- Passover (Bubbles make us happy. Before their bubble pops, they say one word that reminds them of something God has done for them, such as: love, protect, mother.)
- Peter's denial (Bubble solution lasts in the pan, but individual bubbles soon disappear. That's why God wants us together in church.)
- The Resurrection of Jesus (To celebrate the resurrection, blow the bubbles upward and talk about Jesus rising from the tomb.)
- The prodigal son (Some children blow bubbles while the rest try to catch them. How is chasing fame and money like catching bubbles?)

Bubble Solution Recipe
- 3 cups water
- 3/8 cup Karo corn syrup
- 1 cup Joy™ dishwashing detergent*

Combine all ingredients in a bowl. Stir well. Let stand awhile before using. The longer it stands, the stronger the bubbles. *Detergent must be Joy™ for this to work.

Growing to the Light
An application activity

Materials
- 2 young, healthy potted plants of about the same size and type
- A small grow light (optional)

Ahead
The week before this lesson, students water the two plants before placing one of them in a dark cupboard that has a single, small light source. If the room is lighted by a window, leaving the cupboard door ajar may provide the required small light source. The other plant can be left near the window.

Activity
Students retrieve their plants and observe the changes.

Let's talk
What changes do you see in the plants? Explain that plants naturally grow towards the light. In what ways are we like plants? What light source keeps our bodies healthy? What light keeps us growing spiritually?

Use with
- Simon asks for power
- Saul's conversion

Experiential Activities

Floating Picks
Application activity

Materials
- Plastic cups, ¾ full of water, one per student
- Plastic drinking straws, one per student
- Toothpicks, 2 per student
- A bar of soap, soft on one side

Activity
Students float in their cup of water two toothpicks, parallel to each other but not touching. They push one end of the straw into the soft side of the soap then touch the same end of the straw to the water between the two toothpicks and observe what happens.

Let's talk
What happened to your toothpicks when you touched the soapy straw to the water? In what way are you and God like the toothpicks? Name some things in your life that act like the soap on your straw to separate you from God.

Use with
- Satan tempts Jesus
- Cain and Abel (What separated Cain from God?)

Mobius Links
An application activity

Materials
- 11x2-inch strips of construction paper, 2 per student
- Individual scissors
- Clear tape

Activity
Students each try to cut one strip into two linked loops; they may use only one piece of tape (but they cannot tape the links to each other). After they try, they watch a teacher demonstrate. Teacher holds a second paper strip by one end, gives the strip one full twist, and tapes the ends together to make a twisted loop, then pokes the pointed tip of a pair of scissors into the center of the paper strip and cuts down the center of the entire strip. The result is two loops, one passing through the other like links in a chain.

Let's talk
You are one of these links; the other is God. We break the tape when we let go of Jesus. What would you have to do to separate these two links?
God will never break the tape or let you go.

Use with
- The golden calf (God loves us so much He will never let go of us. Only we can break away our link.)
- The prodigal son
- Worship in heaven (Jesus is doing all He can to help us be in heaven, worshiping with Him forever.)

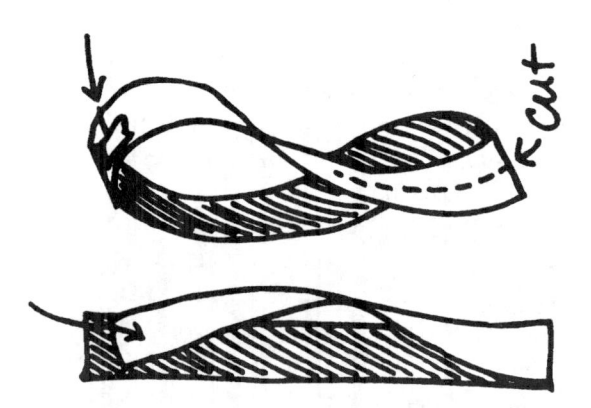

84 Experiential Activities

Perfect Flip
An application activity

Materials
- An old newspaper
- A yardstick or ruler
- Inexpensive prizes, one per student

Activity
Students place the yardstick/ruler on a table so that half the ruler extends over the edge. They place three opened out sheets of newspaper over the yardstick, lining up the edge of the newspaper with the edge of the table (see illustration), and centering the fold over the ruler before smoothing out the paper so it is perfectly flat. They try to hit the yardstick so it flips the newspaper into the air.

Hint
Offer a prize for the first person to flip the paper. Don't forget to flatten the paper between each try.

Let's talk
What happened? This newspaper isn't going anywhere because it has the weight of all the air above resting on it. So no matter how hard you try, you can't win this prize. [*Give everyone a prize anyway.*]

Use with
- Naaman's leprosy (God's grace is for everyone.)
- Barnabas and Saul in Antioch (Grace is a gift that you cannot earn and it is for everyone.)
- Samson (God still loves me though I don't measure up.)
- Any story about grace being unearned, undeserved

Ouch Bags
An application activity

Materials
- Re-sealable sandwich bags, one per student
- Sharpened pencils, one per student
- Water

Activity
Students each partly fill their sandwich bag with water and reseal it. Before poking the bag with their sharpened pencil, they predict what will happen if they do. (They will probably expect the water to pour out.) Following the teacher's instructions, they poke the pencil right through the bag and out the other side, being careful to leave the pencil in place.

Hint
Be sure to try this at home first!

Let's talk
What happened? Was it what you expected? Why didn't the water spill out? Just as the bag uses the pencil to block the holes, God can use sharp things that happen in our lives to bring about good and make us stronger.

Use with
- Elisha and the woman of Shunem
- Elijah and the widow
- Samson

Experiential Activities

TRUST ACTIVITIES

Trust activities require students to complete a task, often while blindfolded, fully dependent upon following directions from someone else. Because there is some risk of being hurt, or of failing to complete the task, leaders give clear directions both for the students performing the task and for those who watch. Primary children will learn that trusting is hard but necessary to learn. They will also know what you mean the next time you talk about trust and guidance. As a side benefit, they also learn the value of dependability and responsibility.

Blind Walk
An application activity

Materials
- Blindfolds for half the children (Rip up an old sheet to make your own.)

Ahead
Plan the route for a blind walk that provides some challenge for an unsighted person. For instance, down the stairs to the furnace room.

Activity
Students pair up. The child within the pair with the closest birthday is the first guide; guides blindfold their partner. The object of the blind walk is to reach the destination without bumping into anything. The guide takes the partner's hand and gives directions. The partners switch roles for the return walk, and for best results, return by another route.

Hint
If you cannot provide blindfolds, unsighted children may shut their eyes tight.

Let's talk
How do you feel about this experience? What did you learn from this activity?

Use with
- Gideon
- Calling the disciples (Have the seeing partners go ahead and call instructions.)

Human Camera
A readiness activity

Activity
Students pair up and decide who will be the camera and who will be the photographer. The camera shuts her eyes tight and allows the photographer to steer her around the room. When the photographer pulls on the camera's ear, she opens and shuts her eyes and tells what she saw. Repeat and then switch roles.

Let's talk
When you were the photographer, did the camera see what you had intended to photograph? Who in today's story could God trust to see things as He does?

Use with
- Jacob deceives Esau (We can always trust God.)
- Simon asks for power

Nerf Test
A readiness activity

Materials
- Nerf ball, bean bag, or soft, non-bouncing object

Activity
Students are told that in this game of catch, they are on their honor to sit down if they miss the ball. But they may not say a word to anyone about any aspect of the game; everyone trusts everyone else to follow these directions. They then throw and catch the ball while staying by their place—no running around.

Let's talk
Did you miss the ball at any point? If so, what did you do and how did you feel? It's more important to be trustworthy than to be right or to look like you are right.

Use with
- God's grace
- Moses strikes the rock (We can always trust God.)

Treat Teaser
A readiness activity

Materials
- A package of wrapped edible treats, containing enough for everyone.

Activity
Students listen while a teacher describes the treat and then reads all the nutrition information on the packet. When asked if they want to know what the treat tastes like, the students will probably decline. So the teacher puts the package away, then has a change of mind and asks if they want to taste it. They get to eat it.

Let's talk
Was it enough for you to know what was in the treats? Did that satisfy you? What did satisfy you? What could this tell us about Jesus? Is talking about Him enough? Read Psalm 34:8. How do we taste God?

Use with
- Josiah leads a revival (Tasting how good Jesus is makes us love Him more.)
- Rahab (Rahab believed what people said about God and she wanted to know Him for herself.)

Trust Chair
An application activity

Materials
- A blindfold
- A chair

Ahead
Send children out of the room and bring back one, or a few, depending on how many blindfolds and pairs of adults you have.

Activity
Students, individually, are invited to sit in the trust chair—but there is no chair there. One adult describes the invisible chair while blindfolding the student, then turns the student around 2-3 times. Meanwhile, the other adult quietly places a chair behind the student. The leader then asks the student to raise his hands and sit down, promising that he will not fall—his word can be trusted. If students trust, they will sit down. The chair will be under them.

Let's talk
How did it feel to be asked to sit when you had not seen or felt a chair? What have you learned about trust?

Use with
- Cities of refuge (In what ways did the people have to trust a city of refuge?)
- Elisha and the invisible army (What does this activity teach you about trusting God?)
- Daniel and friends taken captive (When doing this activity, blindfolded students choose a trusted friend to advise them about their safety.)
- Saul's blindness healed

Experiential Activities

Trust Maze
A readiness activity

Materials
- A blindfold

Activity
A student volunteers to be blindfolded in readiness to walk from the front of the room to the back, without bumping into anything and guided only by voice. The volunteer gets to choose a guide. After the blindfold is applied, motion for everyone else to put obstacles in the way and change the path to the door. As the guide starts giving directions and the volunteer starts walking, motion for the class to offer wrong directions, keeping up a distracting noise throughout the activity. After several minutes stop the activity and talk about it.

Let's talk
Ask the volunteer: How did you feel? Why did you choose the guide you did? What did you learn about trust? Ask the guide: How did you feel? What happened? What did you learn?

Use with
- The plagues on Egypt (Sometimes we can't see the future, but God always can.)
- Elijah and the still small voice

TEAM BUILDING ACTIVITIES
Primaries are joiners—they like to belong to teams, clubs, close knit families. But they don't always know how to welcome other children into their group. Preaching to them about making friends with other children is rarely productive. But leaders can help by letting children experience team-building and confidence boosting activities. Begin by helping them know each other's names and preferences. As you affirm and build up each child, they learn to respect and value each other.

Affirmation Circle
A team building activity

Activity
Students sit in a circle with their crew leader (or class teacher). The teacher begins by saying, "We're going to take turns telling the person to our left what we especially like about them." The crew leader then compliments the child to his left. That child then compliments the child on the other side of her, and so on around the circle. After each compliment, the teacher adds his affirmation of that child. By the time everyone has been affirmed, the children are glowing and more than ready to affirm their leader.

Let's talk
There is one person in our room whom we have left out; can you think Who He might be? Let's bow our heads and tell Him how special He is.

Use with
- The Upper Room experience
- Bitter waters made sweet (Affirming God is called praise)
- Daniel comes out of the lion's den
- Paul and Silas praise at midnight

Balloon Circle
A team building activity

Materials
- Balloons

Activity
Students and teachers form a circle and link arms (the circle should have at least 5-6 children and no more than 10-12; in a large church, divide into groups of 10-12). A balloon is tossed into the circle; keeping arms linked, the children try to keep it aloft using only their feet. To make the activity more challenging, more balloons can be added.

Let's talk
What happened? Did you lose your balance? Why not? What happened when the balloon touched the ground? How is this activity like being part of a family? Like the church?

Use with
- God's community
- United in service
- Any time you want to build team spirit

New Name Game
A readiness activity

Activity
Students take turns telling their first name and favorite food. Each successive student must tell the names and foods of the preceding students before telling their own. The first student finishes by naming all the preceding students and foods.

Let's talk
How do you feel about your name? Did you know that Jesus knows you by name? Read John 10:3. How does that make you feel?

Use with
- The lost sheep (Jesus called the sheep by name; He comes looking for us.)
- Use on promotion Sabbath to get to know the new children

Teamwork Puzzle
A readiness puzzle

Materials
- Simple jigsaw puzzles, one per group of 5-6 students
- Water soluble markers in several colors

Ahead
Draw stripes across the backs of assembled puzzles, using a different color marker for each puzzle (make different patterns if you don't have enough colors), and making sure that the stripe or pattern marks each piece of the puzzle. Return the pieces to their boxes and mix them so that each box is minus one piece of its own puzzle and plus one piece of some other puzzle.

Activity
Students form groups of no more than six and race the clock to see how quickly they can complete the puzzle. When they come up with a puzzle piece they figure out by themselves what to do. (They will all have to work together to get the extra pieces where they belong.) When done, they race to the timekeeper to find out how long they took. The timekeeper gives everyone the time of the slowest group.

Let's talk
How long did your group take? Actually, this was not a race against each other, but a race against the clock. So everyone took as long as it took to get the very last puzzle completed. Looking back, what could you have done to bring down the time?

Use with
- Lydia (Lydia has a part to play in ministry too. She serves Paul and Silas and Barnabas.)
- Cain and Abel (Have 3 puzzle pieces wrongly placed and have the teams competing with each other, not against the clock; talk about working peaceably.)
- Jesus calls Matthew (Do not premix the pieces. Teacher secretly gives each child a puzzle piece but to one child he gives the box with the remaining pieces. This child can invite anyone he likes to help put the puzzle together. If anyone is left out the puzzle will not be complete. God leaves nobody out.)
- Mary anoints Jesus

Experiential Activities

MISCELLANEOUS EXPERIENTIAL ACTIVITIES

The activities that follow do not share a common purpose; each makes a specific point relevant to multiple Bible lessons.

Popcorn Time Saver
An application activity

Materials
- An air corn popper
- Un-popped corn, 2 packets
- A large, empty can
- Napkins for everyone

Ahead
Set up an air popcorn popper ready to go.

Activity
Teacher holds the bag of un-popped corn, explains that the kernels of corn represent the minutes in a typical day, and invites students to name things/activities that can waste their time. For each time-wasting activity, the teacher throws spoonfuls of popcorn in the garbage, until there is not enough left to pop for the class. Because there's still time left in their day to make good use of, the teacher brings out more corn and pops enough for everyone to enjoy a taste.

Hint
Don't worry about adding butter; it makes a mess and kids will eat the popcorn without it.

Let's talk
What will you remember from this activity? Who in today's lesson made good use of time? What was the result?

Use with
- Enoch
- Daniel prays

Balloon Stomp
A readiness activity

Materials
- Balloons
- Ribbon or string

Activity
Students each inflate their balloon and tie it to their ankle. The object of the game is to stomp and pop others' balloons without getting your own stomped. The game ends when all balloons are popped.

Let's talk
How did you feel when your balloon got popped? Whose balloon did you pop? How might that person have felt?

Use with
- Cain and Abel (If you made someone feel bad by stomping his balloon, what can *you* say to be a peacemaker?)
- Elijah and the widow (Ask: When in your life have you felt "stomped on"? No matter what happens, God loves us.)

Marble Scoop
An application activity

Materials
- 2 large glass bowls
- Marbles or dried beans
- A teaspoon, a ¼ cup measure

Ahead
Fill one bowl with marbles or beans.

Activity
Two volunteers come up; one works with the ¼ cup measure to transfer marbles from the full bowl to the empty bowl. The second student works with the teaspoon to refill the full bowl by taking marbles from the empty bowl. The object for both students is to empty their bowl.

Hint
It is not necessary for students to complete this activity to learn from it.

Let's talk
What was happening in this activity? Who was winning? Was the contest fair? Why or why not? What if I had stepped in with a one-cup measure or larger to refill the full bowl?

Use with
- Offerings to build the tabernacle (The building costs keep emptying the church budget; our offerings try to replace the money in the budget. But God works with a much bigger scoop. This is how grace works.)
- The fall of Jericho (Have extra teaspoons and encourage several children to help before you step in to empty the bowl and turn it upside down.)
- Altar to unknown God (Spreading the story of Jesus is like us using one teaspoon—unless we work with God.)
- Water in the desert (The ¼ cup scoop is like God giving so many blessings we can't keep up with them.)

Egg Timer Watch
A readiness activity

Materials
- Egg timer or stop watch
- Calendar

Activity
Children hold their breath while sand passes through an egg timer to get the feel for how long a minute is. They talk about a day they look forward to, such as Christmas, and then turn pages in a calendar to find out how many months until December 25.

Let's talk
Does your family have rules about waiting for the right time to do certain things? Can you share one with the class? Read Ecclesiastes 3:11. God does everything in its time.

Use with
- Ezra or Nehemiah waiting for God
- Elijah running away
- Jesus coming on time
- Second Coming, waiting time
- Pentecost (What did believers do while waiting for the Holy Spirit?)

Body Wrap
An application activity

Materials
- Toilet paper

Activity
Children write their sins (things they've done wrong) on strips of toilet paper at least 18" long, then wrap them around a volunteer mummy. They can wrap the toilet paper around the body part involved in the sin (e.g. mouth, hands, feet). As the teacher leads them in saying the memory verse, they tear off the toilet paper and someone goes to the washroom to flush it away.

Let's talk
Did you think of every sin you need forgiveness for? Might there be some you forgot? What does God do with our sins? Read Micah 7:19.

Use with
- Isaiah's vision
- Prodigal son (We are prodigals when we choose to go our own way. God is waiting to tear off our sins and wash them away.)
- Esther saves her people (Children write different ways they can serve God on strips of toilet paper and then wrap the paper around the appropriate part of the body. (e.g. Helping around the house: wrap around hands. Telling others about Jesus: wrap around mouth.)
- Raising Lazarus (As a readiness activity children wrap a volunteer in toilet paper as a teacher explains that in Jesus' time, this was how dead bodies were prepared for burial.)

Sober Sides
An application activity

Materials
- A feather, or grass stem

Activity
Children sit on the floor hugging their knees and trying to sit as still as possible, without moving, smiling or laughing. Teacher gently draws a feather or stalk of grass across each child's face.

Let's talk
What happened? What were you tempted to do? This temptation did not hurt anyone. But if someone made a joke that hurt somebody else's feelings, what would be the temptation? Would it matter to the person if you laughed at them?

Use with
- The Temptations of Jesus
- Peter's denial

Minute Minders
An application activity

Materials
- Egg timer

Activity
Using a stopwatch or egg timer, children discover how long a minute is. They experiment to see how many of each of the following happens in a minute: heart beats, how far they can walk, bubble gum bubbles they can blow, how much of a Bible passage they can read or write out. Finally, they see how many minutes they can hold their hands in the air.

Let's talk
How fast does a minute go by when you are having fun? When you are waiting?

Use with
- Ten bridesmaids (Waiting takes forever, unless you stay busy or sleep.)
- Second Coming (Waiting for Jesus seems to take forever; maybe that's why Jesus gave us work to do.)

The Weakest Link
An application activity

Materials
- Typing paper
- Rulers (optional)
- Scissors

Activity
Students are challenged to fold the paper into thirds, cut along both folds to exactly one inch from the same edge, and grasp the two corners, also on the edge. They then tug on both corners so as to tear both folds at the exact same time—and end up with three pieces. But they will find this impossible to do. Why?

Let's talk
What happened? Did anyone manage to tear both places with one tug? You should be able to do that, right? Yes, but nobody can. Why? Because no matter how carefully you measure, your cuts are not exactly the same distance from the edge of the paper. So the slightly longer cut makes for a weaker link. And when you tug at the ends, the force goes to work on the weaker spot first. What can we learn about ourselves from this? What weak spots might kids your age have?

Use with
- Peter's denial (What weak spot did Peter have?)
- Temptations of Jesus (What was Jesus' weakest spot after his long fast? Did He give in to temptation?)
- The Law of God (James 2:10 – if you stumble in one point you break the whole law.)

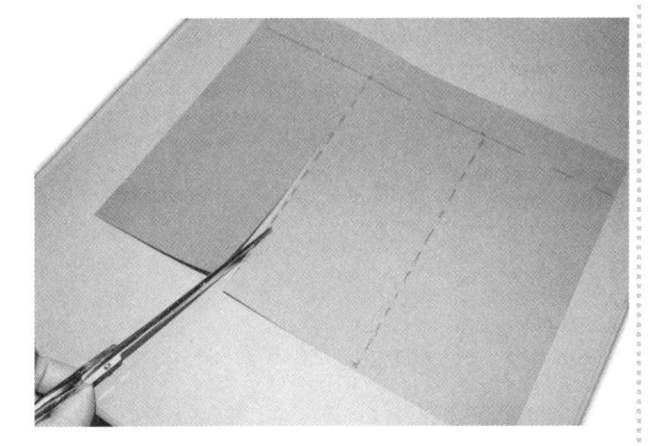

Trampled Rose
An application activity

Materials
- Red roses (one for each child)
- Copies of the song, "Amazing Grace" sung from the hymn book.

Activity
Students listen to the crucifixion story, before receiving a rose, representing Jesus, the perfect Son of God who was willing to die for our sins. Children take their roses, admire them, and trample them underfoot while listening to "Amazing Grace." They each take home a rose petal to remind them of Jesus and His sacrifice for them.

Hint
If only one rose is available, let everyone smell it and ask for a volunteer to trample it. Or ask children individually if they will do it.

Let's talk
What is there about the rose that reminds you of Jesus? How did you feel about trampling the rose? Why did you feel that way? How do you think the disciples felt when Jesus was crucified? How do you feel about this activity?

Use with
- The Crucifixion
- Abraham offering Isaac

Experiential Activities

Trinity Cord
An application activity

Materials
- 3 one-yard lengths of yarn, each in a different color

Ahead
Cut the yarn, enough for each group to have a set of the three strands.

Activity
Two students from the group, one at each end of the yarn, bring the three strands together and knot them. They then face each other, each twisting the yarn in a clockwise direction, until the yarn is tight. A third student pinches the twisted line of yarn at its center, while the first two students, keeping the line taut, walk toward each other until the two ends of the line are touching. The third person, holding the line with only one finger, then slowly moves toward the other two students. The two sides of the line will then twine themselves into a cord.

Let's talk
We now have a cord instead of three lengths of yarn. Can you still see the three strands? What color were the separate strands of yarn? What color is the cord? How are the strands and the cords like God? (Three separate parts make one whole.)

Use with
- Transfiguration
- Jesus' baptism (All three members of the Trinity were at Jesus' baptism.)

Trinity Streamers
A readiness activity

Materials
- Coffee stirrers
- Ribbon of three separate colors: red, white, blue (narrow, curling ribbon for tying gifts is fine)

Ahead
Cut 9-inch lengths of ribbon from each color, one ribbon per student, with the colors evenly distributed.

Activity
Students tie their length of ribbon to the coffee stirrer. They listen to the explanation and wave their ribbon at the appropriate time.

Let's talk
The white ribbon stands for the Holy Spirit, Who is like a dove. When someone mentions the Holy Spirit, please wave your white ribbon. The red ribbon stands for Jesus, the Son of God who died for me. Whenever someone mentions Jesus or the Son, please wave your red ribbon. The blue ribbon stands for the Father, King of the universe. When you hear anyone mention God the Father, please wave the blue ribbon.
Now sometimes we talk about the Trinity, the three people of the Godhead: The Father [WAVE BLUE], the Son [WAVE RED], and the Holy Spirit [WAVE WHITE]. These three are called the Trinity. So what will you wave for Trinity? All three colors together. (*Students practice listening and waving as you talk more about the Trinity.*)

Use with
- Children's Church presentations about the Trinity
- Children's evangelistic lessons on the Trinity
- Children's baptismal classes

Experiential Activities

TEAM ACTIVITIES

Working in cooperation and mutual trust are important biblical concepts children need to practice in everyday life. These skills can be learned through team activities. The following team activities will give children the opportunities to learn to cooperate and trust each other. They may be used either as readiness activities to prepare for the Bible lesson, or as application activities after the lesson.

Balloon Burst
A memory verse activity

Materials
- Index cards

Ahead
Write the words of the Bible verse, one word per index card. Roll and stuff the cards inside a balloon. Blow up and tie the balloons. Write the Bible reference on the board.

Activity
Students get one balloon each, in random order. The class competes against the clock to pop the balloons and to each hold their word in the right order in a straight line so everyone else can read it.

Let's talk
For you, who was the key person in this activity? What word did that person have? Was there anyone doing the activity that we didn't need? Neither is there anyone here that Jesus doesn't need on His team.

Use with
- Jesus calls Matthew (Jesus wants you on His team.)
- Joshua sends out 12 spies (We encourage each other to stay on God's team.)
- Josiah restores temple worship

Balloon Circle
An application activity

Materials
- Balloons

Activity
Students and teachers stand in a large circle. Someone tosses a balloon into the circle, and the group sees how long they can keep it aloft.

Let's talk
What happened? When you put the balloon up, what were you trusting would happen? Did you let down the team at any point? How did you feel? What did the team do to help you not feel bad? What could the team do to be more effective at keeping the balloon in the air?

Use with
- Jericho falls (Where was the teamwork in this story?)
- Gideon

Team Sculpture
An application activity

Activity
Students form into teams of four or five. When the teacher calls out the name of an object from the Bible story: (chair, etc.) teams try to form a "sculpture" of that object using all their team members.

Let's talk
Was anyone left out? If so, ask how it felt. Was anyone hoping we would judge your team as the best? God is just as interested in seeing us work as a team (or a family) as He is in having us do our best.

Use with
- Esther's challenge (What if Esther was not given her part to play in serving God?)
- Joseph's family moves to Egypt

Team Story
An application activity

Activity
Students in their crew groups take turns making up the next word of a one-sentence team story, without coaching from the team. The object is to see how long their sentence can be.

Hint
The focus of this activity is on teamwork skills, not on the story. The leader of each team can keep a record of the team sentence.

Let's talk
What happened? How good were your team skills? To find out, raise a finger for each yes answer to the following questions.
1. Did you affirm the efforts of others on your team? (Affirm means making them feel good about the word they thought of.)
2. Did you listen to what each person on your team said?
3. Were you trying to help your team win?
4. Did you have a good attitude about winning and losing?
5. Do you feel good about your team?

Use with
- Joseph and his brothers reunited (Joseph helps his family feel like a team when he forgives his brothers.)
- Jonah in the whale (Did you make mistakes in this activity? Yes, if your word ended the story, yes if you weren't a good team player. Like Jonah, we admit our mistakes and make them right.)
- Jacob's ladder (We want you on the team no matter what your team skills score was.)

Airplane Accident
Application activity

Materials
- A stopwatch (optional)
- A bowl of M&Ms (optional)

Ahead
Decide where to stage the activity—preferably in the fellowship room or a long hallway.

Activity
Students each take an M&M™ and remember what color it was. The teacher assigns handicaps from the following list, according to the color of their M&Ms™ or at random: Brown—broken arm; blue—comatose; red—broken leg; yellow—completely deaf; green—completely blind; they forgot the color—Alzheimer's. They will act out their handicap throughout the activity. In addition to the handicaps, they are told only three things.

1. They are in an airplane accident.
2. There is spilled fuel and a fire working its way toward the fuel.
3. They will be timed to see how long it takes them to get to the safe area down the hallway (explain where it is).

Some students will rush to the safe area, not noticing that others cannot move. At this point they learn that you are timing the team, not individuals. Eventually they figure out that they need to work together to save everyone.

Use with
- Sheep and goats parable (When we are on Jesus' team we take care of those in need.)
- Abram and Melchizedek (We serve others out of love for God and for them.)

WITNESSING ACTIVITIES

Witnessing activities provide opportunities for children to share what they have learned in Sabbath School, and in a broader sense share their faith with others. Primary children are not too young to tell what they have learned about God and what His friendship means to them. These simple activities can get them sharing in a natural and winsome way.

Sharing Balloon
An application activity

Materials
- Balloons, one per student
- String or ribbon
- 3x5 index cards (in neon colors, if possible)
- Pencil, marker

Activity
Students write the memory verse on a card, roll the card up tight, and stuff it inside the balloon. They then blow up their balloon and tie a string to it. They take the balloons home to share with a friend or neighbor before the air goes out of the balloon.

Let's talk
Do you know neighbors who are elderly and don't get out much? Tell us about them. Could you take your balloon to one of them as soon as you get home? Ask an adult to go with you.

Use with
- Paul and Silas (Paul and Silas shared Jesus by preaching. You can do the same with your balloon.)

Sharing Flower
An application activity

Materials
- Paper coffee filters
- Construction paper
- Pipe cleaners
- Scissors
- Glue

Activity
Students draw a large leaf on construction paper and cut it out. They write the memory verse on it, and glue it to the pipe cleaner. They twist the center of the filter and wrap the pipe cleaner around the flower. They take the flower home to share with a neighbor before asking if they can pray for them.

Let's talk
Who served others in today's Bible story? How can you use this flower to serve others? You serve when you share a Bible verse and when you pray for people. Pretend I am your neighbor. What will you say before you give me your flower?

Use with
- Belshazzar's feast (Telling people about Jesus is one way to serve them.)
- Sabbath (Serving through a sharing flower is a great thing you can do at home on Sabbath.)
- Any Bible story that features service or prayer.

Hint
Squeeze food coloring into saucers of water. Dip the edges of the water filter into the colored water and allow to dry before starting this project.

Experiential Activities

Neighborhood House of Prayer
An application activity

Activity
Students go two-by-two in the neighborhood of the church saying, "We're from the Seventh-day Adventist church and we'd like to pray for the families on your street. Is there anything you want us to pray about today?" Children take note of prayer requests and then pray about them with the neighbor. They can also ask if the neighbor would be willing to act as a "Neighborhood House of Prayer," praying for the needs of others on their street. Children can then share the neighborhood prayer requests with the family in that home. As with any door-to-door activity, parents, teachers or other adults should stay on the street nearby while children visit homes.

Let's talk
Who would be willing to come do this up front pretending I am your neighbor? (Role play a short visit.) Who will come and do this with me? (Take two students while another adult continues Sabbath School.)

Use with
- Stephen (Who is willing to show love like Stephen did?)
- Timothy

Fist Topple
A readiness activity

Activity
Students make fists and hold them at arm's length, one above the other so nobody can lift them apart. (They may not bend their elbows.) The teacher warns that she will get their fists apart, using only her two index fingers to do it. She quickly swipes at the fists from opposite directions. Provided the elbows are not bent, the fists quickly topple, because while students concentrate their forces in a vertical direction, the fingers attack from the horizontal.

Let's talk
How is this like the way Satan attacks us? Jesus can make you strong against attack. Make a fist but hold up the thumb. Your thumb represents Jesus. Now grab the thumb with your other fist. Who can topple your fists now? [Allow time to try.] What are you going to remember from this activity?

Use with
- Peter and John before Sanhedrin
- Peter's denial (Peter would have been strong if He had held tight to Jesus.)

Waters of Forgiveness
A readiness activity

Materials
- A clear glass or plastic container
- Water
- Food coloring or Kool-aid
- Bleach
- Spoon

Ahead
Try out this activity to make sure it works for you. Set up the container partly filled with water.

Activity
The students name specific temptations, such as not listening, being disrespectful, etc., which other children their age face. For each wrong that students name, the leader adds a drop of coloring to the container. As the leader talks about asking God's forgiveness, she adds a little chlorine bleach, and stirs. The water becomes clear if enough bleach has been added.

Let's talk
What happened to the water? Read 1 John 1:9. How did the activity help you understand this verse?

Use with
- Adam and Eve sin
- Through the roof (I can help someone else find Jesus and find forgiveness.)
- The prodigal son (When we truly care for someone, we will forgive them; God helps us forget what they did when we forgive them.)

Experiential Activities

Class Management Activities

While children learn best and remember what they learn when actively involved, their classrooms consequently sound noisier. The noise may signal that learning is taking place, but a noisy classroom can easily get out of control. Instead of yelling above the noise, teachers can come prepared with activities to facilitate learning and transition students from one activity to another. This chapter offers a variety of facilitation activities which work for many different situations.

ATTENTION GETTERS

At church, all that happens in class is meant to contribute to a meaningful worship experience. Students learn about God because they worship Him. So when in their exuberance they become noisy, instead of raised voices or whistles, teachers use signals to bring the class to attention. Leaders introduce the new signal at the beginning of class and practice it with the students several times. Then when needed, the teacher does the signal softly. Those students who hear it come to attention and are affirmed. As the signal sounds louder, the other students hear it and pay attention. If the signal fails, as a last resort, flip the light switch off until silence is restored.

Rhythmic Signals

Try at first a signal with words, such as: Listen up! (snap twice) Look at me! (clap three times) Next week do a rhythm only. Here are some rhythmic signals to try.

- Two slow claps followed by two fast slaps on the thigh followed by a long whispered "Yeah!"
- Tap with pencils on their chair or table a rhythm that matches the syllables in the words, "Tap a little rhythm" (four fast, two slow).
- Make up your own interesting rhythm. Try: clapping, tapping, snapping, slapping hands on thigh or table, tapping feet, stamping one foot, in any combination.

Echo Signals

Clap or tap a lively rhythm; the kids immediately stop what they are doing and mimic the rhythm you clapped.

Tune Snatches

Teacher starts singing a phrase from a song the students know well. The kids join in and finish it by stomping right foot, left foot, right foot, etc., without missing a beat. For instance, use the last phrase from "My God Is So Big!"

[Musical notation: "My God is so big, so strong and so mighty, There's no-thing my God can-not do! (clap, clap)"]

Jonah Says

Play Jonah Says the same way you do Simon Says. The leader does a series of motions, saying either "Jonah says do this," or "do this!" If someone imitates the teacher's action and Jonah has not said to do so, they go to Nineveh (they sit down or go stand by the wall but continue doing the actions).

BOREDOM CHASERS

"Boring!" is the primary-age student's favorite put down. Teachers can always respond in a pained tone of voice: "Oh, no! People who say that are (whisper) boring!" But more gracefully, why not plan ahead so things don't get boring. Have boredom chasers up your sleeve ready at a moment's notice to introduce variety and change of pace when the lesson seems to have bombed. Boredom chasers change the mood and bring laughter in seconds. Select a couple of these activities before class; if you don't need them, great! When students enjoy a boredom chaser, promise to do it again later after their class is finished—if there is time. This motivates kids to get busy.

StopandPopBibleStory

Ahead, the teacher writes the Bible story in outline form, each part of the outline being a complete sentence. She cuts apart the pieces, rolls them up and stuffs them inside deflated balloons, one per balloon. Students each receive a balloon, blow it up, and tie it off. (Large group: Some of the balloons will not have a paper inside.) Students bat the balloons around until the teacher calls, "Stop and Pop!" They then pop their balloons and read the paper.

As the teacher begins the Bible story, the student with the first part of the outline stands up front to the left of the teacher. Others, hearing their part of the story, come up and join the line. When the story is done, those with the papers take turns reading them, beginning at the start of the line. Those who did not get a balloon can help with the sequencing if anyone is wrongly placed in the line.

Disguises

Students cover their faces with masks, scarves or jackets, and guess who is who. After the game, the teacher debriefs with the children, reminding them that no matter who they are or what they're doing, God always knows them and can always use them.

Use with:
- Joseph sold into Egypt
- Esther saves her people
- Samson
- Balaam and the donkey

Balloon Smileys

Teacher tosses an inflated balloon up in the air with a smiley face drawn on it. When the balloon is in the air, children jump up and down; when it touches the floor, they freeze. Play for no longer than 90 seconds, then return to the lesson.

Balloon Chuckles

Play as for Balloon Smileys, except that students laugh loudly when the balloon is up and gradually laugh softer as it floats down. They remain quiet when the balloon touches down.

Class Cheer

Give your class a change of pace after they have been working hard. Affirm their great work and lead them in a class cheer. The cheer can be different each week, but do the cheer many times during the week you use it. A cheer might begin with one clap and two thigh slaps, followed by a long, joyful "Oooo!" with hands cupped around either side of their mouth.

Giggle Wipers

Teacher uses his/her arm as a giant windshield wiper (elbow resting in the other hand, hand and arm raised in front of face). When the wiper is raised, children laugh hard; when the arm is lowered, they stop. Teacher keeps the "wiping" going, sometimes fast, but finally very slow, until children's giggles have subsided and they are ready to stop and return to the lesson.

Magnetic Pull

Children act like "magnets," bunching together in a group around a designated adult when teacher calls out a description, such as: "Everyone wearing white socks!" or "Everyone who drove here in a minivan today!" or "Everyone who likes pizza!"

Popcorn Answers

To get children talking, a teacher asks a question with several possible one-word answers, and children call out their answers. For instance, name some good feelings that kids have. Name some bad feelings. If you were standing in front of (name of place in lesson, such as, Saul's tent), what might you see? What colors might Adam have seen when he first opened his eyes? Gear your questions to the lesson at hand.

Giggles Buster

Children take off their shoes, pile them in a heap, and form a circle lying head to toe on their backs, with one child's feet near the head of the next child. Children each hold the feet nearest their head and on the count of three gently tickle the feet. Then again at the count of three, they change direction and get ready to tickle the feet of the person on the other side. Keep counting so that the children change their position several times. Then ask them to show you which group can be first to find their shoes, put them on, and be ready for the next activity.

Hello, Partner

Children form pairs by grabbing the hand of the person sitting next to them. Partners stand up and go to an area where they can move around. When the teacher says "Goodbye," partners run away from each other. When the teacher says "Hello," they run toward each other. Teacher switches frequently between "Hello" and "Goodbye," keeping the energy level high. Follow this activity with a listening time, such as a story or discussion.

If You Hear Me

Whenever students are milling about noisily, the facilitator says in a low, normal voice, "If you can hear me, clap once." The students nearby who can hear will clap once. The facilitator continues in the same quiet voice: "If you can hear me, clap three times." (Any low number will do.) This time, more students will catch on. Repeat as necessary. Usually you'll have the whole group's attention by the third repetition. After you've used this several times, kids will be alert to others clapping and quiet down right away.

Paper Cut

The teacher writes the lesson theme in the middle of a sheet of 11" x 17" paper. Children sit or stand in a circle; the teacher cuts a piece off the paper and passes scissors and paper to the next child. Each child in turn cuts a section off the paper; the first person to cut into the written part has to recite the memory verse. Continue until everyone has said the verse or ask everyone to say the verse together.

CROWD MANAGERS
Instead of yelling or begging the children to sit down, wait, or form groups, teachers can use fun ways to facilitate the group. Obviously, crowd control is less of an issue in small churches, but some of these activities might still be fun to try. Any of these could become boring if used too often.

Hats Off
Keep a hat handy up front. When you want children to pay attention, put on the hat. When you raise it from your head, everyone stands up. When you use the hat to fan your face, they move quietly toward you. Use this when you want them to come sit on a mat or quilt to hear the story.

Puzzle Grouper
You need separate puzzles with pieces of distinctly different size or color for each group you want to form. Mix all the pieces together. Students reach in and take one piece. When you give the signal, they look for others with pieces to the same puzzle. If time allows, they put the puzzles together. (The leader gives each group the remaining pieces of their puzzle.)

Count Off
This is a popular method of grouping children (having them count off 1-2-3, 1-2-3, then putting all 1's together, all 2's together, etc). Counting off can be varied by using animal names. For instance, children count off "tiger, bear, elephant, tiger, bear, elephant..." then put all the tigers together, all the bears together, and all the elephants together.

Grab Bag Grouper
Teacher passes around a bag filled with pieces of colored crayon in as many colors as the number of groups needed. Children take one, then all children with the same color crayon group together. (Someone in each group collects the crayons!) As a variation, this can also be done with different coins (quarters, dimes, nickels, pennies) or M&Ms.™

Team Line Ups
When you need students to form teams for an activity, ask them to listen carefully and form lines behind the appointed team leaders who come to stand in front of you. (Name the children, one for each team you plan to have.) When the leaders are in place, simply holding out your arm above a team leader's head cues everyone to make straight lines. Call options from one of the following categories.
- Birth months
  2 teams: January-June, July-December
  3 teams: Jan-Apr, May-Aug, Sep-Dec
  4 teams: Jan-Mar, Apr-Jun, Jul-Sep, Oct-Dec
- Seasons (winter, spring, summer, autumn)
- Cookies (peanut butter, oatmeal, sugar, chocolate chip)
- Fruit (apple, banana, grapes, watermelon)

Team Circles
Circles work well for some activities. Up to 20 students can form one circle easily if you just clear floor space, hold open your arms, and say, "Let's form a circle." Adult helpers can join the circle at any point where the circle is going out of shape. To make the circle larger, tell everyone to drop hands and take two steps back. Take steps toward the center for a smaller circle.
If you want several small circles, divide the children with Team Line Ups, adjust the team for size, assign an adult to each team, and ask them to simply form circles.
Tell crews of 5 students plus a crew leader to sit knee to knee, if you want them seated in a circle.

Clusters
Teacher calls out a number and a body part; children form groups of that number, connected with that body part. For example: "Twos, shoulder-to-shoulder!" or "Threes, feet-to-feet." Try: wrist-to-wrist, hand-to-shoulder, knee-to-seat (they sit on the knees of the person behind them). Try a few rounds before settling into your group activity.

Mystery Chairs
Teacher puts colored sticky notes under the children's chairs ahead of time (as many colors as the number of groups needed). The teacher tells children to look under their chairs and groups them together by color.

Class Management Activities

Stand If

Use this activity when you need everyone to stand ready for grouping or for the next activity. By the end, everyone should be standing. Ask everyone to close their eyes and keep them closed until you call, "Open!" After each stand if statement, pause for kids to react. Do not comment, but simply read the next statement. Say: Stand if... you think you might be too tall (pause); too quick (pause), too old (pause), too serious (pause); too funny (pause); too happy (pause); too long sitting down! Open your eyes and... (tell them what to do next).

Optional Stand Ifs
- If you are wearing (turquoise, plaid, red, white, black, blue, brown, or many colors).
- If you are wearing (footwear with buckles, snow boots, lace-up shoes, button-down shoes, slip-on shoes, shoes with Velcro).
- If you like (shots, back rubs, pills, medicine, ointment, cough drops).
- If your favorite ice cream flavor is (licorice, prune, pumpkin, vanilla, strawberry, chocolate, bubble gum).

Jelly Bean Count

Each child guesses how many jellybeans (or chocolate coated raisins or almonds) are in a small jar. After everyone has guessed, children count the jelly-beans and the teacher congratulates the person closest to the correct number. As children share the treat, talk about how God knows everything about us and cares about even the smallest things in our lives.

Use with
- Elisha and the borrowed axe head
- Jesus and the children
- Saul's conversion
- Woman at the well

ICE BREAKERS

Ice breakers are meant to warm the atmosphere at a meeting or gathering where people may not all know each other. This type of activity is usually not too serious and gives people a reason to mix and talk about something of common interest or experience, or to achieve something simple as a group. Even children who worship among friends can arrive at Sabbath School not wanting to talk. After the ice breaker melts their reserve, by getting them to talk to each other, they are ready to talk to their teacher. Because ice breakers contribute little to the lesson, many teachers use them only occasionally, preferring instead the GraceLink readiness activities.

Name-Caller Cheer

The leader calls the name of one child at a time. After a name is called, the whole class calls, "Hello (name)!" followed by a class cheer. Repeat for each child. In a smaller church, do this with the whole group; in a larger church, do it with visitors and new members and a few regular members.

Name Game

Children sit in a circle. Teacher introduces herself by saying her name with a positive descriptive word that starts with the same letter (e.g. "Happy Harry"). The child to the teacher's left repeats the teacher's two words and introduces himself the same way (Nice Nick). The child to his left says the teacher's name, Nick's, and then her own. Children can help each other when they get stuck.

Shuffle Hoops

Students see how many people can fit inside a hula-hoop at one time. When no one else can fit in, the teacher calls out directions, such as, "Go to the door!" The group shuffles in that direction. Before the group reaches the door, they are directed to some other destination that requires them to shuffle backward or sideways. Directions get faster and faster until either the children tire or time is up.

Newspaper Pileup

Children lay a sheet of typing paper on the floor and see how many people can fit on it. (Variations include, how many shoes, hands, or heads. It's OK if someone thinks of piling them one above another, but let them think of that. Another variation is to see how many fingers fit on a Post-It note™.)

Use with:
- Jonah and the gourd (Talk about how much fun it is when others join our church family.)
- Pentecost
- Heaven
- Rahab (Israelites welcomed her into their community.)

Odd or Even

Give everyone five dried beans. They may remove a bean to their other hand if they wish. Then they move around the room holding out their fist and asking, "Odd or even?" The person to whom they direct this question must guess whether the fist holds an even number of beans or an odd number. If they guess correctly, they get to keep one of the beans. The object is to ask as many people as possible. Those with zero beans continue to play (zero is even).

Who Has the Bug?

Students move around the room shaking hands and greeting each other by name. The leader joins in the activity, but has a small bug, made from a pistachio nut, or a ladybird pin hidden in his hand. When he shakes hands the bug passes into the hand of the other person. The leader whispers, "Sssh! Pass it on." After 2-3 minutes, the leader calls for everyone to return to their seats and asks: "Who has the bug?" The leader tells about losing track of the bug, just like we sometimes lose track of God. But God always knows where we are and comes looking for us. Welcome everyone and ask them to look around and figure who might be absent from class.

Use with
- The Fall
- Saul's conversion
- Elijah hides from Ahab

Class Management Activities

Memory Motivators

Children have amazing memories; their minds soak up information, songs, and Scripture like little sponges. Primaries memorize easily, provided they hear the material many times. The challenge to teachers is to make memorization so much fun that children have a reason to recall the verse again and again. If we make the memorization of Scripture into a game or challenge, they willingly commit whole verses to memory.

Memory games, songs, and activities may take longer than five minutes. However, if the class reads or hears the verse after each activity throughout Sabbath School, the words and meaning become familiar, and the memorization games and songs quickly catch on. Remember, making it fun is the key.

A Maze Verse
You need 3 x 5" index cards with the words of the verse, one on each card. Students see the cards in correct order and read the verse 2-3 times. The teacher then takes up the cards and puts them down again in the wrong order, in close proximity. Students step from the first word to the next correct word, trying to complete the verse in the right order and without stepping on any wrong cards in between. Give child a chance to complete the maze.

Add a Word
Children sit in a circle to say the memory verse a word at a time. The teacher says the first word, the child to his left says the next word, and so on around the circle. If some children do not have a chance to contribute, the next child starts the verse over. When they know it well, teacher can tell every other child to think, rather than say, their word, to see if the next child will know "their" word even without hearing the word before it.

Around the World
Children stand in a circle while one child walks "around the world" (outside the circle). He/she taps someone on the head and races "around the world," trying to make it back before the chosen child can finish saying the Bible verse with reference.

Books of the Bible Run
A boredom busting activity

Materials
- A large Bible

Activity
Students are told which wall is designated as the Old Testament wall and which, the New Testament wall. They then take turns finding a book of the Bible in the index of the teacher's Bible. When a person calls the book, everyone must decide which testament, the old or the new, the book belongs in. When the teacher calls, "Books of the Bible," they run to the wall representing the testament of their choice. The child who chose the book now chooses another child to come up and check the Bible index to confirm the correct answer. The same child stays up front to choose the next book.

Hint
Play for 2-3 minutes before settling everyone down again. Promising to play again when they complete their work will be a great incentive to them.

Use with
- Any lesson when children look disinterested
- Students who are beginning to learn the books of the Bible

Ball of Yarn Reminders
Teacher writes memory verse words on individual slips of paper and tapes them in order to a long piece of yarn, then winds the yarn into a ball starting at the end of the verse. Children unwind the ball and pass the yarn around, each child reading the next word. They all say the whole verse while the teacher rewinds the ball. This time they try to say the word before they unwind the yarn and read the next word.

Beanbag Toss
Children stand in a circle and repeat the Bible verse together. Teacher tosses a beanbag to one child, who says the first word in the verse and tosses the beanbag to someone else, who says the next word. Continue to the end of the verse.

Hang-a-Word
Children each cut a piece of construction paper in the shape of an item of clothing and write one word from the memory verse on it. They then pin their clothing to a line that has been strung up in the room. They take turns touching the words with a ruler as they say the memory verse. If the words are out of order, they must run back and forth to touch the correct words.

Balloon Pop
Teacher blows up a balloon for each word of the Bible verse and writes one word on each balloon. Children help line up the balloons on the floor in the right order, securing each balloon with a piece of tape. Children then say the verse, tapping each balloon as they say that word. One child then pops a balloon with a pencil, and the class again reads the verse together, pausing at the empty spot until they remember the missing word. Children continue popping balloons one at a time until they can say the entire memory verse without help.

Color Code
Teacher calls out a color. All the children wearing that color stand and repeat the Bible verse together.

How Many Friends?

One child comes up front and turns a spinner on a numbered board. If the spinner stops on "3", the class gathers in groups of three to say the Bible verse, etc. Adults can join in to complete groups as needed.

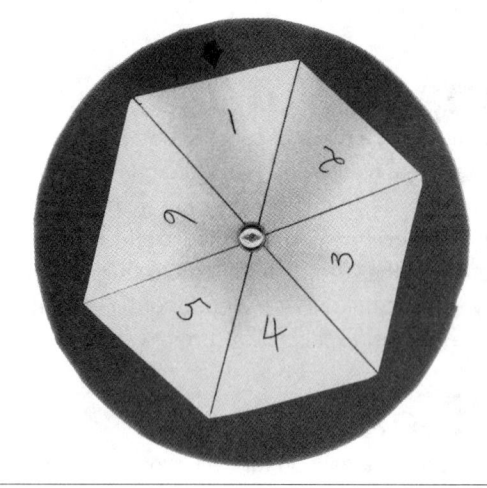

see Appendix A16

Last One Standing

Children stand and the teacher goes around the class asking each student to say a Bible verse from memory, without anyone using the same verse twice. Children who can't quote a new verse go to an adult "coach" to learn one; they re-enter the game when ready. This activity works well at the end of the quarter, reviewing the 13 verses. At the start of a new quarter, they may review the verses for the previous month.

Use with
- Houses on rock and sand

Memory

You need pairs of identical cards, made from index cards with pictures from the student guides glued on one side. The cards are laid face down in rows. Players turn them over two at a time, taking turns. If the cards match, the player gets to keep them. Otherwise, he or she turns them back down in the same place he or she picked them up and the next player takes a turn. The game ends when all the cards are gone.

Variations: Pair the memory verse on one card with matching Bible reference on the other. Or write one book of the Bible on each card, matching one Bible book with another from the same Testament. Or match a book with the one that comes before or after it in the Bible order.

Memory Hunt

Teacher writes the words to the memory verse on separate pieces of paper and hides them around the room. Children find the words and put them in order to make the memory verse.

Memory Verse Songs

Primary memory verses have been set to music. For more information about memory verse songs, go to www.childmin.com.

Muffin Cup Flowers

Students rearrange paper muffin cups that each have a word from the memory verse written inside. They place the cups on stems that have been drawn on banner paper. After saying the verse 2-3 times, they mix up the cups for the next person to sort.

Memory Tray
A readiness activity

Materials
- A tray
- 10 objects: a small toy, a piece of candy, scissors, a box of matches, a bottle of perfume, a piece of fruit, a cotton ball, soap, a comb, a pen
- A dishtowel to cover the tray

Ahead
Set the 10 objects on the tray so that all can be clearly seen. Cover with the cloth and set aside.

Activity
Students observe the uncovered tray for 2-3 minutes at which time the cover is replaced. Alone or in pairs, they try to remember all the objects that were on the tray.

Let's talk
Who remembered all 10 objects correctly? Though we sometimes forget things, God never forgets us.

Use with
- Elisha and the invisible army
- Deborah judges

Pop Up
Teacher assigns each child one word in the memory verse. Children crouch on the floor (not in the correct order). Teacher says the verse several times (using different voices, e.g. high, low, loud, soft for variety) and children pop up as their word is said. At the end, children arrange themselves in the correct order and say the verse.

Walk the Talk
Students can help cut out large footprints from construction paper. The teacher writes the words of the Bible verse words on the footprints, one word on each footprint. The footprints are laid down in order on the floor and secured with tape, and children take turns repeating the Bible verse as they step on the footprints. Turn over some of the words and see if the children can remember those words as they do the walk. You will need a set of footprints for each crew of five students. The crew leaders can keep their crews on task.

Prayer Experiences

To prevent prayer time in Sabbath School from becoming routine, repetitive, or boring, use a variety of prayer activities from week to week. And instead of praying only at the start and close of your session, stop and pray whenever a need is highlighted. Use a prayer activity when your program runs out before the clock does.

PRAYER EXPERIENCES

We do not so much teach children to pray as we facilitate prayer experiences so that prayer becomes natural for them. When prayer is a daily part of the home and church experience, children open up to God and continue to be open to Him as they grow up. Those who do not learn to pray while they are young may later resist attempts to bring them to God. The activities that follow not only help get children praying, they also give children a chance to teach their family new ways to pray.

Prayer Partners

Students buddy up and pray with a partner, each taking a turn to pray for the other. Children can encourage each other by praying together during the week, at school, or by phone. When comfortable with prayer, they can ask people they don't know if they may pray for them.

Use with
- Sending out the twelve
- Houses on rock and sand

Hand-Squeeze Prayers

Form pairs and have partners gently hold hands. One partner prays aloud or silently for the other partner. When finished, he or she firmly squeezes the partner's hand and the other partner prays. Try this when you know your students are confident, comfortable, and serious about prayer.

Use with
- Esther prays

Prayer Walks

Students, supervised by an adult, walk in twos and threes around the block, praying for the people in the houses that they pass. Families might be challenged to pray as they walk the halls of their apartment building or as they ride the elevator. Encourage the kids to always take an adult with them when prayer walking.

Use with
- Jericho falls

Church Prayer Prowl

Students, alone or with a partner, walk through the church complex, pausing outside Sabbath School rooms, the janitor's closet, fellowship room, etc., to pray for the people either in the room or associated with the room. Encourage them to come early next week and prayer walk with a teacher before class. Alert the deacons and some trusted adults to also walk the halls for the safety of the children.

Use with
- Nehemiah rebuilds

ACTS Prayer

Students learn to construct their prayers around a standard formula summarized by the acronym, ACTS, where the letters stand for the following.

    A= adoring God—adoring is like giving God a compliment
    C= confessing what we've done wrong
    T= thanksgiving
    S= supplication (asking God for something)

An ACTS prayer may consist of just one sentence for each letter of the acronym or many.

Use with
- Praying for power

PART Prayers

PART prayers are like ACTS prayers, but easier to pronounce. PART is an acronym formed as follows.

    P—praise
    A—ask
    R—repent
    T—thanks

Until they get used to a PART prayer, primaries need adult help and modeling—or a written worksheet to cue them. When praying in groups, a facilitator begins praying and says, "Now we will offer praise." Persons in the group then offer a sentence or two, giving everyone a chance to take part. When a long pause occurs, the leader might pray or move to the next part of the prayer.

ACTS Hats
An application activity

Materials
- Construction paper or foil
- Marker
- Tape, scissors

Activity
As a way to learn the ACTS prayer students draw on the construction paper a large outline of a hat worn by a community helper, such as a firefighter, construction worker, cowboy, or airline pilot. Inside the hat shape they write an ACTS prayer. Or they make a tiny hat out of foil to sit on their index finger. They say the ACTS prayer that the owner of the hat might pray.

Let's talk
Which part of an ACTS prayer is easiest for you? (Probably thanksgiving.) Which is the hardest? (Adoring God—because they want to just say thank you. Confession, because we don't like admitting that we did wrong.)

Use with
- Daniel and the lions (write Daniel's ACTS prayer)
- Jesus prays (write Jesus' ACTS prayer)

Hint
When just two people pray an acts prayer, they can go back and forth each adding short statements of adoration, until they are ready to move to confession.

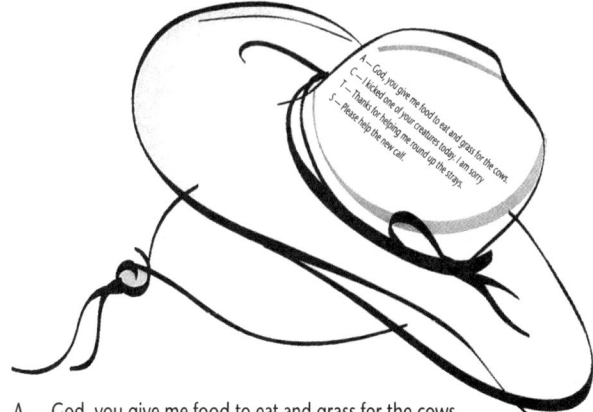

A — God, you give me food to eat and grass for the cows.
C — I kicked one of your creatures today. I am sorry
T — Thanks for helping me round up the strays.
S — Please help the new calf.

Prayer Activities

Prayer Journal

Students make the journal by folding sheets of paper in half and gathering them into a book tied with yarn. Or they can purchase a notebook and decorate the cover. They write their prayer in the journal each morning or night. Older children can reflect on their daily lesson study and record their thoughts in their journal.
In a specific part of the journal, such as along the bottom of each page, they write names of people they are praying for.

Use with
- Any lesson, early in the new year.

Prayer Maps

Students walk the neighborhood, counting the houses. Upon their return they draw a map of their street or the block around the church. They then pray for the people who live in each house, by turn, as their fingers do the walking from house to house. They keep the maps handy so they can pray for the neighborhood even when they cannot get out and prayer walk.

Use with
- Jonah in Ninevah

Apple Prayers

Students nibble on a small segment cut from an apple as the teacher reads Psalm 17:8, "Keep me as the apple of your eye; hide me in the shadow of your wings." Explain that when someone is very special to us, we say that they are the apple of our eye. Read the text again, inserting the names of the children in place of "me." (Keep Janie as the apple, etc.) Then read Zechariah 2:8, "Whoever touches you touches the apple of (God's) eye."
Invite children who are done chewing to pray, telling God how they feel about being the apple of His eye.
Option: Young children can tell God how they feel about apples and about God. They may not be able to make the connection between the apple and their own special selves, but they can remember every time they eat an apple that they are special to God. Challenge them to do this activity for their family.

Use with
- Samuel speaks for God

Prayer Vespers

Encourage your class to write down and keep their favorite prayers and prayer activities. The children can plan a prayer vespers for the church or take over prayer meeting. This can be like a prayer concert or a prayer program where the songs, the scripture, the sermon, and special features are all prayers. Children can read their creative prayers from the past month or months, play tapes of past prayer sessions, and involve the audience in some of their favorite prayer activities. The theme might be centered around a season of the year or pertaining to something in the church calendar. Or the prayers and activities might be random subjects. Include a time where children recount answers to prayer and take prayer requests from the audience.

Prayer Letters

Have children write their own prayers, or "letters," to God. (Non-readers may draw a picture.) Afterward, students volunteer to read their letters or pictures as verbal prayers to God. More reserved children can explain what they had in mind, and other students can volunteer to pray the prayer for them.

Sensory Prayers

This prayer works best in silence as a response to the continuing experience of God's goodness. Students silently soak in the warmth of the sun, stroke a feather, or chew a piece of fruit. They silently talk to God during their sensory experience.

GROUP PRAYERS

Usually when a group worships, one or two students pray while everyone else listens. But having the whole group participate can be a memorable experience and keep minds from wandering to other things. A teacher leads the group prayer and weaves group instructions into it, so prayer and giving directions are seamless. For best results, the prayer leader needs to anticipate the student reactions and attention spans. For instance, tell students what to do when they are finished praying—remain kneeling, begin humming, "Whisper a Prayer," etc.

Warm Water Prayers
A prayer activity

Materials
- Bowls of comfortably warm water
- Hand towels

Ahead
Invite assistants and crew leaders to come early to prepare for this activity. At class time, present the leaders who participated with a bowl, warm water and a copy of this activity. They then lead their own small groups.

Activity
A student soaks her hands in freshly poured water while someone reads Jeremiah 29:11-13. Each person in the group then prays for the "warm water student" by name. After the prayers, hand the child a dry towel and ask how she felt. (Warm, loved, OK, etc.) Encourage her to be ready for God's blessing. Pour a fresh bowl of water for the next child and repeat the activity.

Use with
- The Last Supper
- The seven deacons
- Naaman cleansed

Popcorn Prayers

This group prayer does not involve eating. The leader names the subject of the prayer, such as revival, families, or whatever your lesson is about. The start of the prayer might be: "Dear God, we know that we need You to be number one in our lives. We know we are safe with you. We plead for revival and hold up our friends and loved ones just now." Pause and wait for everyone to respond. One at a time, students around the group say one word or name that comes into their minds. (For instance, for growing closer to God, students might say one of the following: John, Sister Smith, family, home, Dad, grandma, etc.). The sound of words popping up here and there reminds one of corn popping. When the popping stops, the leader closes the prayer.

Keep popcorn prayer exercises short and upbeat. Do them at any point but no more than once in a program. Once your group gets the idea, they will enjoy this type of prayer.

Use with
- Elijah on Mt. Carmel
- Josiah's revival
- Any time kids need to pray

Prayer Chains

You need strips of paper about 12 inches wide and 8 inches long to make the links. The children write a prayer request, one per strip, pass one end of the strip through the last link in the prayer chain, and then staple the ends of their strip together. They then stand in a circle holding the prayer chain in their hands and praying link by link for each request.

Use with
- Peter escapes prison

Thanks Banks

Give children a facial tissue box, which they decorate and label "Thanks Bank." (All the decoration some boxes will need is the addition of a simple bow, heart, or flower.) Instruct the children to look each day for something that they are extra thankful for. They put a clue, a specimen, or a written description of the blessing in their thanks banks the next week. At prayer time, they draw something from their bank and take turns praying about what they drew out.

Prayer Activities

Lord's Prayer Chain

Students are each assigned a phrase from the Lord's Prayer. They write their phrases, each on a separate link, and then link them together in order. The phrases could be 1) Our Father, 2) Who art in heaven, 3) Hallowed be thy name, 4) Thy kingdom come, 5) Thy will be done on earth as it is in heaven, 6) Give us today our daily bread, 7) And forgive us our debts as we forgive our debtors, 8) Lead us not into temptation 9) But deliver us from evil, 10) For Thine is the kingdom and the power, 11) And the glory forever, Amen (Let it be so).

Use With
- Jesus prays

Names of Jesus Chain

On each strip of paper write a name of Jesus. The kids may want to collect the names for several weeks before taping them together as links in a chain. It is fun to order the links alphabetically. At prayer time for the next couple months, children stand in a circle each holding the chain at some place. They pray something based on the name written on the link that they are holding. For instance, the child holding "Rock" might say: "Be with Danny in the hospital, please be like a solid rock for him to hold onto." Alphabet Names of Jesus: Alpha, Beginning, Creator, Counselor, End, Everlasting Father, Father, God, King, Lion, Lamb, Lily, Life-giver, Mighty God, Omega, Prince of Peace, Savior, Son, Victor, Vine, Word, etc.

Use with
- New Testament fulfills prophecies

Intercessory Prayer Chain

The children write the name of a person on each link and a special request for that person. Each week for the entire quarter, they keep adding to the chain. At prayer time, they bring down the chain and take turns praying for the link. To celebrate answers to prayer, they put stickers on the links.

Use with
- Eutychus falls
- Gethsemane

Telephone Prayer Chain

Kids agree that if anything important comes up that needs immediate prayer, they will be notified by telephone to call and tell one other person and then pray about the special concern. Organize so that the leader needs to make only 1-3 calls. Each person calls the next person on the prayer chain. Large churches can divide into more than one chain.

Use with
- The early church

Pocket Prayers

The whole class participates in pocket prayers. You need an envelope for each child with their name written on the front and the open flap cut off. When kids arrive at the door, give them a blank card to write out their prayer request. They then place their request in somebody's envelope on the prayer bulletin board. At prayer time, the children retrieve the contents of their pockets and pray for the requests they find there. Use every week for one month.

Memory Verse Prayer

Students are given a verse or assigned the memory verse. They read the verse several times, think about its meaning, and consider the time, place, or story that the verse was connected with. They then take turns saying a prayer of their own that is based on their text. Teach children to do this when they study their lesson. Soon they can do it for themselves.

Use with
- Any lesson, early in the year

Add-on Prayers

Begin a sentence and have children complete it as a prayer, keeping one thought in focus at a time. For instance: "God, we thank You for . . ." and "God, please help . . ." Responses can be audible or silent.

Empty Chair Prayers

Kids who have a problem staying awake when they pray or who feel like God is not listening can pray while seated with an empty chair opposite them. They think of God as sitting in that chair.

In Sabbath School place an empty chair up front or in the circle for Him. Begin by singing songs to Him, such as, "I'm gonna sing, sing, sing." (*He Is My Song*, #10). Change the words so that instead of saying, "I'm gonna sit by Jesus' side," you sing, "Jesus gonna sit here by your side." They then pray with their eyes open, each telling God what they like best about Him, while addressing the empty chair.

Position Prayers

Children can experience prayer in many positions. For a prayer of thanks, have children stand and clap their hands after a thought that they feel strongly about, or they can sit with heads bowed. For a prayer of confession, have kids kneel or sit on the floor and hug their bent knees. For adoration, have kids lie outdoors on the grass and look up into the sky as they adore God and reflect on His majesty.

Moving Prayers

Young children are interested in things their bodies can do. Stretching, bending, smiling, breathing, and flexing actions can be prayers. For example, children can stretch to say, "Thank You, Jesus for causing me to grow." Children can pretend to swing a bat to say, "Thank you, Lord, for strong arms."—Karen Neussle

M&M™ Prayers

Children divide into groups of four. Dump a handful of M&Ms™ on the table in front of each group. Each child chooses one color of the M&M's™. The person who chooses yellow, for instance, may see that there are four yellow M&Ms™, so he tells God four things he adores about God.

    Yellow = adoring God
    Brown = confession, telling God sorry
    Green = thanking God
    Red = making special requests of God

Prayer Collage

Students snip words, letters and pictures from magazines to form a prayer. At prayer time they pray with eyes open as they share their collage.

Prayer Activities

Inventories

Inventories are photocopiable sheets that challenge children to examine their feelings or to assess their strengths and weaknesses. Inventories are high interest, low-risk activities that involve students in evaluating their growth, progress, or preferences. Inventories work well as either readiness or application activities and should be chosen to either fit the theme of the lesson or to boost a child's walk with Jesus. For best results, photocopy the inventory for each student, enlarging them on the copier.

To use an inventory to their advantage, have the students fill it out and write their name on it. After collecting up the completed sheets, read some responses from a sheet while everyone guesses whose it is. Affirm kids for their responses so nobody feels their responses were wrong in any way. The process gets students thinking and leaves them wanting to talk. One of the side effects is helping students realize that they share many of the same fears, concerns, and joys.

Note
For the following inventories, the teacher's help is listed first with class presentation notes. A photocopiable master for each activity is provided on the following page.

About Me
Readiness Activity

Hint
Take notice of students' responses so that you can adapt your class presentations to address different personal situations and preferences.

About Me

My name is _____

My age is _____ My birthday is _____

My family is _____

I live at _____

My pets are _____

My best friend is _____

I wish that _____

See next page for photocopy master

Let's talk
Did someone else have the same pet you have? Or the same wish? Did anyone else answer every question the same way you did? Why not?

Use with
- Newly promoted class in the fall
- Jesus dedicated at the temple

Inventories

About Me

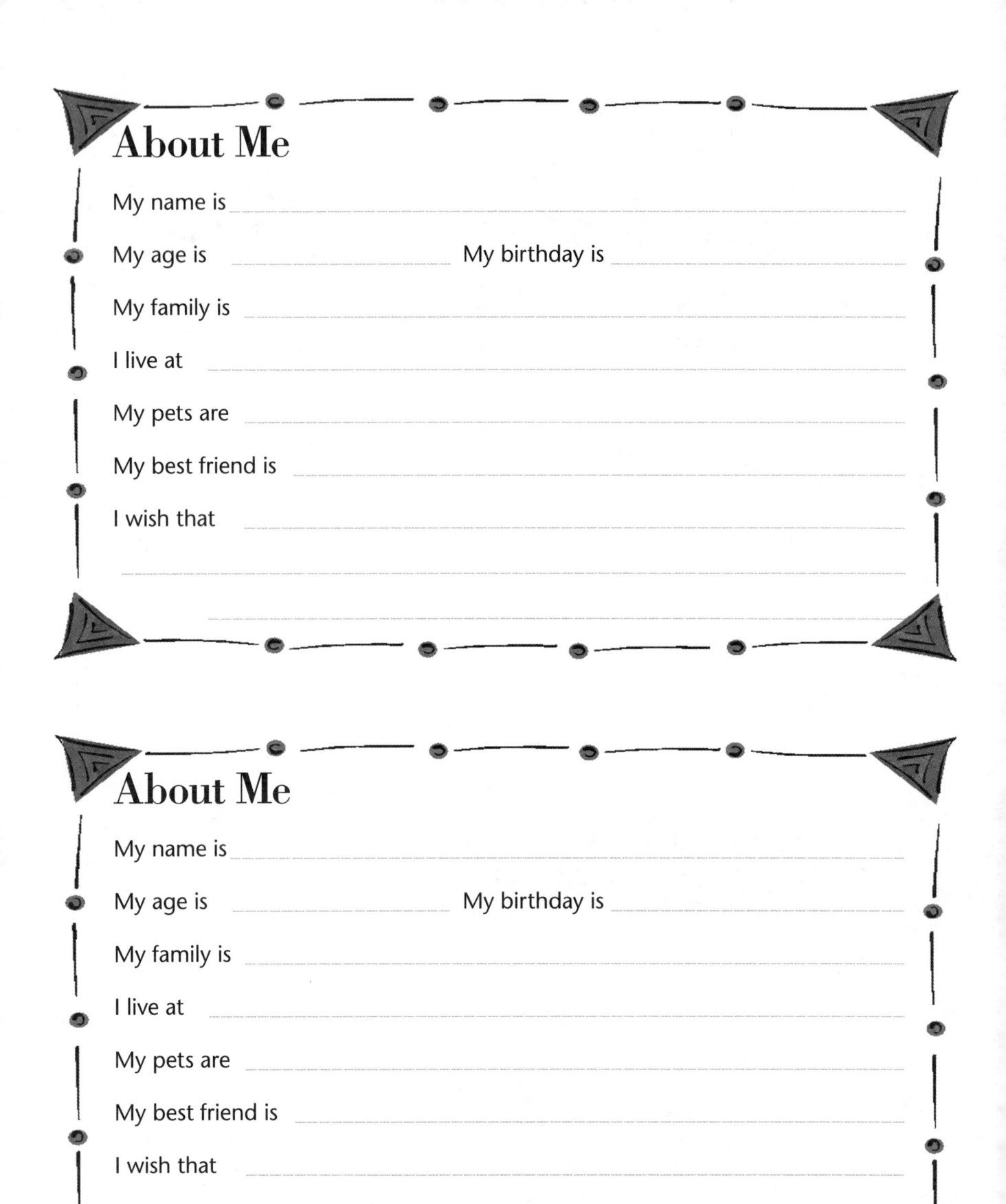

My name is _____

My age is _____ My birthday is _____

My family is _____

I live at _____

My pets are _____

My best friend is _____

I wish that _____

_____

About Me

My name is _____

My age is _____ My birthday is _____

My family is _____

I live at _____

My pets are _____

My best friend is _____

I wish that _____

_____

Favorite Things
A readiness inventory

Activity
Students circle one item per row, beginning before class starts. Later in class, the teacher reads aloud some responses from an inventory. The class tries to guess whose inventory is being read.

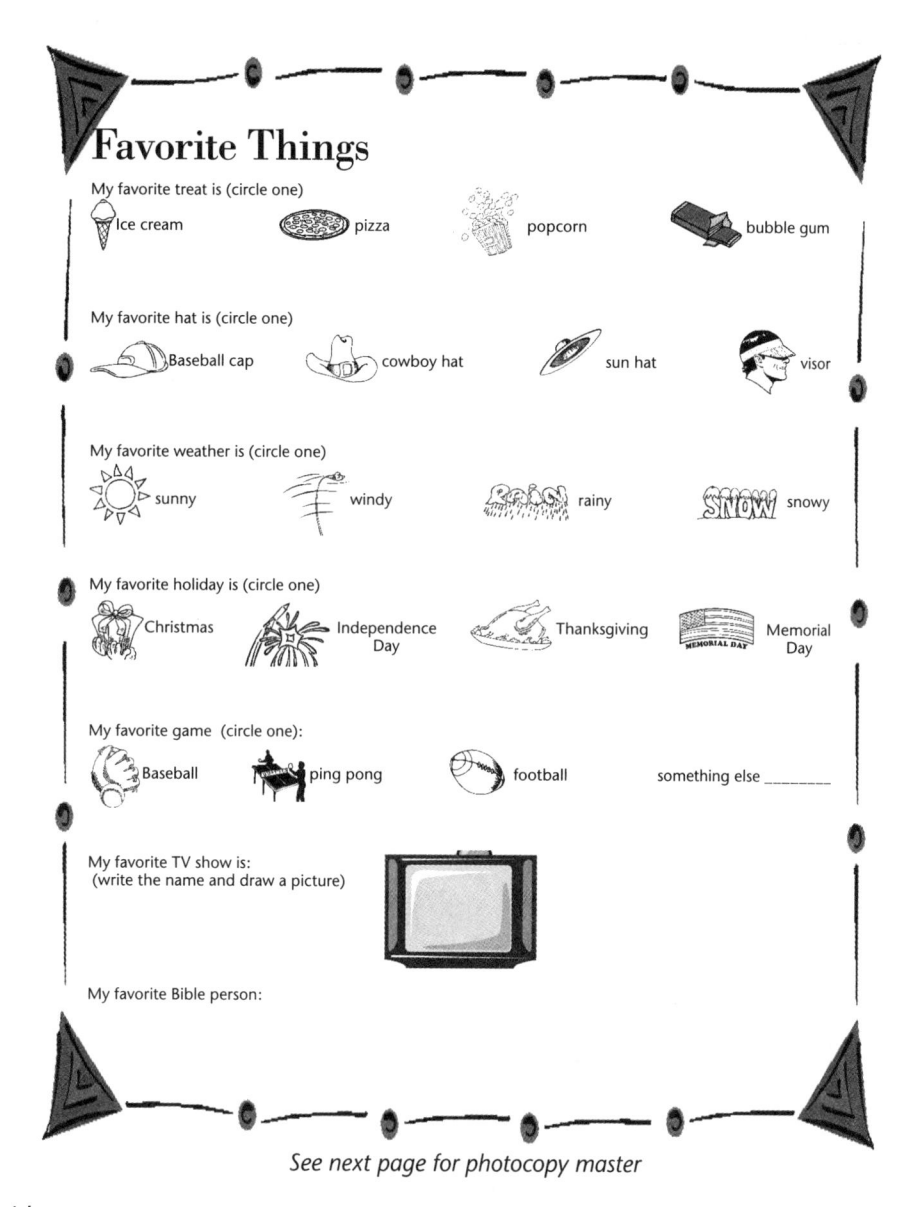

Favorite Things

My favorite treat is (circle one)
- Ice cream
- pizza
- popcorn
- bubble gum

My favorite hat is (circle one)
- Baseball cap
- cowboy hat
- sun hat
- visor

My favorite weather is (circle one)
- sunny
- windy
- rainy
- snowy

My favorite holiday is (circle one)
- Christmas
- Independence Day
- Thanksgiving
- Memorial Day

My favorite game (circle one):
- Baseball
- ping pong
- football
- something else _____

My favorite TV show is:
(write the name and draw a picture)

My favorite Bible person:

See next page for photocopy master

Use with
- Tower of Babel (Everyone is different.)
- Any time you want kids to get to know each other better.

Inventories — 119

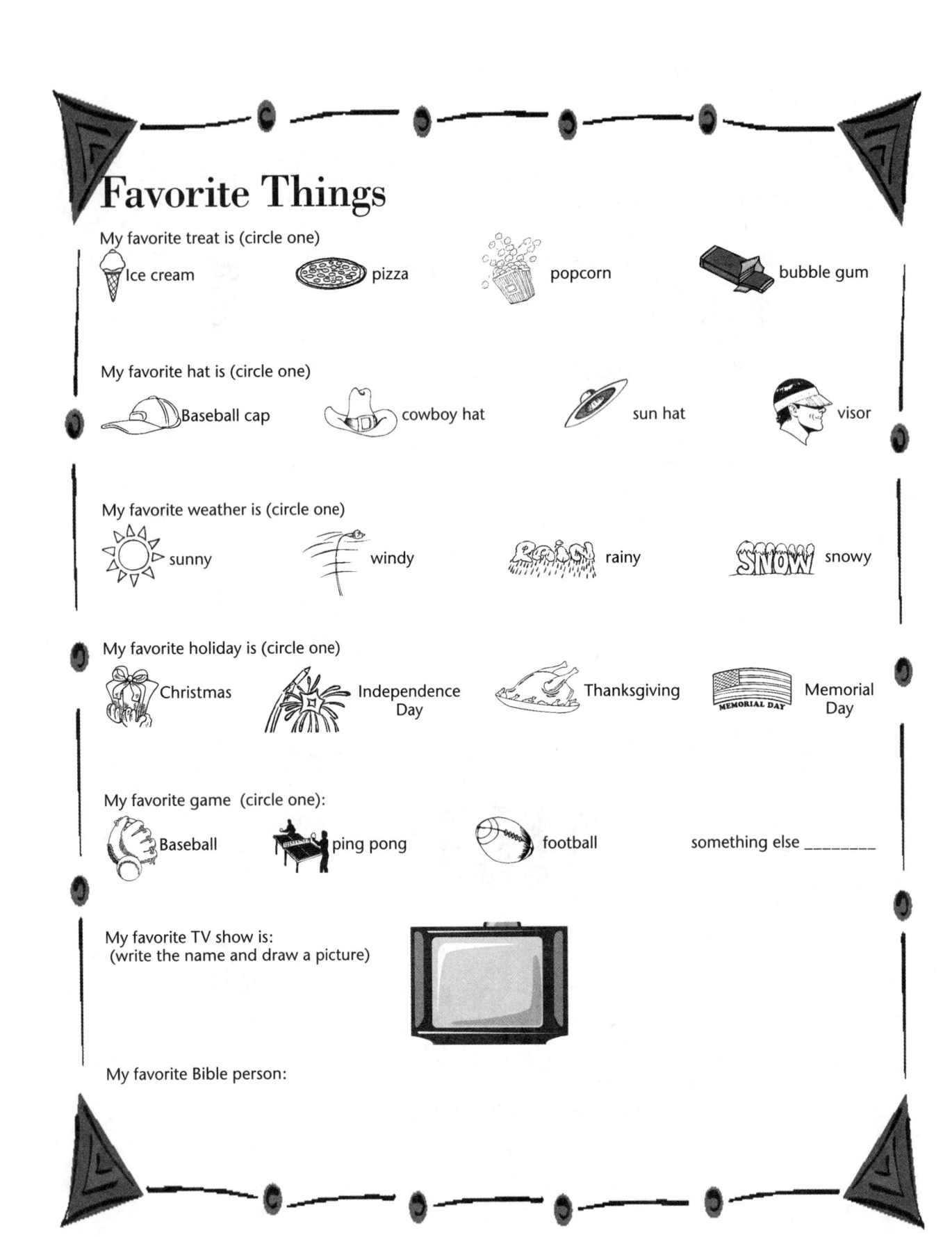

Favorite Things

My favorite treat is (circle one)

Ice cream　　pizza　　popcorn　　bubble gum

My favorite hat is (circle one)

Baseball cap　　cowboy hat　　sun hat　　visor

My favorite weather is (circle one)

sunny　　windy　　rainy　　snowy

My favorite holiday is (circle one)

Christmas　　Independence Day　　Thanksgiving　　Memorial Day

My favorite game (circle one):

Baseball　　ping pong　　football　　something else _____

My favorite TV show is:
(write the name and draw a picture)

My favorite Bible person:

Friends
An application activity

Friends

My best friends are _____

What I like best about my friends _____

The most fun thing I've ever done with my friends _____

I really need my friends when _____

I like to be with my friends because _____

A friend who encourages me is _____

See next page for photocopy master

Let's talk
Why are friends important to us? Does anyone here have too many friends? What are some things that friends do?

Use with
- Stephen and the deacons

Friends

My best friends are _____

What I like best about my friends _____
_____

The most fun thing I've ever done with my friends _____
_____

I really need my friends when _____
_____

I like to be with my friends because _____
_____

A friend who encourages me is _____
_____

Friends

My best friends are _____

What I like best about my friends _____
_____

The most fun thing I've ever done with my friends _____
_____

I really need my friends when _____
_____

I like to be with my friends because _____
_____

A friend who encourages me is _____
_____

Fearful Stuff
A readiness activity

Fearful Stuff
Below is a list of things that kids can be scared of. Choose 3 that you think are the scariest for kids.

Missing the school bus	Moving to a new city
A parent leaving the family	Losing a lot of money
Getting a bad grade	Having everyone laugh at you
Getting lost in a strange city	Dying
Not being ready when Jesus comes	Bullies

Talk with a friend about one response he or she chose.

Draw a sad face beside the response you think would be worst.

See next page for photocopy master

Let's talk
Why do you think scary things happen? How can you help kids from being scared? Who was probably scared in today's lesson?

Use with
- Ten plagues
- The Ascension
- Death of Moses

Fearful Stuff

Below is a list of things that kids can be scared of. Choose 3 that you think are the scariest for kids.

- Missing the school bus
- A parent leaving the family
- Getting a bad grade
- Getting lost in a strange city
- Not being ready when Jesus comes
- Moving to a new city
- Losing a lot of money
- Having everyone laugh at you
- Dying
- Bullies

Talk with a friend about one response he or she chose.

Draw a sad face beside the response you think would be worst.

Fearful Stuff

Below is a list of things that kids can be scared of. Choose 3 that you think are the scariest for kids.

- Missing the school bus
- A parent leaving the family
- Getting a bad grade
- Getting lost in a strange city
- Not being ready when Jesus comes
- Moving to a new city
- Losing a lot of money
- Having everyone laugh at you
- Dying
- Bullies

Talk with a friend about one response he or she chose.

Draw a sad face beside the response you think would be worst.

Feelings Inventory
An application activity

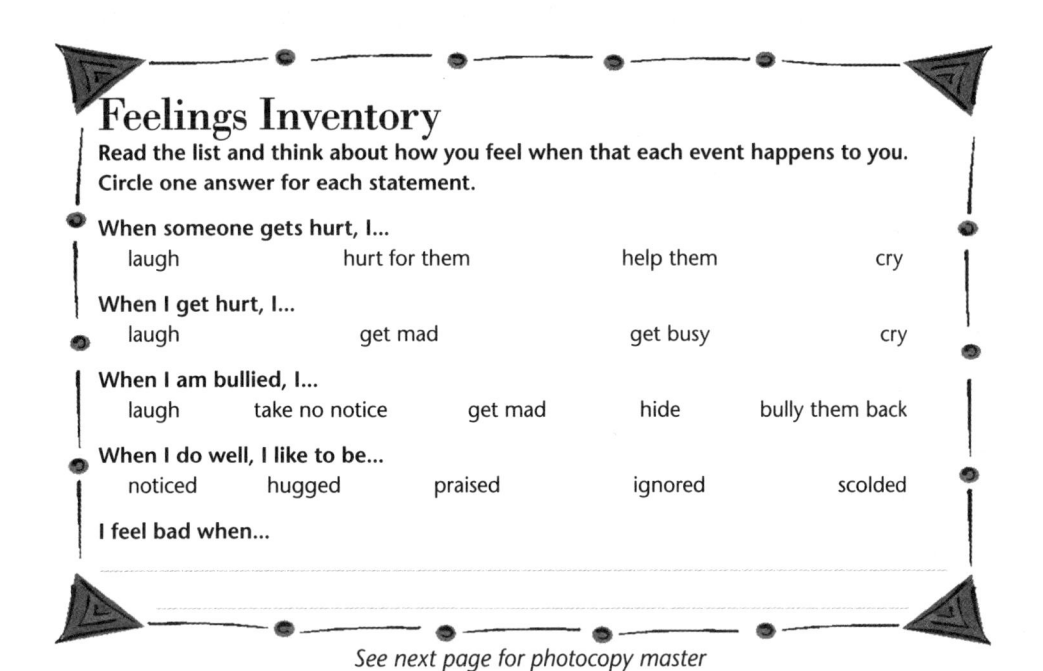

Feelings Inventory
Read the list and think about how you feel when that each event happens to you. Circle one answer for each statement.

When someone gets hurt, I...
laugh   hurt for them   help them   cry

When I get hurt, I...
laugh   get mad   get busy   cry

When I am bullied, I...
laugh   take no notice   get mad   hide   bully them back

When I do well, I like to be...
noticed   hugged   praised   ignored   scolded

I feel bad when...
_____

See next page for photocopy master

Let's talk
Do you think Jesus had real feelings like we do? How do you think Jesus felt when He was on the cross? Having a nail driven into your hand is a bad feeling, right? So does that mean you are bad when you have a bad feeling? [What you do about a bad feeling is what matters.]

Use with
- Death of Jesus
- Dorcas

Feelings Inventory

Read the list and think about how you feel when that each event happens to you. Circle one answer for each statement.

When someone gets hurt, I...

   laugh   hurt for them   help them   cry

When I get hurt, I...

   laugh   get mad   get busy   cry

When I am bullied, I...

   laugh   take no notice   get mad   hide   bully them back

When I do well, I like to be...

   noticed   hugged   praised   ignored   scolded

I feel bad when...

_____

_____

Feelings Inventory

Read the list and think about how you feel when that each event happens to you. Circle one answer for each statement.

When someone gets hurt, I...

   laugh   hurt for them   help them   cry

When I get hurt, I...

   laugh   get mad   get busy   cry

When I am bullied, I...

   laugh   take no notice   get mad   hide   bully them back

When I do well, I like to be...

   noticed   hugged   praised   ignored   scolded

I feel bad when...

_____

_____

I Give Thanks
A readiness activity

Activity
Students fill out their inventories and try to imagine what they would have to praise God for in heaven.

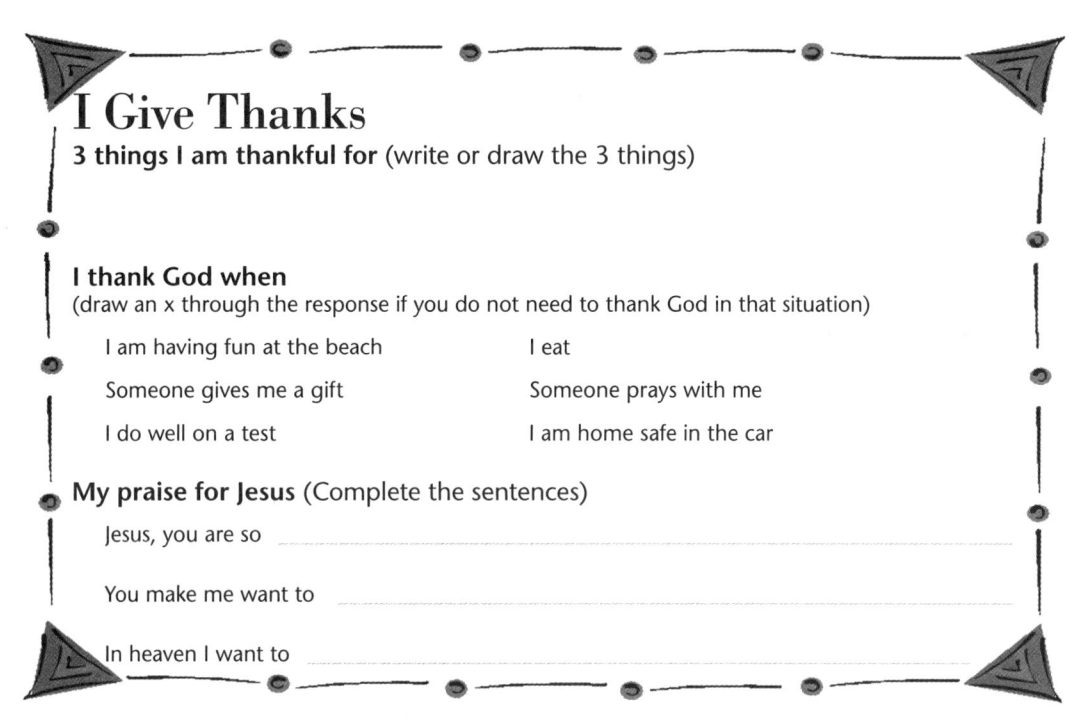

I Give Thanks

3 things I am thankful for (write or draw the 3 things)

I thank God when
(draw an x through the response if you do not need to thank God in that situation)

I am having fun at the beach	I eat
Someone gives me a gift	Someone prays with me
I do well on a test	I am home safe in the car

My praise for Jesus (Complete the sentences)

Jesus, you are so _____

You make me want to _____

In heaven I want to _____

See next page for photocopy master

Let's talk
Why do we praise Jesus? How does God feel about our praise?

Use with
- Songs of praise in heaven

Inventories

I Give Thanks

3 things I am thankful for (write or draw the 3 things)

I thank God when
(draw an x through the response if you do not need to thank God in that situation)

- I am having fun at the beach
- Someone gives me a gift
- I do well on a test
- I eat
- Someone prays with me
- I am home safe in the car

My praise for Jesus (Complete the sentences)

Jesus, you are so _____

You make me want to _____

In heaven I want to _____

I Give Thanks

3 things I am thankful for (write or draw the 3 things)

I thank God when
(draw an x through the response if you do not need to thank God in that situation)

- I am having fun at the beach
- Someone gives me a gift
- I do well on a test
- I eat
- Someone prays with me
- I am home safe in the car

My praise for Jesus (Complete the sentences)

Jesus, you are so _____

You make me want to _____

In heaven I want to _____

My Bible and Me
A readiness activity

My Bible and Me
Choose one response that best completes the statement about you. Underline your response.

The thing I like best about the Bible is . . .
God talks to me   I like the stories   I like the people in the Bible

I think the Bible is mostly about . . .
People long ago   God's story   Rules

The Bible words are mostly . . .
From Jews   From old men   From God

The Bible has in it . . . (circle more than one)
A record of long ago   Poems   Telling about the future   Letters   Sermons

What are the two parts of the Bible called? (circle one)
Books   Letters   Testaments

Do you have a Bible of your own? Yes No

See next page for photocopy master

Let's talk
What do you like best about the Bible? How is the Bible different from other books? What if we didn't have any Bibles?

Use with
- Bereans study Scripture
- Fulfilled prophecies

My Bible and Me

Choose one response that best completes the statement about you. Underline your response.

The thing I like best about the Bible is . . .
God talks to me   I like the stories   I like the people in the Bible

I think the Bible is mostly about . . .
People long ago   God's story   Rules

The Bible words are mostly . . .
From Jews   From old men   From God

The Bible has in it . . . (circle more than one)
A record of long ago   Poems   Telling about the future   Letters   Sermons

What are the two parts of the Bible called? (circle one)
Books   Letters   Testaments

Do you have a Bible of your own? Yes No

My Bible and Me

Choose one response that best completes the statement about you. Underline your response.

The thing I like best about the Bible is . . .
God talks to me   I like the stories   I like the people in the Bible

I think the Bible is mostly about . . .
People long ago   God's story   Rules

The Bible words are mostly . . .
From Jews   From old men   From God

The Bible has in it . . . (circle more than one)
A record of long ago   Poems   Telling about the future   Letters   Sermons

What are the two parts of the Bible called? (circle one)
Books   Letters   Testaments

Do you have a Bible of your own? Yes No

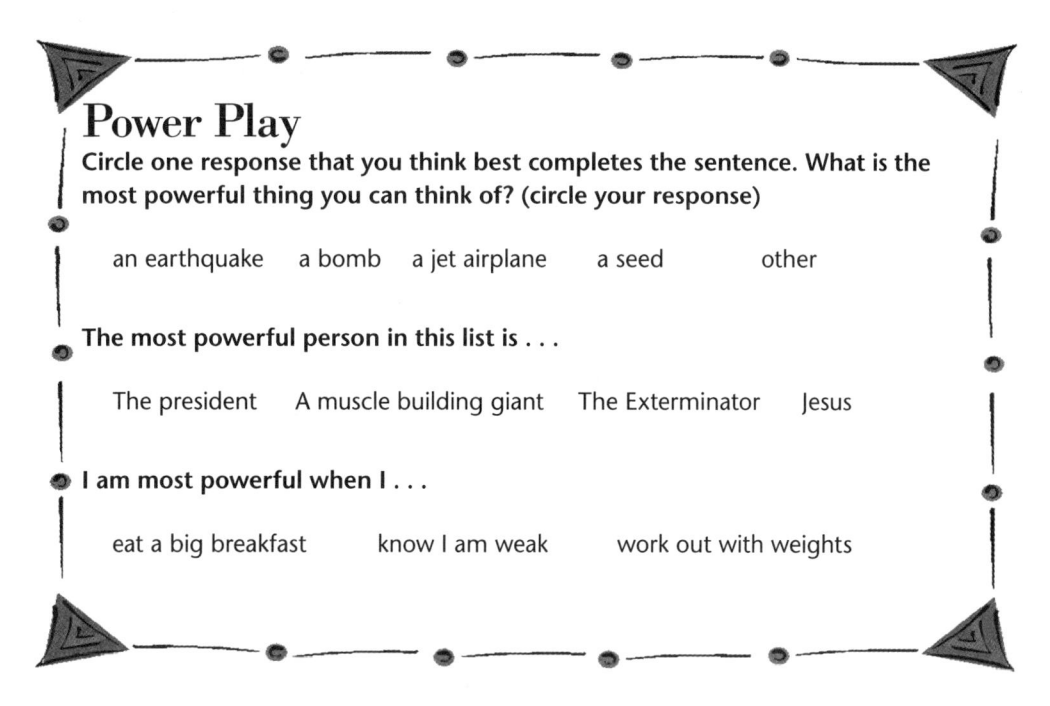

Power Play
A readiness inventory

Power Play

Circle one response that you think best completes the sentence. What is the most powerful thing you can think of? (circle your response)

an earthquake   a bomb   a jet airplane   a seed   other

The most powerful person in this list is . . .

The president   A muscle building giant   The Exterminator   Jesus

I am most powerful when I . . .

eat a big breakfast   know I am weak   work out with weights

See next page for photocopy master

Let's talk
Read 2 Corinthians 12:10. What does Paul say about feeling weak? How can we be both weak and strong at the same time?

Use with
- Nehemiah rebuilds the temple
- Saul's conversion
- Jonathan's victory

Power Play

Circle one response that you think best completes the sentence. What is the most powerful thing you can think of? (circle your response)

    an earthquake   a bomb   a jet airplane   a seed   other

The most powerful person in this list is . . .

    The president   A muscle building giant   The Exterminator   Jesus

I am most powerful when I . . .

    eat a big breakfast   know I am weak   work out with weights

---

Power Play

Circle one response that you think best completes the sentence. What is the most powerful thing you can think of? (circle your response)

    an earthquake   a bomb   a jet airplane   a seed   other

The most powerful person in this list is . . .

    The president   A muscle building giant   The Exterminator   Jesus

I am most powerful when I . . .

    eat a big breakfast   know I am weak   work out with weights

Prayer Inventory
A readiness activity

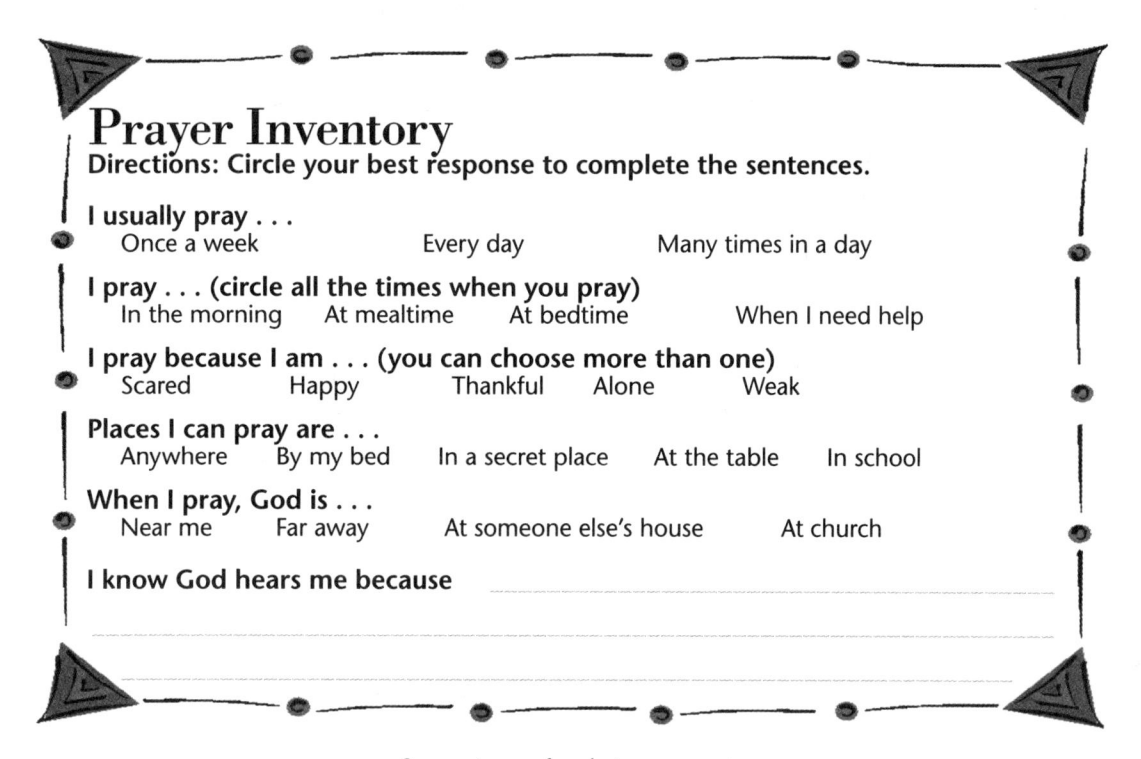

Prayer Inventory
Directions: Circle your best response to complete the sentences.

I usually pray . . .
  Once a week   Every day   Many times in a day

I pray . . . (circle all the times when you pray)
  In the morning   At mealtime   At bedtime   When I need help

I pray because I am . . . (you can choose more than one)
  Scared   Happy   Thankful   Alone   Weak

Places I can pray are . . .
  Anywhere   By my bed   In a secret place   At the table   In school

When I pray, God is . . .
  Near me   Far away   At someone else's house   At church

I know God hears me because _____

See next page for photocopy master

Use with
- Jesus prays
- Dedicating the temple
- As preparation for prayer

Inventories

Prayer Inventory

Directions: Circle your best response to complete the sentences.

I usually pray . . .
    Once a week   Every day   Many times in a day

I pray . . . (circle all the times when you pray)
    In the morning   At mealtime   At bedtime   When I need help

I pray because I am . . . (you can choose more than one)
    Scared   Happy   Thankful   Alone   Weak

Places I can pray are . . .
    Anywhere   By my bed   In a secret place   At the table   In school

When I pray, God is . . .
    Near me   Far away   At someone else's house   At church

I know God hears me because _____

_____

Prayer Inventory

Directions: Circle your best response to complete the sentences.

I usually pray . . .
    Once a week   Every day   Many times in a day

I pray . . . (circle all the times when you pray)
    In the morning   At mealtime   At bedtime   When I need help

I pray because I am . . . (you can choose more than one)
    Scared   Happy   Thankful   Alone   Weak

Places I can pray are . . .
    Anywhere   By my bed   In a secret place   At the table   In school

When I pray, God is . . .
    Near me   Far away   At someone else's house   At church

I know God hears me because _____

_____

Temperaments
An application activity

TEMPERAMENT INVENTORY

1. As a person, I am most like...
   - a. A lion
   - b. An otter
   - c. A panda
   - d. A beaver

2. When I play, I am most like...
   - a. A fire engine
   - b. A bulldozer
   - c. A dump truck
   - d. A steam roller

3. When I am at Sabbath School, I am most like a...
   - a. Buzzing bee
   - b. Wiggle worm
   - c. Lady bug
   - d. Butterfly

4. When I think about my feelings, they are mostly...
   - a. Sunny
   - b. Wet
   - c. Cold
   - d. Stormy

5. When I wake up in the morning, I am most like a...
   - a. Kitten
   - b. Snail
   - c. Frog
   - d. Crab

6. When I am by myself, I am most like a...
   - a. Teddy bear
   - b. Puzzle
   - c. Coloring book
   - d. Building block

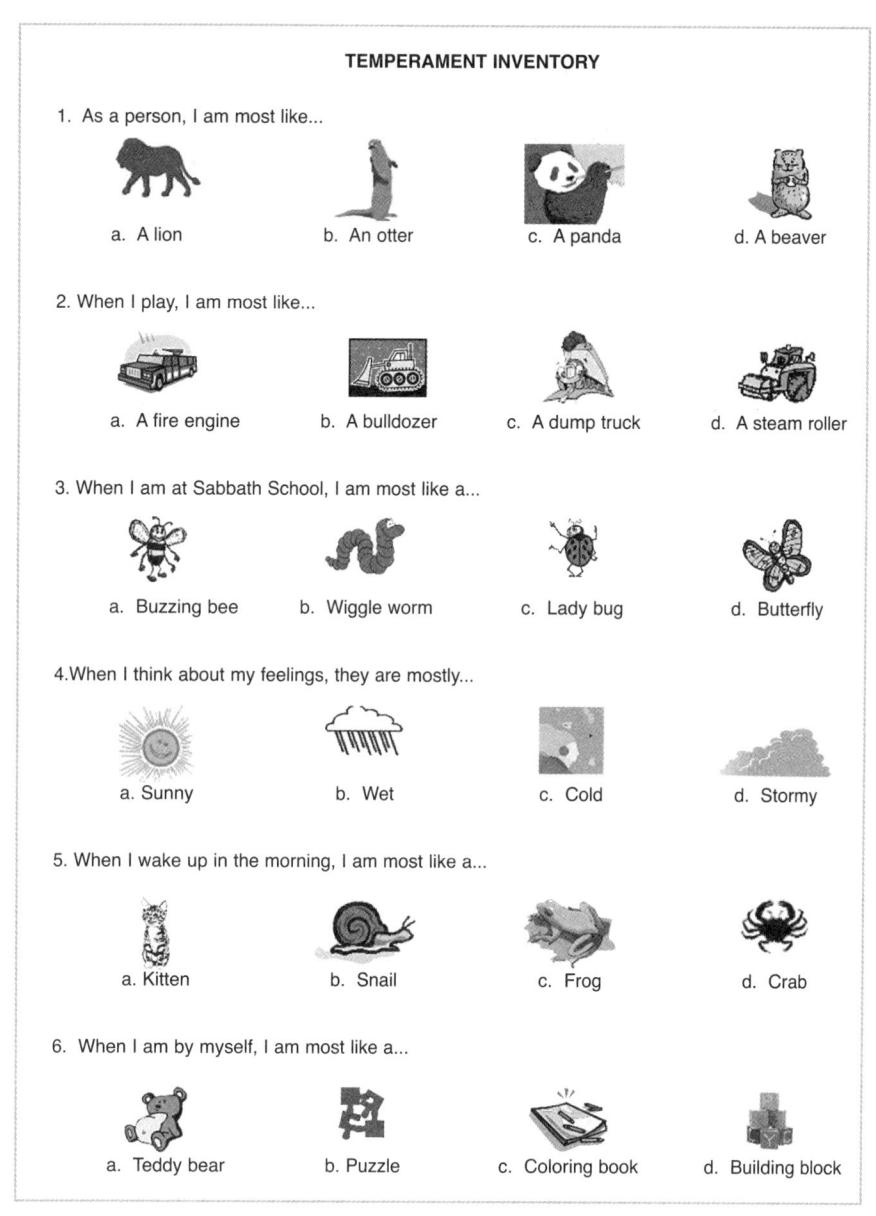

See next page for photocopy master

Let's Talk
Which animal did you like best? In what ways might you be like the animal you just chose? Which animal do you think (name a character from the lesson) is most like?

Use with
- Jacob leaves home (Choose an animal that is like Jacob, Esau, Isaac, Rebekah; accept animals not included in the inventory.)
- Escape to Egypt (choose for Jesus, Joseph, Mary, Magi, etc.)

Inventories

TEMPERAMENT INVENTORY

1. As a person, I am most like...

   a. A lion   b. An otter   c. A panda   d. A beaver

2. When I play, I am most like...

   a. A fire engine   b. A bulldozer   c. A dump truck   d. A steam roller

3. When I am at Sabbath School, I am most like a...

   a. Buzzing bee   b. Wiggle worm   c. Lady bug   d. Butterfly

4. When I think about my feelings, they are mostly...

   a. Sunny   b. Wet   c. Cold   d. Stormy

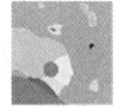

5. When I wake up in the morning, I am most like a...

   a. Kitten   b. Snail   c. Frog   d. Crab

6. When I am by myself, I am most like a...

   a. Teddy bear   b. Puzzle   c. Coloring book   d. Building block

Spiritual Gifts Treasure Hunt
An application activity

Activity

This simplified spiritual gifts inventory introduces children to just four of the many spiritual gifts talked about in the Bible: the gifts of leadership, knowledge, helping, and evangelism. This inventory works best for children age 9 and older.

Give each child a copy of the Spiritual Gifts Treasure Hunt. Once they have completed their inventory help them total and score their inventory.

Spiritual Gifts Treasure Hunt

Directions: Choose the response that is most true for you.

1. **A friend seems to be feeling sad and lonely. So I would....**
   a. talk to some other friends about planning a special event to cheer her up.
   b. tell her a story and Bible verse I learned that made me feel better.
   c. invite her to my house and give her one of my toys to play with.
   d. tell her about Jesus and pray with her.

2. **Everyone has to help with our Sabbath School class party. I would choose to:**
   a. be the one who organizes others and makes sure they have their jobs done.
   b. keep lists of what needs to be done and make sure nothing is forgotten.
   c. decorate the room and bake cookies.
   d. invite neighborhood friends to come and join us for the party.

3. **At the end of the school year, I'd be most likely to get a prize for:**
   a. being a class leader.
   b. getting high grades.
   c. helping others.
   d. being friendly and outgoing.

4. **I discover that a friend is stealing from stores. So I...**
   a. talk to an adult to find out what's the right thing to do.
   b. find out everything I could about shoplifting and study the Bible so I could explain to him why it's wrong.
   c. spend some time with him and see if I could get him involved in other things.
   d. tell him that I know what he's doing and offer to pray with him that God will help him stop.

5. **My idea of a perfect day would be:**
   a. organizing a group of my friends to go do something special.
   b. spending some time alone reading a favorite book.
   c. doing a project around the house with my mom or dad.
   d. getting to know the kids who just moved in down the street.

6. **My friends really want me to watch a movie with them, but I know my parents would not approve. So I would:**
   a. suggest another video we could all watch.
   b. help myself grow strong by memorizing a chapter of the Bible.
   c. find something else useful to do with my time, like making or fixing something.
   d. suggest to my friends that we play some games together instead.

7. **A younger child is hurt on the playground. I would:**
   a. send someone to call an adult while I stayed with the child.
   b. remember what I learned in class about first aid.
   c. do what I could to make the child feel better while holding her hand.
   d. say a prayer for the child.

8. **I most often get praised for:**
   a. taking charge of a situation.
   b. always knowing the right answer.
   c. being helpful.
   d. telling others about Jesus.

9. **A classmate who doesn't believe in God makes fun of my friends and me because we do. So I:**
   a. tell her she's being mean and has to stop it.
   b. explain the reasons why I believe there is a God.
   c. get to know this person and try to become a friend so she won't be so unkind.
   d. invite her to come to a fun children's event at our church so she can find out what it's all about.

10. **When I grow up, I think a perfect job would be:**
    a. running my own business or being in charge of a big company.
    b. being a teacher or a college professor.
    c. working as a nurse or doctor so I could make people better.
    d. going overseas as a missionary.

Score	Gift Type
a _____	Leader
b _____	Knowledge
c _____	Helper
d _____	Friend

To score: Count the number of "a." responses and write the number in the space beside a. Do the same for b, c, and d. The gift with the highest score could be your spiritual gift.

See next page for photocopy master

Scoring

If most or many of your answers were "A", you may have the gift of **LEADERSHIP**. You understand what needs to be done and can get others working together to do it. God needs people like you to run the many programs and organizations of the church.

If most or many of your answers were "B," you may have the gift of **KNOWLEDGE**. You like learning and can understand things well, especially things to do with the Bible. God can use you to help others understand His Word better

If most or many of your answers were "C," you may have the gift of **HELPING**. You are good at doing practical things to serve others. God needs people like you in many ways to help others.

If most or many of your answers were "D," you may have the gift of **EVANGELISM**. You are comfortable with all kinds of people, like meeting new people, and love telling others about Jesus. God can use you to spread His message in your own community and maybe someday even in other countries.

Use with
- Lessons about service
- The tongues of fire
- Abraham and Melchizedek
- Sending disciples two by two
- Esther saves her people

Inventories

Spiritual Gifts Treasure Hunt

Directions: Choose the response that is most true for you.

1. **A friend seems to be feeling sad and lonely. So I would....**
   a. talk to some other friends about planning a special event to cheer her up.
   b. tell her a story and Bible verse I learned that made me feel better.
   c. invite her to my house and give her one of my toys to play with.
   d. tell her about Jesus and pray with her.

2. **Everyone has to help with our Sabbath School class party. I would choose to:**
   a. be the one who organizes others and makes sure they have their jobs done.
   b. keep lists of what needs to be done and make sure nothing is forgotten.
   c. decorate the room and bake cookies.
   d. invite neighborhood friends to come and join us for the party.

3. **At the end of the school year, I'd be most likely to get a prize for:**
   a. being a class leader.
   b. getting high grades.
   c. helping others.
   d. being friendly and outgoing.

4. **I discover that a friend is stealing from stores. So I...**
   a. talk to an adult to find out what's the right thing to do.
   b. find out everything I could about shoplifting and study the Bible so I could explain to him why it's wrong.
   c. spend some time with him and see if I could get him involved in other things.
   d. tell him that I know what he's doing and offer to pray with him that God will help him stop.

5. **My idea of a perfect day would be:**
   a. organizing a group of my friends to go do something special.
   b. spending some time alone reading a favorite book.
   c. doing a project around the house with my mom or dad.
   d. getting to know the kids who just moved in down the street.

To score: Count the number of "a." responses and write the number in the space beside a. Do the same for b, c, and d. The gift with the highest score could be your spiritual gift.

6. **My friends really want me to watch a movie with them, but I know my parents would not approve. So I would:**
   a. suggest another video we could all watch.
   b. help myself grow strong by memorizing a chapter of the Bible.
   c. find something else useful to do with my time, like making or fixing something.
   d. suggest to my friends that we play some games together instead.

7. **A younger child is hurt on the playground. I would:**
   a. send someone to call an adult while I stayed with the child.
   b. remember what I learned in class about first aid.
   c. do what I could to make the child feel better while holding her hand.
   d. say a prayer for the child.

8. **I most often get praised for:**
   a. taking charge of a situation.
   b. always knowing the right answer.
   c. being helpful.
   d. telling others about Jesus.

9. **A classmate who doesn't believe in God makes fun of my friends and me because we do. So I:**
   a. tell her she's being mean and has to stop it.
   b. explain the reasons why I believe there is a God.
   c. get to know this person and try to become a friend so she won't be so unkind.
   d. invite her to come to a fun children's event at our church so she can find out what it's all about.

10. **When I grow up, I think a perfect job would be:**
    a. running my own business or being in charge of a big company.
    b. being a teacher or a college professor.
    c. working as a nurse or doctor so I could make people better.
    d. going overseas as a missionary.

Score	Gift Type
a _____	Leader
b _____	Knowledge
c _____	Helper
d _____	Friend

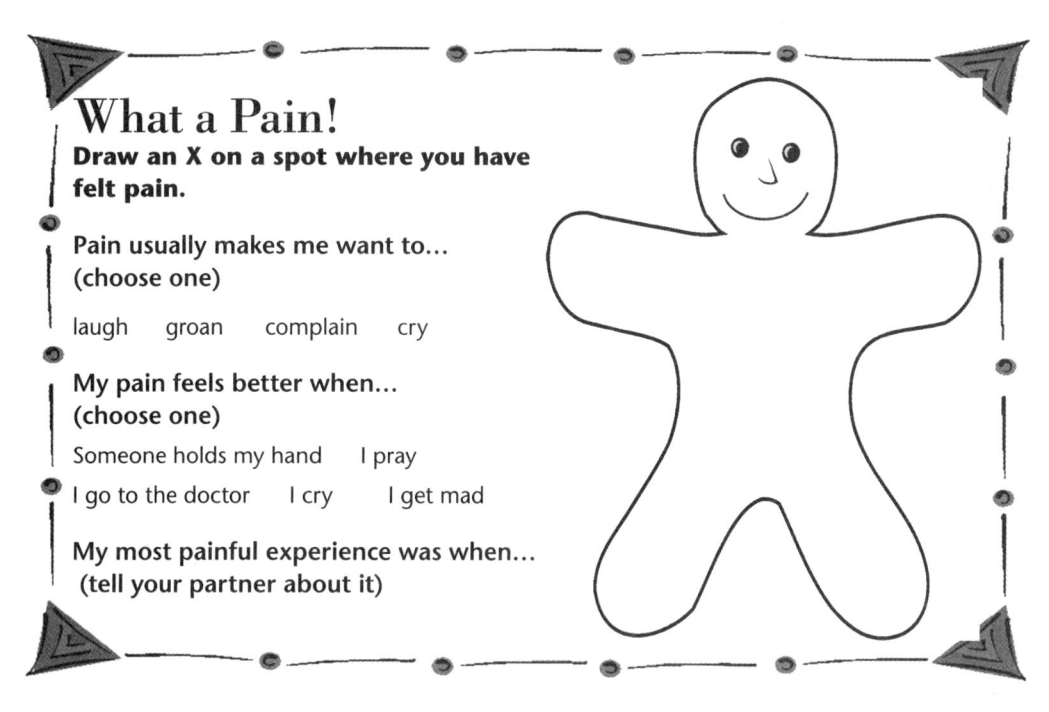

What a Pain!
A readiness activity

What a Pain!
Draw an X on a spot where you have felt pain.

Pain usually makes me want to...
(choose one)

laugh   groan   complain   cry

My pain feels better when...
(choose one)

Someone holds my hand   I pray

I go to the doctor   I cry   I get mad

My most painful experience was when...
(tell your partner about it)

See next page for photocopy master

Let's talk
Have you ever had a sharp pain? A throbbing pain? A dull ache? Where does it hurt when you feel sad? How can we serve people who are in pain?

Use with
- Eutycus falls from a window
- Healing in the streets
- Hezekiah healed

Inventories

What a Pain!
Draw an X on a spot where you have felt pain.

Pain usually makes me want to...
(choose one)

laugh   groan   complain   cry

My pain feels better when...
(choose one)

Someone holds my hand   I pray

I go to the doctor   I cry   I get mad

My most painful experience was when...
 (tell your partner about it)

What a Pain!
Draw an X on a spot where you have felt pain.

Pain usually makes me want to...
(choose one)

laugh   groan   complain   cry

My pain feels better when...
(choose one)

Someone holds my hand   I pray

I go to the doctor   I cry   I get mad

My most painful experience was when...
 (tell your partner about it)

What I Know About God
A readiness activity

What I Know About God

Directions: Put an X on the line to show how well you know God.

How well do you know God?
____ Not at all ____ A little ____ A lot ____ Really well

What do you think God is most like?
____ An old person ____ A father ____ Jesus ____ A young person

How much do you love God?
____ Not at all ____ A little ____ A lot ____ With my whole heart

How would you feel if Jesus came back today?
____ Happy ____ I'm not sure ____ Scared ____ Sad

If you could, what would you want to ask God? _____

What do you want God to know about you? _____

See next page for photocopy master

Let's talk
Do you know anyone who is scared of God? What can you tell them so they won't be scared of Him? Who do you know who rejoices in God's presence? Ask them why they feel so good about Him.

Use with
- The Transfiguration
- The burning bush
- Ten Commandments

What I Know About God

Directions: Put an X on the line to show how well you know God.

How well do you know God?
___ Not at all   ___ A little   ___ A lot   ___ Really well

What do you think God is most like?
___ An old person   ___ A father   ___ Jesus   ___ A young person

How much do you love God?
___ Not at all   ___ A little   ___ A lot   ___ With my whole heart

How would you feel if Jesus came back today?
___ Happy   ___ I'm not sure   ___ Scared   ___ Sad

If you could, what would you want to ask God? _____
_____

What do you want God to know about you? _____
_____

What I Know About God

Directions: Put an X on the line to show how well you know God.

How well do you know God?
___ Not at all   ___ A little   ___ A lot   ___ Really well

What do you think God is most like?
___ An old person   ___ A father   ___ Jesus   ___ A young person

How much do you love God?
___ Not at all   ___ A little   ___ A lot   ___ With my whole heart

How would you feel if Jesus came back today?
___ Happy   ___ I'm not sure   ___ Scared   ___ Sad

If you could, what would you want to ask God? _____
_____

What do you want God to know about you? _____
_____

use with **Introduction (page 1)**

UNDERSTANDING OURSELVES AND HOW GOD IS AT WORK IN US

How we learn to better understand ourselves and our Christian experience with God may be thought of in terms of our life-long process of growth, learning, and "inner change" as we become more aware of the message and meaning of Jesus Christ as it "crosses with" our persistent life concerns and stages of growth from age to age. The following "Life-Span Curve"* provides a way for us to interpret this.

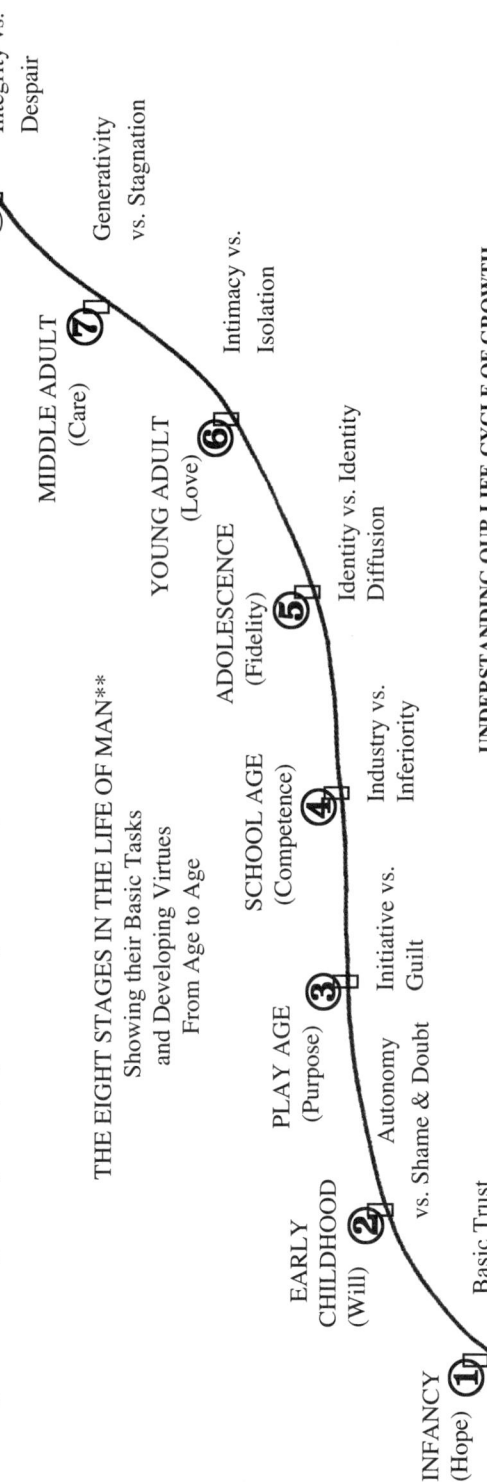

THE EIGHT STAGES IN THE LIFE OF MAN**
Showing their Basic Tasks
and Developing Virtues
From Age to Age

① INFANCY (Hope) — Basic Trust vs. Mistrust

② EARLY CHILDHOOD (Will) — Autonomy vs. Shame & Doubt

③ PLAY AGE (Purpose) — Initiative vs. Guilt

④ SCHOOL AGE (Competence) — Industry vs. Inferiority

⑤ ADOLESCENCE (Fidelity) — Identity vs. Identity Diffusion

⑥ YOUNG ADULT (Love) — Intimacy vs. Isolation

⑦ MIDDLE ADULT (Care) — Generativity vs. Stagnation

⑧ MATURE ADULT (Wisdom) — Integrity vs. Despair

BIRTH

UNDERSTANDING OUR LIFE-CYCLE OF GROWTH

A. In our lives, God is as personally being present in us as an active creative spirit or force affecting an unfolding process of creation in us through each stage of our life-long process of growth, learning and "inner change."

B. As we come to resolve each "developmental task" at its time of crucial importance, we develop certain "inner strengths" or VIRTUES which help to give our lives direction and contribute toward the development of character.

C. How well our sense of character and feeling of personal identity come into being is dependent upon how well we resolve each developmental task at its earlier critical stage of development as well as when each reappears later in life.

D. With our belief in God as our Creator who continues to be at work within us, we see Jesus as the Christ--the One whose spirit in us enables us to grow and learn and change--as the HOPE, POSSIBILITY, and THE WAY of life.

* Developed by Dr. Paul Irwin, Professor of Religious Education at the School of Theology in Claremont, CA.
** Adapted from Erik Erikson in his book, *Childhood and Society*.

Appendix   A1

use with **Introduction (page 2)**

Faith Development

"And Jesus grew in wisdom and stature and in favor with God and man." Luke 2:52

1. Four Areas of Development
   Luke 2:52 suggests that Jesus developed in four basic areas:
   a. Mental--"wisdom"
   b. Physical--"stature"
   c. Spiritual--"in favor with God"
   d. Social--"in favor with . . . man"

2. What is Faith? "Faith is a living, growing relationship with God that develops throughout life."
   a. Hebrews 11:1, 12:2
   b. James 2:14, 26
   c. Romans 10:17
   d. 2 Corinthians 10:15
   e. James 1:3
   f. Ephesians 3:17

   Growing in faith is growing in "trustful dependence on Jesus."
   "Let us have more confidence in our Redeemer. . . . Have faith in God. Trustful dependence on Jesus makes victory not only possible but certain" (Ellen White, *In Heavenly Places*, p. 17).

3. Stages of Faith Development: Faith grows like a tree trunk. And just as you can count the rings on a trunk, so you can identify stages of faith growth.

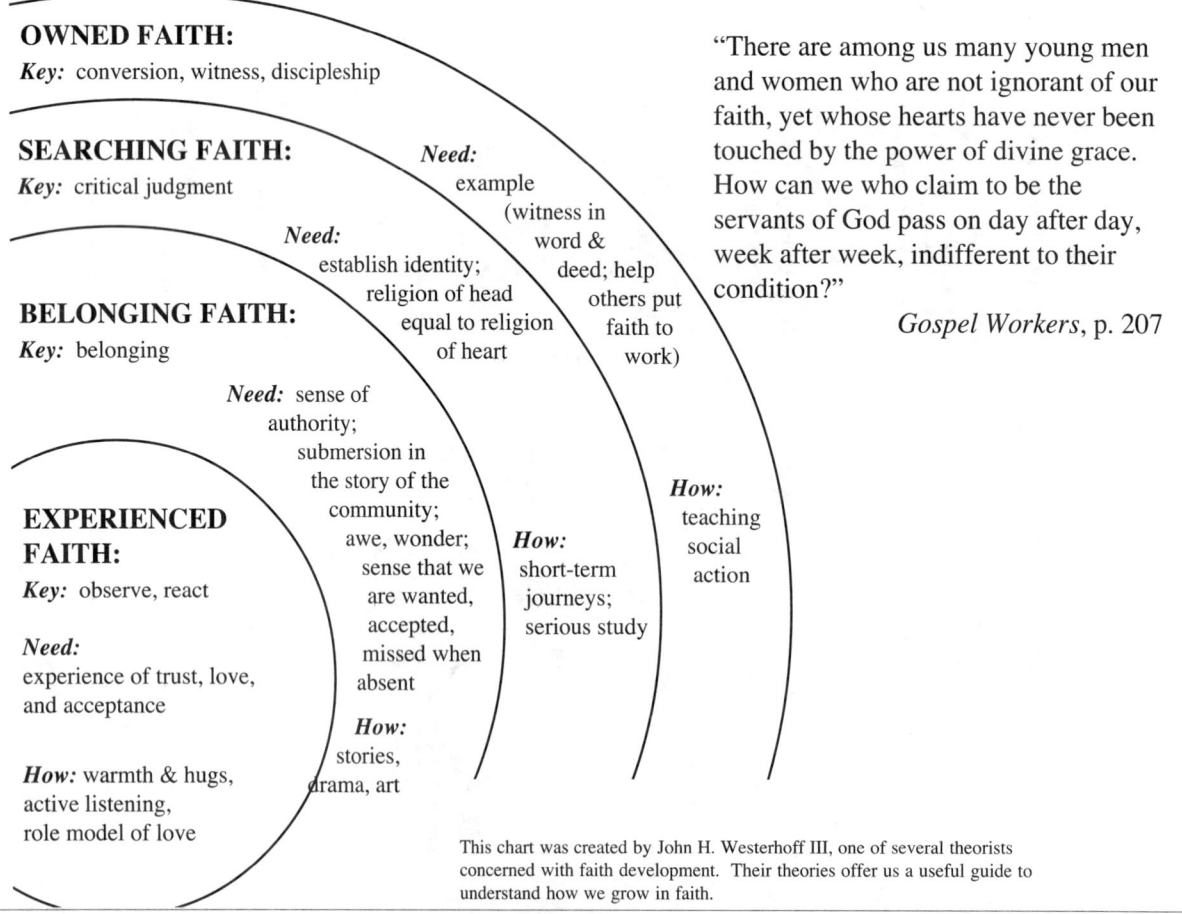

OWNED FAITH:
Key: conversion, witness, discipleship

SEARCHING FAITH:
Key: critical judgment

BELONGING FAITH:
Key: belonging

EXPERIENCED FAITH:
Key: observe, react

Need: experience of trust, love, and acceptance

How: warmth & hugs, active listening, role model of love

Need: sense of authority; submersion in the story of the community; awe, wonder; sense that we are wanted, accepted, missed when absent

How: stories, drama, art

Need: establish identity; religion of head equal to religion of heart

How: short-term journeys; serious study

Need: example (witness in word & deed; help others put faith to work)

How: teaching social action

"There are among us many young men and women who are not ignorant of our faith, yet whose hearts have never been touched by the power of divine grace. How can we who claim to be the servants of God pass on day after day, week after week, indifferent to their condition?"

Gospel Workers, p. 207

This chart was created by John H. Westerhoff III, one of several theorists concerned with faith development. Their theories offer us a useful guide to understand how we grow in faith.

use with **Doorknob Hanger (page 17)**

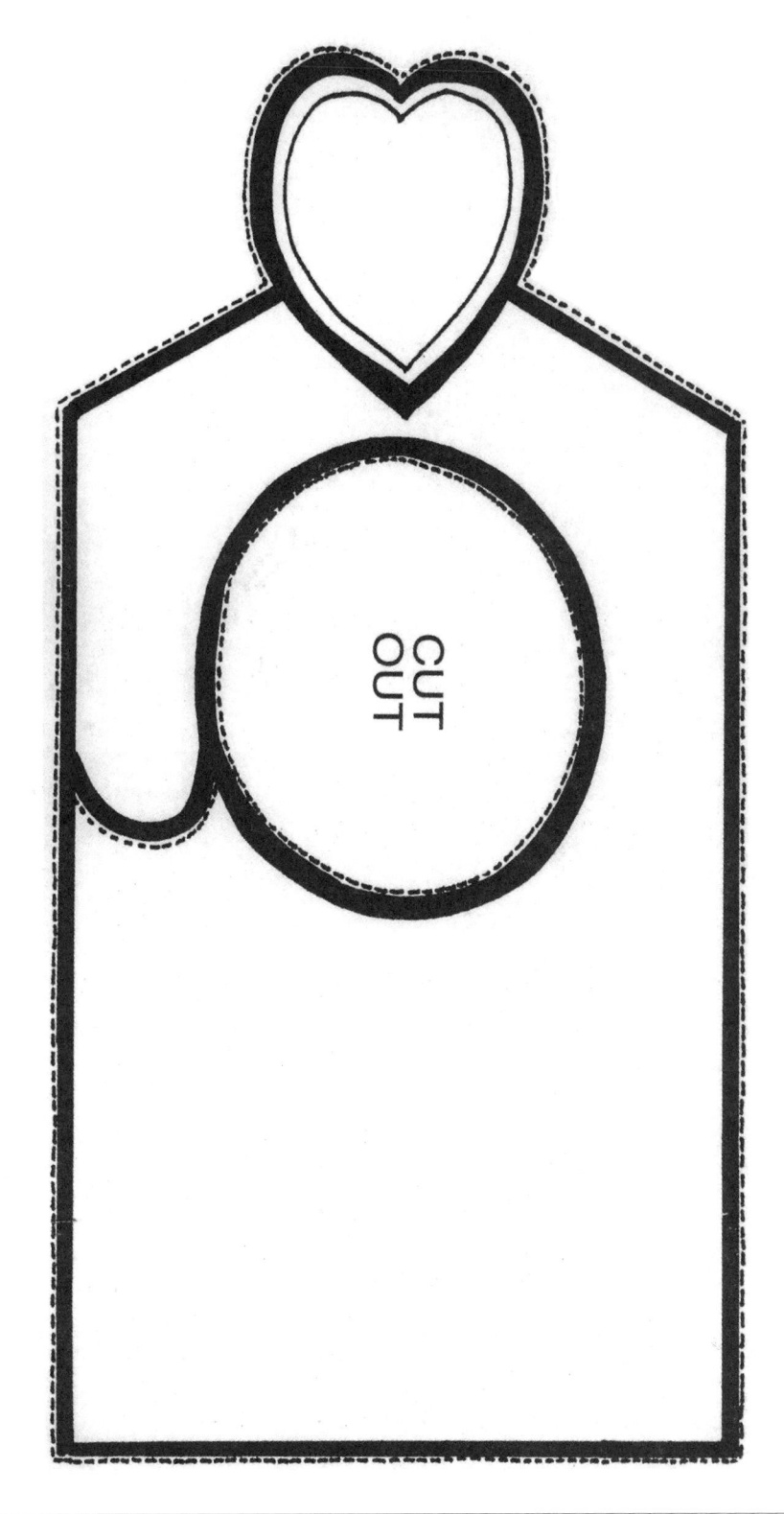

CUT OUT

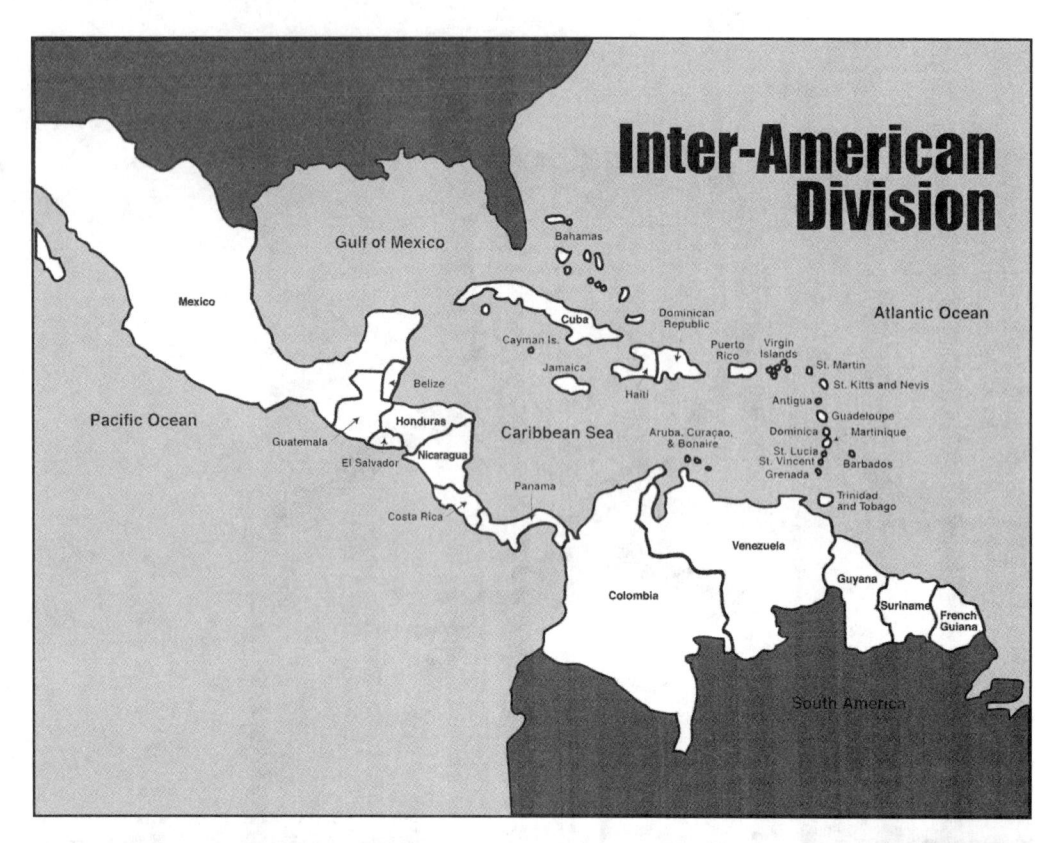

use with **Mission Maps** (page 24)

Inter-American Division

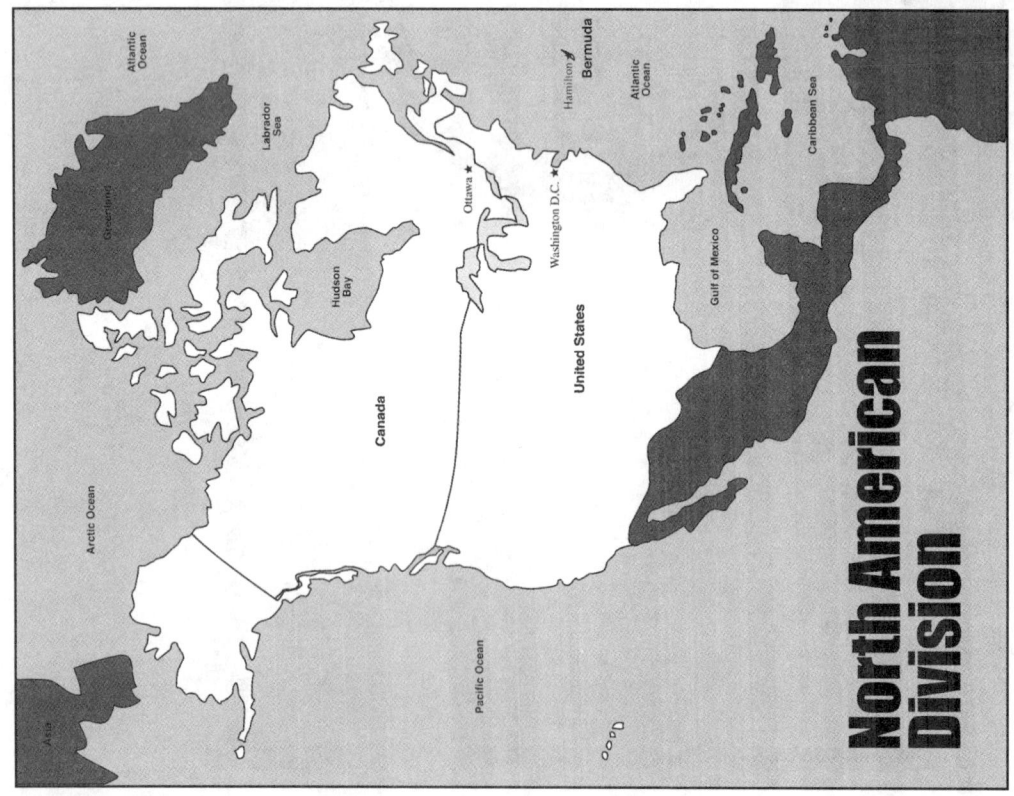

North American Division

Appendix

use with **Mission Maps (page 24)**

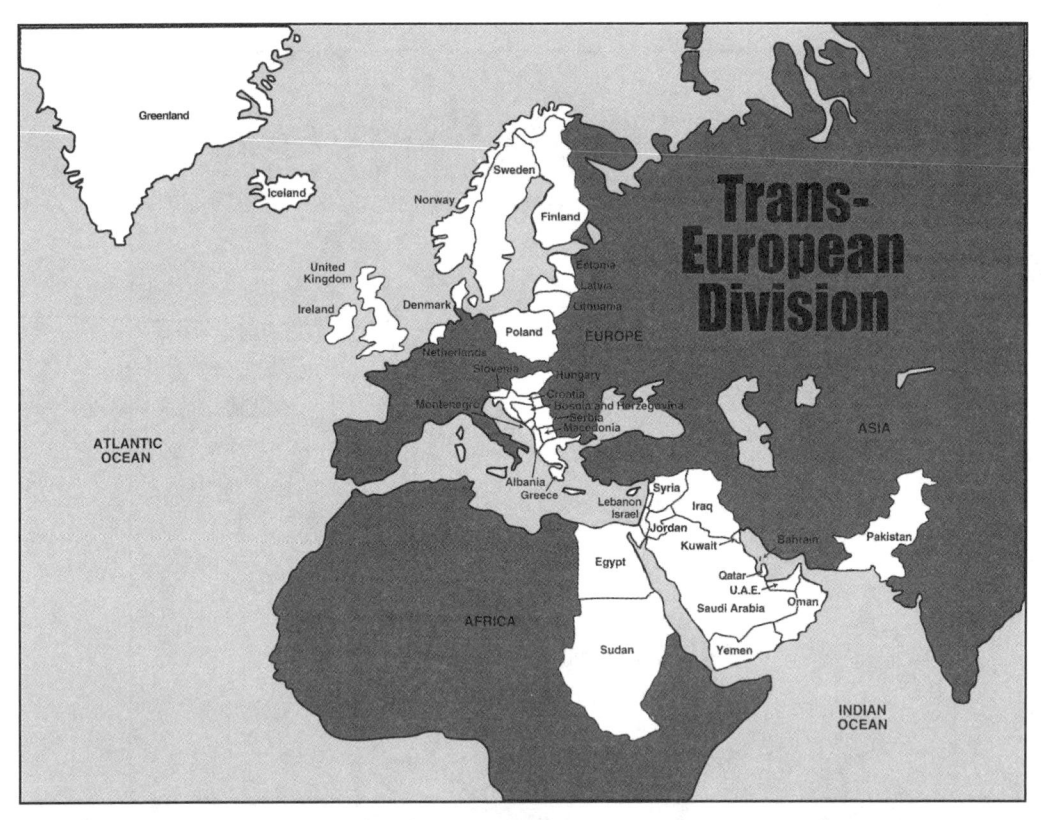

Trans-European Division

Euro-Asia Division

use with **Mission Maps (page 24)**

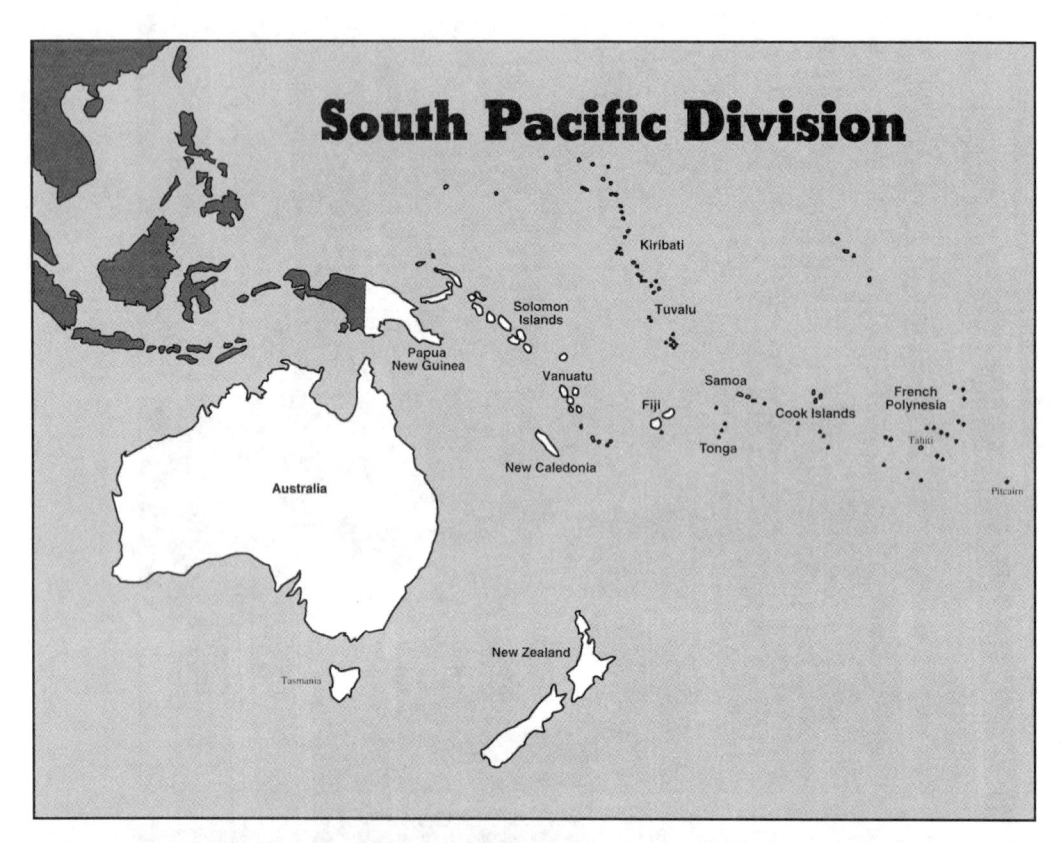

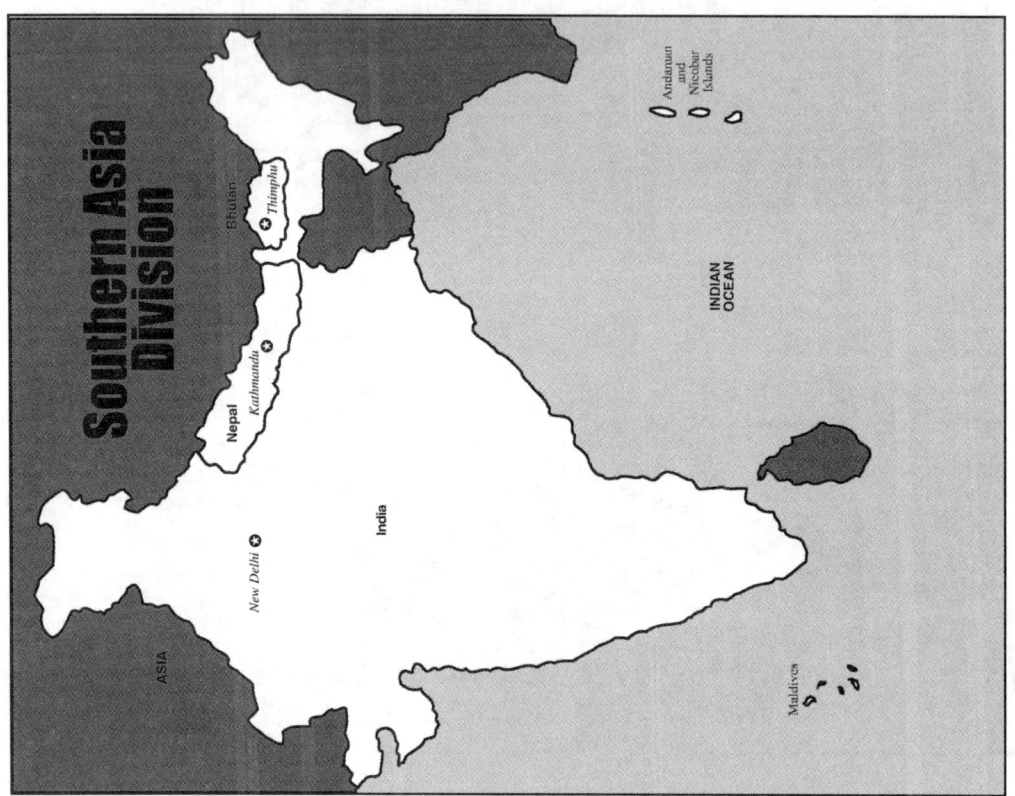

South Pacific Division

Southern Asia Division

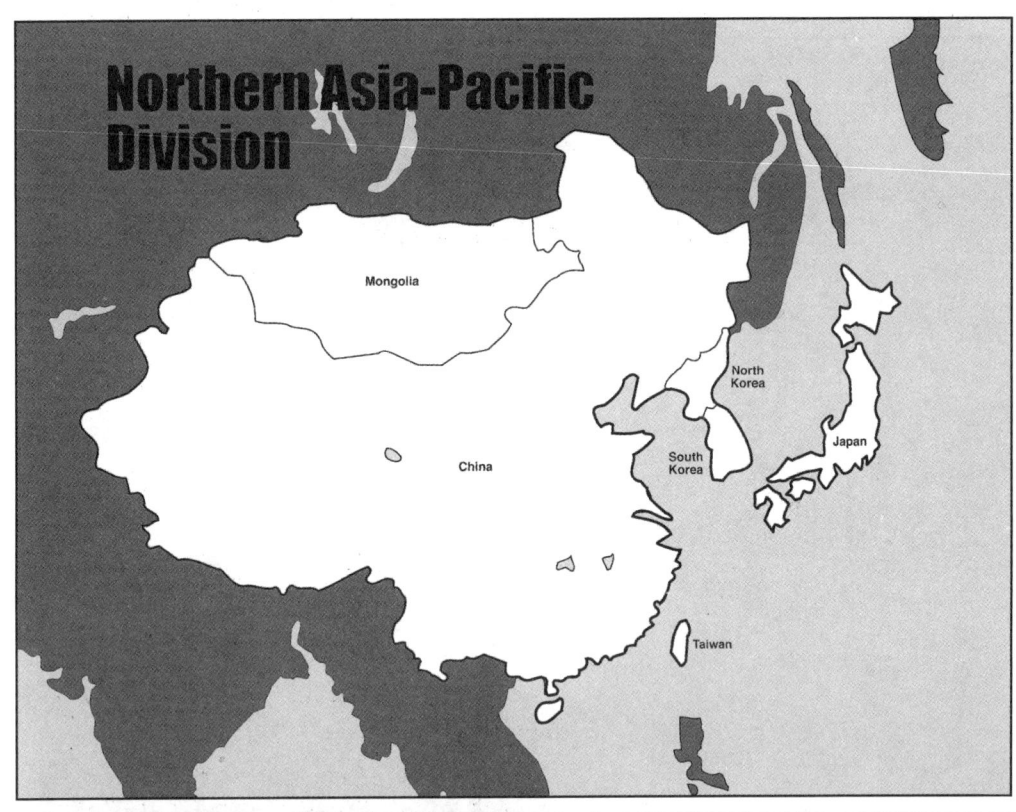

use with **Mission Maps (page 24)**

Northern Asia-Pacific Division

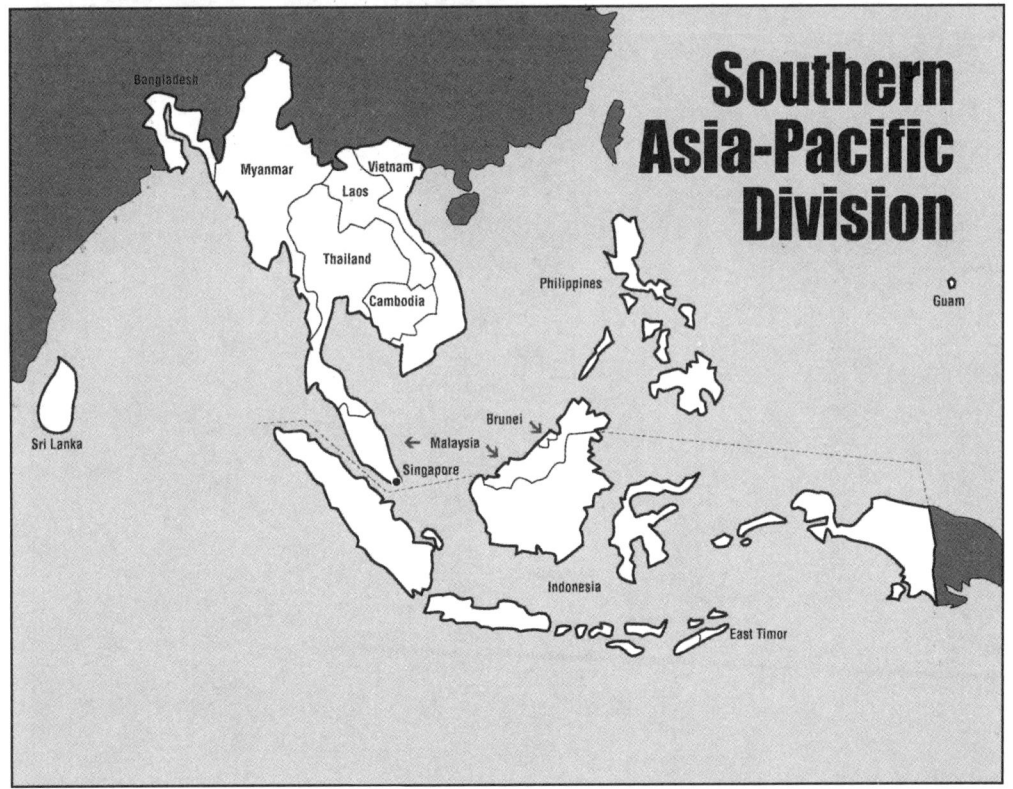

Southern Asia-Pacific Division

Appendix

use with **Mission Maps** (page 24)

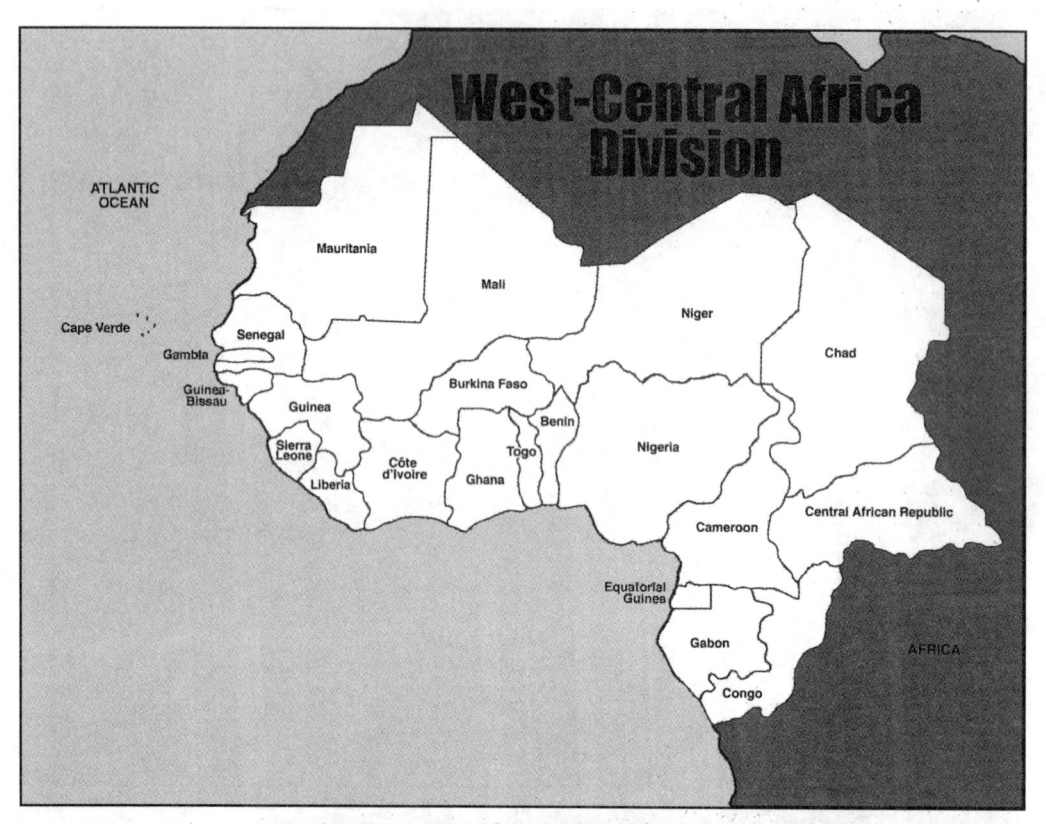

use with **Mission Maps (page 24)**

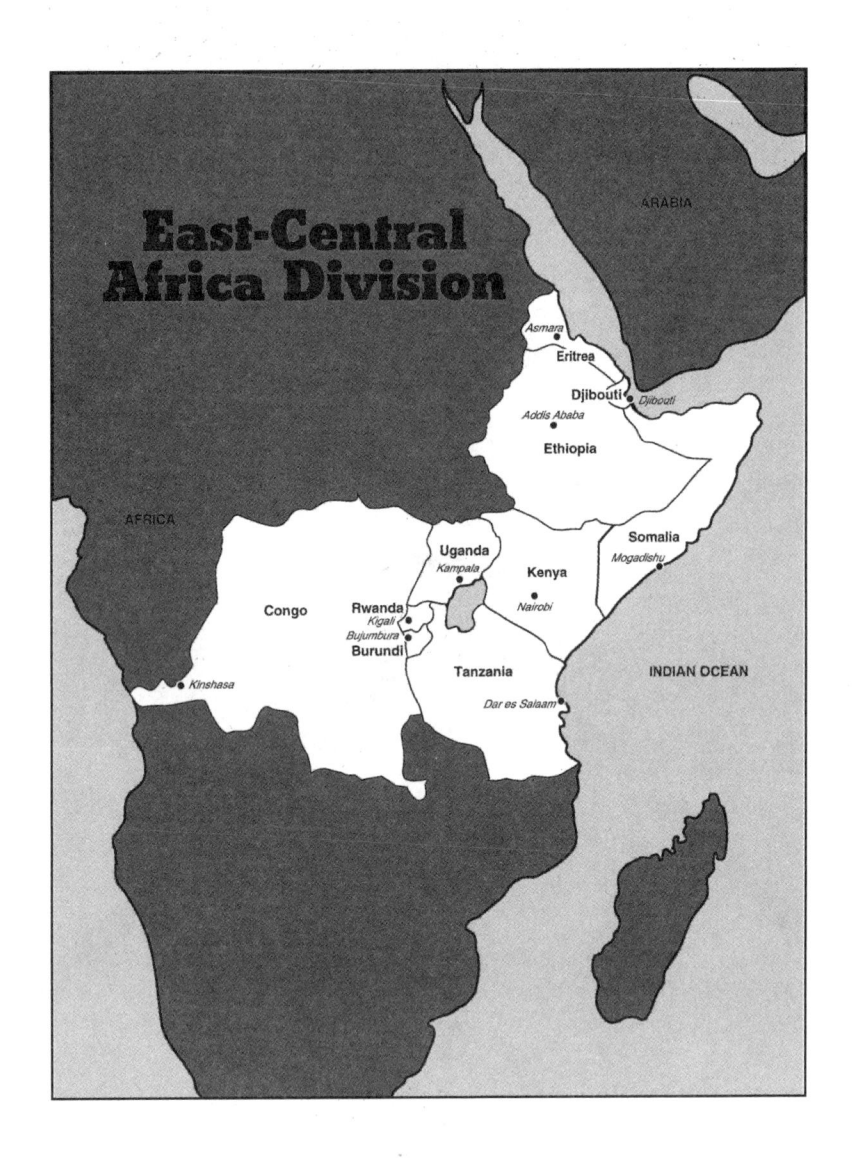

East-Central Africa Division

use with **Pay Day at Church** (page 48)

use with **Tin Can Prints** (page 33):

Appendix

A11

use with **Paper Bag Animals** (page 69):

use with **Paper Bag Animals (page 69)**

Appendix

use with **Money Pouch and Coins (page 74)**

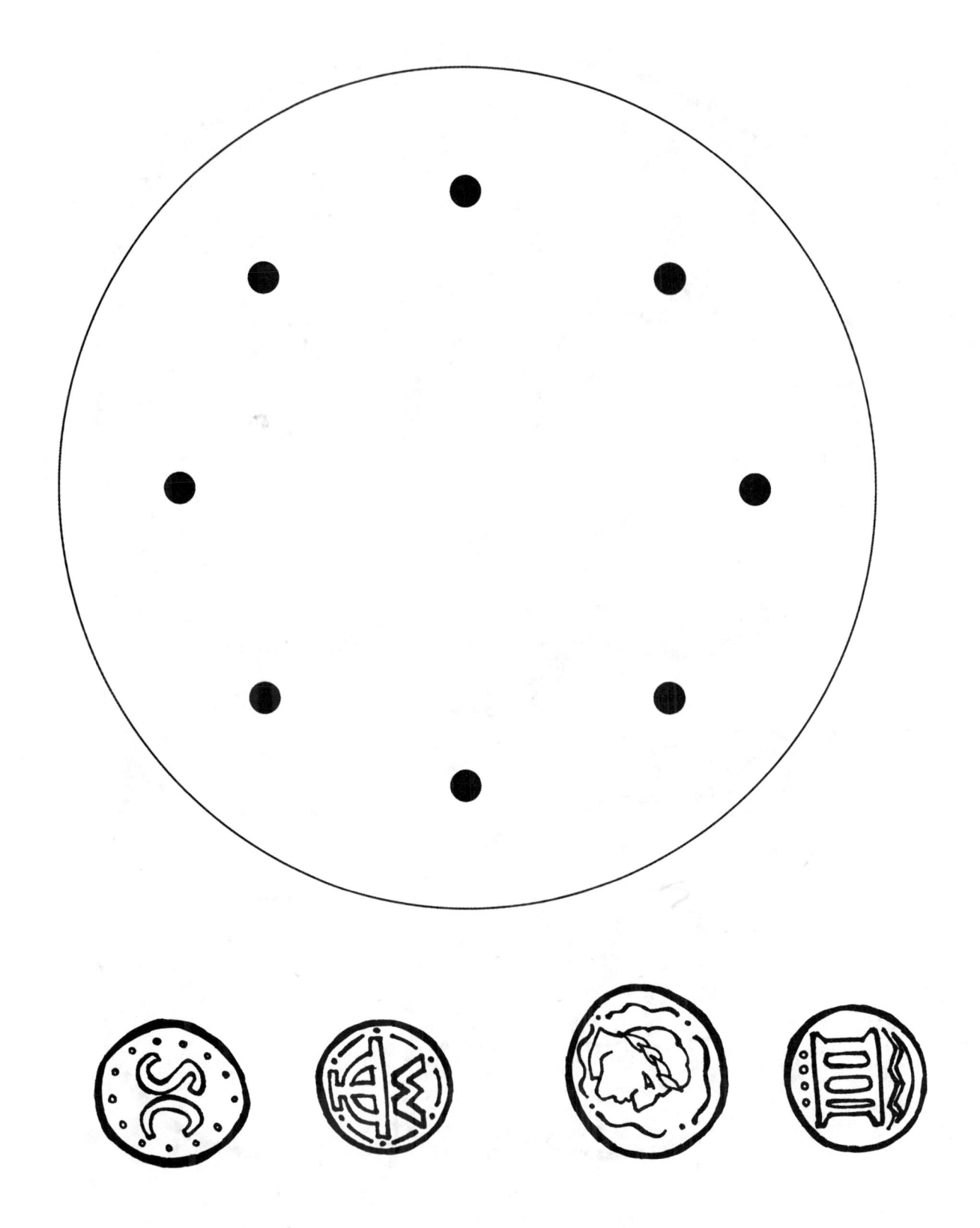

A14 Appendix

use with **Bible Times Potpourri** (page 74)

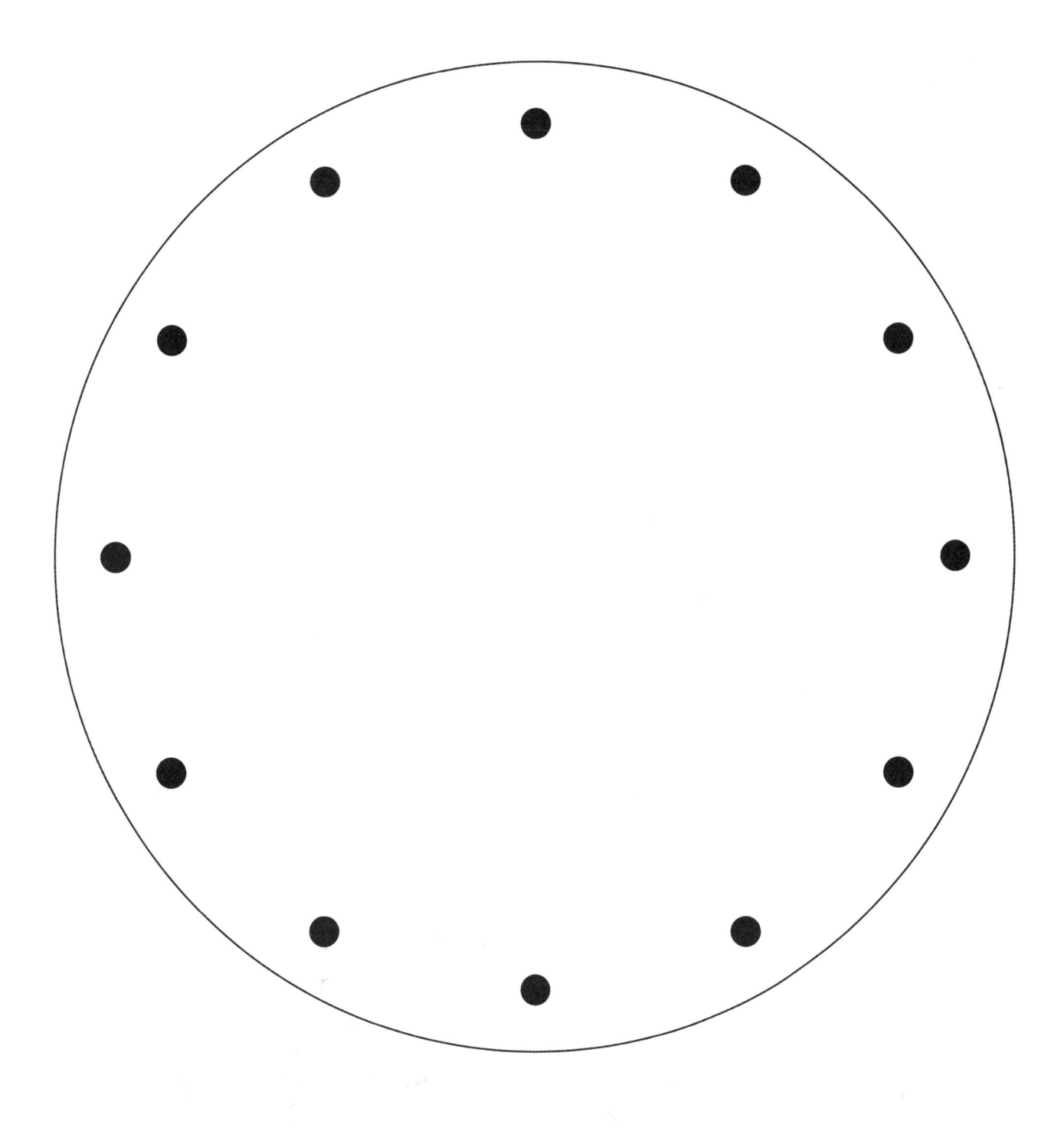

use with **How Many Friends?** (page 108)

Materials
- Poster board or empty cereal box
- Scissors
- Brass paper fastener

Directions for making a spinner
- Photocopy this page.
- Use the shaded circle pattern to draw and cut out a circle from poster board—or from a cereal box.
- Cut out the white numbers on the dashed line and push a brass brad through the center, and then through the center of the cardboard circle.
- Draw an arrow on the cardboard circle as shown.

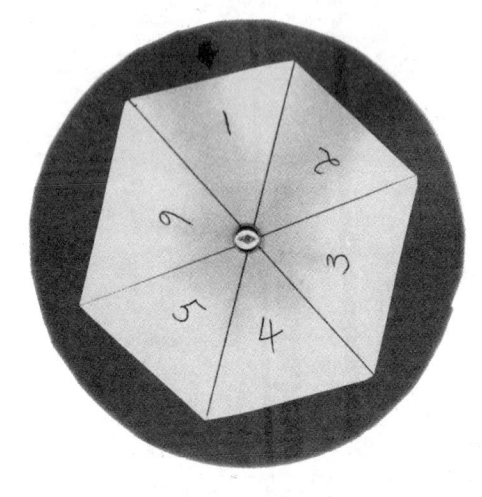

- Twist the brad until it can turn easily.
- Flick the white circle so it spins. Call the number closest to the point of the arrow.

Note: The spinner works best if the brass paper fastener is somewhat loose

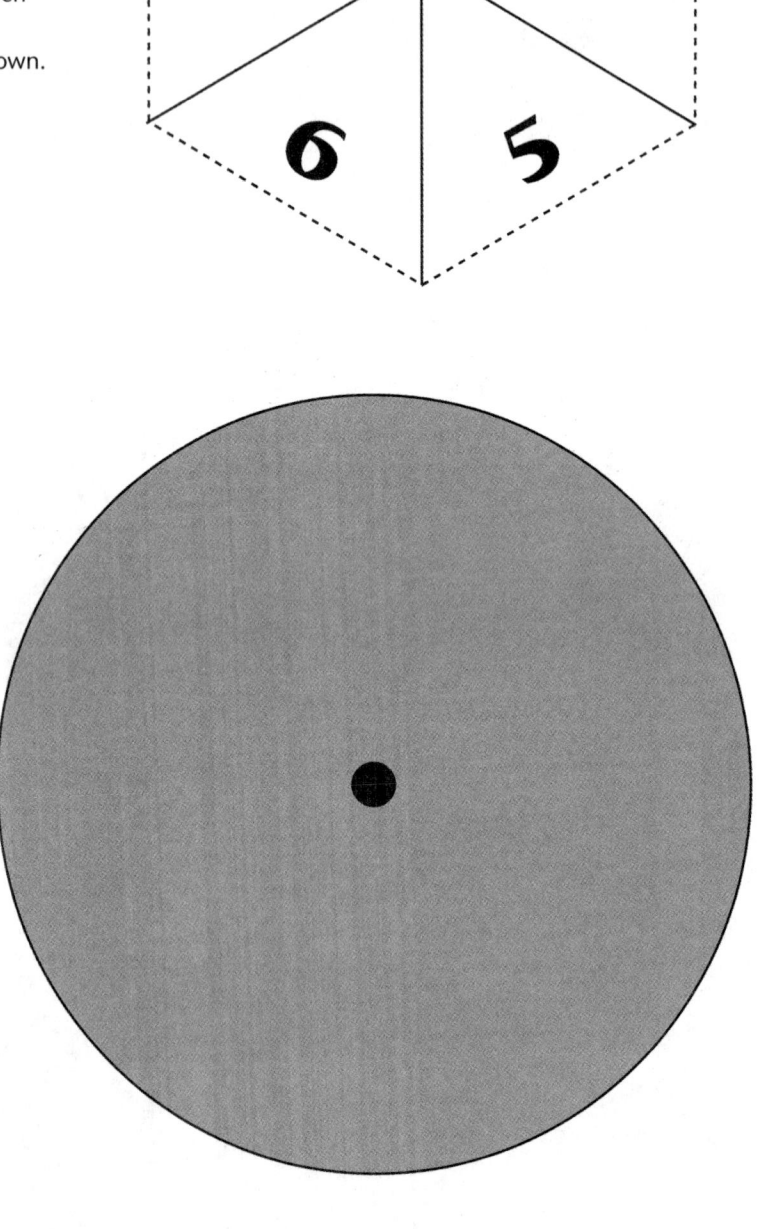

A16   Appendix

GraceLink Curriculum Index

Year A
First Quarter
Week 1- Creation days 1-6 (Gen 1:1-25)
Week 2- Adam and Eve (Gen 1:26-2:23)
Week 3- The Sabbath (Gen 2:1-3)
Week 4- Adam and Eve hide (Gen 2:8,9, 16, 17)
Week 5- Moses' early life (Ex 1,2)
Week 6- Moses at burning bush (Ex 3)
Week, 7- First nine plagues (Ex 7-10)
Week 8- Passover; last plague (Ex 11-12)
Week 9- Water from the rock (Ex 17:1-7)
Week 10- Jesus calls disciples (Mt 4:18-22)
Week 11- Matthew called (Mt 9:9-13)
Week 12- Jesus and children (Lk 18:15-17)
Week 13- Zacchaeus (Lk 19:1-10)

Second Quarter
Week 1- The Last Supper (Jn. 13:1 17)
Week 2- Simon carries cross (Mt 27:27 32)
Week 3- The Crucifixion (Mt 27)
Week 4- Resurrection (Mt 27:57 28:10)
Week 5- Feed My Sheep (Jn 21:1-17)
Week 6- Manna falls from heaven (Ex 16)
Week 7- Bronze snake (Num 21:4-9)
Week 8- Moses' Last Words (Dt 4-6, 28)
Week 9- Balaam & Donkey (Num 22-24)
Week 10- Noah builds a boat (Gen 6)
Week 11- Animals enter ark (Gen 7)
Week 12- Waiting in the ark (Gen 8:1-14)
Week 13- Rainbow promise (Gen 8:15-22)

Third Quarter
Week 1- Matthias replaces Judas (Acts 1)
Week 2- Upper room experience: Tongues of fire (Acts 1-2)
Week 3- Pentecost (Acts 2)
Week 4- The early church (Acts 2:42 47)
Week 5- The seven deacons (Acts 6:1 7)
Week 6- Saul's conversion (Acts 9:1 9)
Week 7- Saul's blindness (Acts 9:10 19)
Week 8- Barnabas believes (Acts 11:19 26)
Week 9- Paul, Barnabas go to Cyprus (Acts 13:1-12)
Week 10- Isaac's wife (Gen 24)
Week 11- Jacob & Esau (Gen 25:19 34)
Week 12- Jacob deceives (Gen 27:1 45)
Week 13- Jacob's ladder (Gen 28:10 22)

Fourth Quarter
Week 1- Rachel at the well (Gen 29:1 14)
Week 2- Laban cheats Jacob (Gen 29:15 28)
Week 3- Jacob leaves (Gen 30:24-43)
Week 4- Jacob, Esau reunited (Gen 32-33)
Week 5- Nicodemus (Jn 3:1 21)
Week 6- Jesus and Peter walk on water (Mt. 14:22 36)
Week 7- Widow's son raised (Lk 7:11 17)
Week 8- Parable of feast (Lk 14:15 24)
Week 9- Paralytic at pool of Bethesda (Jn 5:1-15)
Week 10- Angels & shepherds (Lk 2:8 15)
Week 11- Shepherds worship Jesus (Lk 2:15 20)
Week 12- Magi worship with gifts (Mt 2:1 12)
Week 13- Worship in heaven (Rev 7,21,22)

Year B
First Quarter
Week 1- Tower of Babel (Gen 11:1 9)
Week 2- Abraham's journey from Ur to Canaan (Gen 12:1 7)
Week 3- Abraham & Melchizedek (Gen 14)
Week 4- Sodom/Gomorrah (Gen 18:20 33)
Week 5- Samuel speaks for God (I Sa 12)
Week 6- Jonathan's victory (I Sa 14:1 23)
Week 7- David, shepherd boy (I Sa 16; 17:34 5)
Week 8- David shares victory (I Sa 30:1 25)
Week 9- House on the rock (Mt 7:12 29)
Week 10- Jairus' daughter (Mt 9:18 26)
Week 11- 10 lepers (Lk 17:11 19)
Week 12- Transfiguration (Mt 17:1 13)
Week 13- Paul & Silas (Ac 16:16-34)

Second Quarter
Week 1- Forgive 70x7 (Mt 18:21-35)
Week 2- Vineyard Workers (Mt 19:27 20:16)
Week 3- Mary's Perfume (Lk 7:36 50)
Week 4- Lazarus's Death/Resurrection (Jn 11)
Week 5- Moses crosses Red Sea (Ex 13:21-14:20)
Week 6- Bitter waters made sweet (Ex 15:22 27)
Week 7- Aaron's rod buds (Num 17)
Week 8- Moses strikes rock (Num 20:1 13)
Week 9- Elijah fed by ravens (I Ki 17:1 6)
Week 10- Widow of Zarephath (I Ki 17:7 24)
Week 11- Elijah on Mt. Carmel (1 Ki 18)
Week 12- Elijah and God's still, small voice (I Ki 19)
Week 13- Elijah taken in fiery chariot (2 Ki 2)

Third Quarter
Week 1- Peter & John, Sanhedrin (Ac 3-4:33)
Week 2- Peter & John escape prison (Ac 5:17)
Week 3- Stephen (Ac 6:1-8:4)
Week 4- Simon the Sorcerer (Ac 8:9-25)
Week 5- Peter heals lame man (Ac 3:1-26)
Week 6- Healing in the streets (Ac 5:12-16)
Week 7- Philip & Ethiopian (Ac 8:26-39)
Week 8- Dorcas (Ac 9:32-42)
Week 9- Moses cannot enter Canaan (Dt 6)
Week 10- Moses dies; Joshua leads (Dt 31-34)
Week 11- Joshua meets the Lord (Jos 5:13-15)
Week 12- Cities of Refuge (Dt 4:41-43, etc.)
Week 13- Offerings build Tabernacle (Ex 35:4-36:7)

Fourth Quarter
Week 1- 12 spies (Num 13:1-3, 17-33)
Week 2- Rahab helps the spies (Josh 2)
Week 3- Israelites crossing Jordan (Josh 3:4)
Week 4- Jericho falls (Josh 6)
Week 5- Boy Jesus in Temple (Luke 2)
Week 6- Jesus' childhood (Lk 2; Mat 13:55)
Week 7- Jesus, wedding at Cana (Jn 2:1-11)
Week 8- John the Baptist (Mk 1:1-12, etc.)
Week 9- Gabriel visits Mary (Lk 1:26-38, etc)
Week 10- Angel messages:Zach/Mary/Shep (Lk 1-2)
Week 11- Birth of Jesus (Lk 2:1-7)
Week 12- Angels' Song (Lk 2:8-20)
Week 13- Baby Jesus' dedication (Lk 2:21-38)

Year C
First Quarter
Week 1- 10 plagues (Ex 3:1-10, 6:28-10:29)
Week 2- Passover (Ex 12)
Week 3- Exodus (Ex 13:17-22; 14)
Week 4- 10 Commandments (Ex 20:1 17)
Week 5- Golden calf (Ex 31:18-32, etc)
Week 6- Wilderness sanctuary (Ex 25:1 9)
Week 7- Bezaleel the builder (Ex 31:1 11)
Week 8- Solomon's temple (I Kings 5 7)
Week 9- Dedicating temple (I Kings 8)
Week 10- Jonah in the boat (Jonah 1)
Week 11- Jonah in the whale (Jonah 1-2)
Week 12- Jonah in Ninevah (Jonah 3)
Week 13- Jonah & gourd (Jonah 4)

Second Quarter
Week 1- Paul worshipped (Acts 14:8 20)
Week 2- Lydia in Macedonia (Acts 16:9 15,40)
Week 3- Paul in Athens (Acts 17:15 34)
Week 4- Eutychus falls (Acts 20:5 12)
Week 5- Sabbath (Gen.2:1 3, Ex 20:8 11)
Week 6- Daniel prays (Dan 6:1 16)
Week 7- Daniel & the lions (Dan 6:10 28)
Week 8- Daniel out of lion's den (Dan.6:25 28)
Week 9- Jesus' baptism (Mt 3:1 17)
Week 10- Good Samaritan (Lk 10:25 37)
Week 11- Prodigal Son (Lk 15:11 32)
Week 12- 10 Bridesmaids (Mt 25:1 13)
Week 13- Sheep & Goats (Mt 25:31-46)

Third Quarter
Week 1- Fishers of men (Mt 4:18-22, etc)
Week 2- Disciples go two by two (Mt 10:1-16, etc)
Week 3- Woman at the well (Jn 4:1-42)
Week 4- Jesus feeds 5000 (Mt 14:13-21, etc)
Week 5- Elisha & Shunemmite (2 Ki 4:8-37)
Week 6- Naaman (2 Ki 5:1-16)
Week 7- Floating Axehead (2 Ki 6:1-7)
Week 8- Elisha and invisible army (2 Ki 6:8-23)
Week 9- Joseph sold (Gen 37)
Week 10- Potiphar's wife (Gen 39)
Week 11- Joseph rules Egypt (Gen 40, 41)
Week 12- Joseph forgives (Gen 42-45)
Week 13- Joseph's family (Gen 45:16-47:12)

Fourth Quarter
Week 1- Priscilla & Aquila (Ac 18)
Week 2- Titus (2 Cor 2:12, 13, etc)
Week 3- Onesimus, Philemon (Philemon)
Week 4- Timothy (2 Tim)
Week 5- Isaiah's vision of throne (Is 6)
Week 6- Hezekiah healed (Is 38:1-21)
Week 7- Jeremiah & potter (Jer 18:1-6)
Week 8- Nehemiah rebuilds (Neh 1-4, 6)
Week 9- New/Old Testament prophecies (Mic 5:2, etc)
Week 10- Zechariah & angel (Lk 1:5-23, etc)
Week 11- Mary & Gabriel (Lk 1:26-56)
Week 12- Angels & shepherds (Lk 2:1-14)
Week 13- Shepherds give news (Lk 2:15-20)

Year D

First Quarter
Week 1- Speck/plank parable (Mt 7:1-12)
Week 2- First in the kingdom (Mt 20:20-28)
Week 3- Paralytic through the roof (Mt 9:1-8)
Week 4- Jesus heals the blind man (Jn 9)
Week 5- Lost sheep (Mt 18:12-14)
Week 6- Lost coin (Lk 15:8-10)
Week 7- Jesus calms the storm (Mt 8:23-27)
Week 8- Jesus does good on the Sabbath (Mt 12:1-13)
Week 9- Gethsemane (Mt 26:36-56)
Week 10- Jesus on trial (Mt 26:57-27:2, etc)
Week 11- Jesus' Crucifixion (Mt 27:15-66, etc)
Week 12- Jesus' Resurrection (Mt 28:1-15, etc)
Week 13- Jesus' Ascension (Lk 24:50-53, Acts 1)

Second Quarter
Week 1- Peter's denial (Mt 26:31-35, 69-75)
Week 2- Pentecost (Ac 2)
Week 3- Cornelius & Peter (Ac 10)
Week 4- Peter escapes prison (Ac 12:1-19)
Week 5- Creation (Gen 1, 2)
Week 6- Creation of man (Gen 1:26-30, etc)
Week 7- The Sabbath (Gen 2:1-3)
Week 8- Cain & Abel (Gen 4)
Week 9- Enoch (Gen 5:21-24)
Week 10- Second Coming (Jn 14:1-3)
Week 11- Heaven (Rev 21:1-6, Is 11:1-9)
Week 12- Tree, River of Life (Rev 22:1-5, etc)
Week 13- Songs of praise in heaven (Rev 5:11-13, etc)

Third Quarter
Week 1- Moses' song (Ex 15; Ps 106:1 12)
Week 2- Josiah restores worship (2 Ki 22)
Week 3- Josiah & revival (2 Ki 22; 2 Chr 34)
Week 4- Josiah & Passover (2 Ki 23:21 25)
Week 5- Esther becomes queen (Es 1, 2)
Week 6- Esther pleads for Jews (Es 2:19 4:17)
Week 7- Esther's banquet (Es 5 7)
Week 8- Esther saves her people (Es 7, 8)
Week 9- Satan tempts Jesus (Mt 4)
Week 10- Jesus heals; prays (Lk 5:12 16, etc)
Week 11- Timothy, Eunice, Lois (2 Tim 1)
Week 12- Paul & Silas in prison (Ac 16:16-40)
Week 13- Bereans study Scripture (Ac 17:1 14)

Fourth Quarter
Week 1- Deborah & Barak (Judges 4, 5)
Week 2- Gideon (Judges 6, 7)
Week 3- Samson (Judges 16)
Week 4- God calls Samuel (I Sa 3)
Week 5- Daniel taken to Babylon (Dan 1:1,2)
Week 6- Daniel & friends (Dan 1:3 20)
Week 7- Daniel & Nebuchadnezzar (Dan 2)
Week 8- Nebuchadnezzar exiled (Dan 4)
Week 9- Daniel & Belshazzar (Dan 5)
Week 10- Gabriel appears to Zechariah, Joseph, Mary (Lk 1:5-38)
Week 11- Birth of Jesus (Lk 2)
Week 12- Shepherds visit Baby Jesus (Lk 2)
Week 13- Magi; escape to Egypt (Mt 2)

Bible Story Index

Aaron, the Priest	63
Aaron's rod buds	31, 42
Abraham and Melchizedek	15, 28, 48, 96
Abraham offers Isaac	93
Abraham pleads for Sodom	16
Abraham's journey from Ur	24
Adam and Eve created	50, 79, 81
Adam and Eve sin	44, 18, 99, 105
Angel visits Mary, Zechariah	9, 27, 60
Angel's song	76
Angels visit shepherds	30, 33, 56
Animals enter ark	9, 23, 25, 46, 66, 68
Apostles escape prison	46, 82
Apostles heal and preach	43, 58
Baby Jesus	22, 38, 41, 80
Baby John	41
Baby Moses	14
Balaam and donkey	101
Belshazzar's feast	28, 44, 49, 97
Bezaleel	15
Birth of Jesus	13, 14, 15, 25
Birthday Sabbath	59
Bitter waters made sweet	57, 88
Boy Jesus in Temple	82
Boy Samuel's coat	35
Bronze snake	68
Cain and Abel	17, 89, 90
Captive maid	75
Christmas story	51, 53
Cities of refuge	31, 44, 87
Communion Sabbath	57
Creation days 1-5	80
Creation	13, 14, 19, 25, 31, 34, 39, 41, 46, 50, 79, 80
Cripple at pool of Bethesda	46
Crossing Jordan	42, 65
Crucifixion	43, 53, 61, 93
Daniel and lions	9, 14, 67, 111
Daniel out of lion's den	77, 88
Daniel prays	17, 29, 48, 66, 77, 90
Daniel, friends at king's table	53, 66
Daniel, friends taken captive	82, 87
David shares the victory	39
David, shepherd boy	21, 45
Death of Moses	19, 83
Deborah and Barak	42, 65
Deborah judges	109

Disciples prepare to serve	65, 110
Disciples want to be first	39, 70, 78
Dorcas	15, 28
Early church	11, 114
Easter story	49
Elijah and Still Small Voice	24, 88
Elijah and widow's oil	73, 85, 90
Elijah fed by ravens	19, 49
Elijah hides from Ahab	91, 105
Elijah on Mt. Carmel	42, 50, 67, 113
Elisha and axe head	9, 47, 76, 104
Elisha and invisible army	49, 87, 109
Elisha and Shunemite	78, 85
Enoch	15, 90
Enoch spends time with God	48
Esther	29
Esther becomes queen	18
Esther prays	110
Esther saves her people	16, 92, 95, 101
Esther's banquet	21, 28, 37, 65
Eutycus falls	69, 114
Exodus	16, 27
Ezra or Nehemiah wait for God	91
Feed my sheep	10, 43
Forgiving 70x7	18, 71
Gethsemane	114
Gideon	39, 86, 95
God calls Abram	17
God's community	89
Golden calf	43, 64, 84
Good Samaritan	50, 54, 63
Grace	18, 43, 85, 86
Healing ten lepers	67
Heaven	58, 60, 79, 80, 105
Hezekiah	15, 47, 53, 71, 81
Houses on rock and sand	108, 110
Isaac's wife	11, 44, 47, 64
Isaiah's vision of temple	17, 39, 71, 92
Jacob and Esau	11, 70
Jacob and Esau reunited	28, 44, 70, 77
Jacob and Rachel	29, 70
Jacob deceives Esau	70, 86
Jacob leaves home	70
Jacob serves Laban	10, 16, 55, 70
Jacob's ladder	36, 70, 76, 96
Jairus' daughter	54

Jeremiah visits potter	65, 71, 73
Jericho falls	11, 23, 54, 61, 91, 95, 110
Jesus and children	15, 39, 104
Jesus and the Samaritans	16
Jesus calls disciples	21, 86
Jesus calls Matthew	64, 89, 95
Jesus calms the storm	12
Jesus does good on Sabbath	15, 51, 55
Jesus feeds the 5,000	16, 22, 50
Jesus heals a leper	9
Jesus heals blind man	22, 49, 70, 78
Jesus on trial	82
Jesus prays	48, 111, 114
Jesus serves disciples	41, 54, 57
Jesus' ascension	33, 51
Jesus' baptism	33, 67, 94
Jesus' childhood	55, 78
Jesus' resurrection	19, 60, 83
Jonah and gourd	64, 105
Jonah and the whale	12, 14, 31, 41, 96
Jonah preaches in Nineveh	82, 112
Jonathan defeats Philistines	41, 66
Joseph and brothers reunited	96
Joseph and Potiphar's wife	46
Joseph becomes ruler	48, 65
Joseph sold into Egypt	77, 101
Joseph's coat	35
Joseph's family moves to Egypt	95
Joshua meets the Captain	17, 53
Josiah	42
Josiah restores worship	81, 95
Josiah's revival	22, 46, 55, 87, 113
Last Supper	47, 75, 113
Law of God	93
Lazarus' death/resurrection	18, 36, 71, 92
Lost coin	11
Lost sheep	14, 16, 17, 76, 89
Lydia	89
Magi worship with gifts	48
Manna in wilderness	9, 28, 36, 53
Mary anoints Jesus with perfume	20, 42, 57, 71, 74, 89
Mary's song	30
Mordecai saves king	34, 45
Moses and burning bush	12, 30, 31
Moses at Red Sea	41
Moses cannot enter Caanan	44

Moses' early life	16
Moses' last words	39, 76
Moses strikes rock	86, 91
Naaman's leprosy	18, 85, 113
Nehemiah rebuilds temple	23, 111
Nicodemus	50, 68
Noah and the animals	14
Noah, family wait in ark	76
Noah's ark	13, 66
Noah's ark rests	25
Offerings build tabernacle	35, 74, 91
Old/New Testament prophecies fulfilled	71, 114
Onesimus, Philemon	33, 55
Parable of vineyard	33
Parable of wedding banquet	42
Paralytic through roof	70, 99
Party on Sea of Glass	47
Passover; Last Plague	17, 83
Paul and Silas	77, 97
Paul in Athens (To the Unknown God)	31, 91
Paul worshipped	24, 58
Paul writes Timothy	58
Paul, Barnabas go to Cyprus	78
Paul, Barnabas in Antioch	85
Paul, Silas in prison	9
Paul, Silas praise at midnight	88
Paul's call to Macedonia	37
Paul's blindness healed	49
Pentecost	21, 23, 78, 91, 105
Peter and Cornelius	34, 46
Peter and John, Sanhedrin	20, 41, 98
Peter escapes prison	27, 40, 113
Peter walks on water	25
Peter, John heal lame man	21, 81
Peter's denial	20, 41, 45, 83, 92, 93, 98
Philip and Ethiopian	39, 81
Praying for power	111
Priscilla and Aquila	42
Prodigal son	83, 84, 92, 99
Promotion Sabbath	58, 89
Rahab and spies	47, 87, 105
Rainbow promise	21, 34
Rachel at the Well	18
Red Sea deliverance	64, 77
Sabbath	21, 22, 30, 33, 39, 47, 55, 57, 66, 97
Samson	65, 69, 78, 80, 85, 101

Samuel speaks for God	112
Sanctuary	13
Satan tempts Jesus	84, 92, 93
Saul's conversion	24, 43, 51, 82, 83, 87, 104, 105
Second coming	64, 91, 92
Serpent tempts Eve	68
Seven deacons	58, 113
Sheep and goats	61, 96
Shepherds tell good news	25, 56, 61
Shepherds visit Jesus	9, 56
Shepherds worship Jesus	51
Simon carries cross	30, 53
Simon tries to buy power	47, 83, 86
Solomon and Queen of Sheba	81
Solomon builds temple	28, 47, 51
Solomon dedicates temple	11, 21, 24
Speck and plank parable	46
Spiritual armor	61
Spiritual gifts	41
Stephen	98
Stephen and deacons	9, 46
Tabernacle or temple	63, 74
Ten bridesmaids	30, 44, 47, 73, 92
Ten Plagues	13, 88
Timothy	98
Tithing	74
Titus visits Corinth	45
Tower of Babel	11, 23, 25
Transfiguration	64, 94
Tree of life	30, 66
Trinity	94
Twelve spies	64, 95
Upper Room experience	88
Vineyard workers	71
Water from the rock	25, 45
Wedding at Cana	10, 16, 73
Widow's son raised	42, 47, 64
Wilderness sanctuary	48
Woman at well	104
Worship in heaven	33, 75, 84
Zacchaeus	46, 67, 68
Zechariah and the angels prophecy	72